READINGS IN FEMINIST PSYCHOLOGY

READINGS IN FEMINIST PSYCHOLOGY

K.S.MOORTHI

CYBER TECH PUBLICATIONS
4264/3, Ansari Road, Daryaganj, New Delhi-110002 (India)
Ph.: 011-23244078, 011-43559448 Fax: 011-23280028
E-Mail: cyberpublicationsdelhi@yahoo.com
Website: www.cybertechpublications.com

READINGS IN FEMINIST PSYCHOLOGY

K.S.MOORTHI

First Edition 2011

Published by :

G.S. Rawat for **Cyber Tech Publications**
4264/3, Ansari Road, Daryaganj, New Delhi-110002 (India)
Ph.: 011-23244078, 011-43559448 Fax: 011-23280028
E-Mail: cyberpublicationsdelhi@yahoo.com
Website: www.cybertechpublications.com

CONTENTS

Preface

This book offers a sampling of the many ways that gender affects experience. Whether the context is domestic or international, a court-room or a business or a clinic, gender matters. It influences ideas and expectations, and they shape behavior and laws. Across settings, the ex-periences of women are shaped by patterns of power and dominance, cultural expectations, economic disparities, and internalized models of social relationships that are defined by gender.

The experiences of women are also shaped by absence and invisibil-ity: what does not get noticed, discussed, valued, or included. This in-cludes invisibility in the workplace. As Fletcher (1999) demonstrates, the relational work that women are expected to do does not quite make it into the job evaluation.

It includes the "second shift" of the average working mother, which occurs after she comes home from her paid em-ployment, when she has the primary responsibility for the care of the emotional and physical needs of family members (children, husband, elderly parents, or parents-in-law). She has this responsibility because she is female. She may ask for "help" in these duties, but that they are her responsibility is not likely to be questioned (Hochschild & Machung, 2003). It includes the routine exclusion of women as subjects in health care and drug research, because their inclusion makes the subject pool less "homogeneous" and more complicated statistically (Epstein, 1996), even when women will be the consumers of the drugs.

In every context, we see the power of language to define experience. When it is men defining the experience of women, the results can be surprising. In the law pregnancy is not seen as a gender-related issue because health benefits divide employees into "pregnant people" and "nonpregnant people" (*Geduldigv. Aiello*, 1974). Using this logic, a company can choose not to pay for the health care costs of pregnancy, even if it does cover illnesses related to the prostate. Under similar logic, erectile dysfunction is viewed as a health disorder for which in-surance should cover the cost of treatments such as Viagra, while preg-nancy is not a health problem and insurers should not be required to cover the cost of birth control pills.

Those psychological and legal schol-ars who use a power and dominance model to explain gender relations will readily note the irony: that we are enabling men to have more sex and simultaneously making it more difficult for women to protect themselves from the consequences of that sex.

—Auhor

1

Introduction

When a baby is born, there is one thing we want to know: Girl or boy? It is good manners to ask about the health of the baby first, and of course we want to know how mother and child fared during the birth. But once we are assured of their health and safety, we want to know: Girl or boy? We have to know, because without that piece of informa-tion, our imaginations are stuck. We want to be able to think about how this new member will fit into the rest of the family. We want to think about how we will interact with the new child. Will she follow in the footsteps of the family business tycoons, or artists, or teachers? Will we identify with him? Will we make a point of giving him career advice so that he can avoid the mistakes we made? Will we want to give her beauty advice? Will he be the shortstop or quarterback we can brag about? Will she be the devoted child who makes up for those times when we did not feel loved? Will he carry on the family name? How will she fit in our models for how families work? Is this a child who will help cook the Thanksgiving turkey? Is this the child who will clean up afterward—or the child who will sit and watch football while others clean? Will we en-courage this child to be nice? Ambitious? Accommodating? Proud?

Our imaginations require that we know the gender of the new per-son. Only with that information can we begin to organize our expec-tations and our perceptions. The classic study of infants by Rubin, Provenzano, and Luria (1974) first documented this process, and the results have been replicated since (Karraker, Lake, & Vogel, 1995). Adults looking at the very same babies will describe them different-ly depending on their belief about the baby's gender. If the adults thought they were looking at a female infant, she was described as sweet, fragile, and fine-featured. If the adults thought they was looking at a male infant, he was described as strong, vigorous, and energetic.

Research on attachment relationships (Main, 1996) has demon-strated that the quality of the relationship between a mother and a child when the child is one year old can be predicted from the mother's responses to an interview about her own relationships with her par-ents. The mother's interview took place during the pregnancy, before the baby was even born and available to influence the relationship. This speaks to the power of our expectations to influence our behavior and, even more subtle, the power of our expectations to influence what we see. The research subjects saw a more vigorous baby when they thought he was male. The interviewed mothers saw their new babies through the lens of their own personal relationship histories.

Gender is a core attribute that organizes our thinking consciously and unconsciously. We know this based on psychological research. We know this based on the history of sex discrimination law. We know this when we see Julia Sweeney's *Saturday Night Live* ambiguously sexed character, Pat. At the heart of every Pat sketch is the determination of the other characters to figure out if Pat is male or female. We relate to their frustration because we also want to know. We laugh with the same frustration at the way Pat's partner, "Chris," is equally ambiguous. We are uncomfortable not knowing.

This book offers a sampling of the many ways that gender affects experience. Whether the context is domestic or international, a court-room or a business or a clinic, gender matters. It influences ideas and expectations, and they shape behavior and laws. Across settings, the ex-periences of women are shaped by patterns of power and dominance, cultural expectations, economic disparities, and internalized models of social relationships that are defined by gender.

The experiences of women are also shaped by absence and invisibil-ity: what does not get noticed, discussed, valued, or included. This in-cludes invisibility in the workplace. As Fletcher (1999) demonstrates, the relational work that women are expected to do does not quite make it into the job evaluation. It includes the "second shift" of the average working mother, which occurs after she comes home from her paid em-ployment, when she has the primary responsibility for the care of the emotional and physical needs of family members (children, husband, elderly parents, or parents-in-law). She has this responsibility because she is female. She may ask for "help" in these duties, but that they are her responsibility is not likely to be questioned (Hochschild & Machung, 2003). It includes the routine exclusion of women as subjects in health care and drug research, because their inclusion makes the subject pool less "homogeneous" and more complicated statistically (Epstein, 1996), even when women will be the consumers of the drugs.

In every context, we see the power of language to define experience. When it is men defining the experience of women, the results can be surprising. In the law pregnancy is not seen as a gender-related issue because health benefits divide employees into "pregnant people" and "nonpregnant people" (*Geduldigv. Aiello*, 1974). Using this logic, a company can choose not to pay for the health care costs of pregnancy, even if it does cover illnesses related to the prostate. Under similar logic, erectile dysfunction is viewed as a health disorder for which in-surance should cover the cost of treatments such as Viagra, while preg-nancy is not a health problem and insurers should not be required to cover the cost of birth control pills. Those psychological and legal schol-ars who use a power and dominance model to explain gender relations will readily note the irony: that we are enabling men to have more sex and simultaneously making it more difficult for women to protect themselves from the consequences of that sex.

Jean Baker Miller (2003), a psychiatrist who has written about the psychological effects of gender, notes the following:

Power is very real and is operating in front of us all the time. Quite amazingly, those who have the most power in our society almost never talk about it, and even more amazingly, they induce many of the rest of us not to recognize it, either. [Through distorted representations of groups in film] we absorbed... untruths routinely every week.... This is one example of how the "cultural materials" of a dominant group mystify its operation of power.

For various historical reasons, a dominant segment in any society tends to divide people with less power into groups by race, class, gen-der, sexual preference, and the like. The dominant group often gains tremendous power over the less powerful groups in economic, social, political, and cultural realms. But dominant groups do not usually say, "I have great power over your life; I want to keep it and, if possible, in-crease it because I'm afraid of losing any of it to you.'

It is important to recognize that there are different kinds of power. We use the term "power-to" to mean the ability to make a change in any situation, large or small, without restricting or forcing others. The term "power-over" we apply to situations or structures in which one group or person has more resources and privileges and more capacity to force or control others. Structural power reinforced by power-over practices obstructs growth and constructive change.

Dominant groups usually manufacture false belief systems that act to perpetuate their power-over position and sustain their separation from subordinate groups. Patricia Hill Collins (1990), an African-American sociologist, discusses the impact of controlling images. She notes that dominant groups tend to create sets of images about them-selves and about each of the "subordinate" groups. These controlling images are always false, yet they exert a powerful influence, holding each group in its place and maintaining the status quo. We absorb these im-ages about others and ourselves, usually without fully realizing it.... This is part of the way dominant groups mystify their power-over practices and entice many of us into cooperation [p. 5].

MYSTIFICATION AND BIOLOGY

The concept of mystification helps us understand how gender stereo-types can be perpetrated, maintained, and internalized, until we are almost convinced they are true. We live in a culture that provides con-tradictory messages about almost everything, and gender is no excep-tion. Any challenge to the status quo is met with opposition. Frequently, that opposition takes the form of biological mandates, or "natural law," which suggest that women are limited by the immutable characteris-tic of sex and it is the result of biology, nature, genetics, or, more re-cently, evolutionary forces that require women to be in a culturally inferior position.

When women began to assert their rights to education, property, and the vote, the science of the times warned of the health dangers of a higher education. The data were clear: women with college educa-tions tended to have fewer children. In the late 1800s, the explanation was biological: education was literally impairing women's fertility, pri-marily by exhausting them with all that thinking (Barnes, 1985).

If the health dangers were not enough to keep women from seek-ing an education, then the genetic explanation was available. The vari-ability hypothesis argued that only males could be expected to achieve great things. This "scientific" hypothesis pointed to the data: the his-torical records demonstrated that only men had made great intellec-tual and societal achievements. It also demonstrated that there were more men than women institutionalized for "mental defects." The conclusion was clear: men were genetically endowed with more po-tential to reach extremes in both directions, while women were resigned to mediocrity. The subtext was, Why bother educating women, who could achieve only modest goals (Barnes, 1985)?

As late at the 1960s, women at Harvard Law School were formally required to justify their presence. Alumnae have described an annual ritual, a dinner hosted by the school's dean, Erwin Griswold, where the guest list included all of the women in each class (and none of the men), along with selected faculty and their wives. After dinner the stu-dents were called upon, one by one, to answer Griswold's horrifying question, "Why are you at Harvard Law School, taking the place of a man?" (Hope, 2003). While the history of legal education in the United States was primarily that of exclusion of women, professional psy-chology was not dramatically more liberal. Women began earning Ph.D.s in psychology in the late 1800s, but they did it at the cost of a personal life. One could choose to be a professional or have a family, but not both. Institutions of higher education, even those most ac-cepting of women as professors, required that they leave teaching once they married (Barnes, 1985).

MYSTIFICATION AND THE PSYCHE

By the early 1900s, psychology was beginning to explain gender in-equalities as the result of intrapsychic conflicts. It was not that there was inherently a problem with women's legal, cultural, or economic status. The problem was that women did not willingly accept their in-feriority. Freud himself had warned his colleagues, "We must not allow ourselves to be deflected... by... the feminists, who are anxious to force us to regard the two sexes as completely equal in position and worth" (quoted in Steinem, 1994, p. 20). Modern psychoanalysis con-tinues to struggle with Freud's concept of penis envy. One strategy is to dismiss it as children's fantasy or magical thinking based on a child's naive understanding of anatomy. This leaves open the opportunity to outgrow the "natural inferiority" that little girls experience at the dis-covery that they are without a penis or to compensate by acquiring a man—and therefore vicarious ownership of a penis.

One strategy is to "equalize" the child's dilemma: girls wish they had a penis, and boys wish they could have babies, because children (and perhaps adults) do not want to acknowledge any limitations. All difference is loss at the preoperational level of cognitive development (Fast, 1990). In classical psychoanalytic theory, the core issue is power: who has the advantage between the sexes and who is lacking and there-fore inferior. Girls make the heartbreaking discovery that they are not "as good as boys," and they spend their lives trying to make up for it. The question of sexual identity is thus complicated by the value judg-ment that says girls are lesser.

Chodorow (1978) redefined the early childhood struggle as one of connection and separation. In this scenario, it is the boys who have the more difficult challenge of separating from the nurturing mother in order to identify with the same-sex parent. Boys have to give up the regressive pull toward mother in order to be "masculine."

Those who do not will face the ultimate criticism from peers: that they are weak, sissies—in other words, like girls. This model offers an explanation for the intensity of feeling around masculinity, and the ever-present fear of being emasculated, as if masculinity were a fragile and precar-ious state of being, subject at any time to being lost or stolen. Women do not worry about "losing" their femininity any more than they worry about misplacing an arm or a leg.

What these theories have in common is the locus of control. Feel-ings about gender identity come from within and are an inherent part of the developmental process of all humans. They are ultimately bio-logically based, the result of millions of years of evolution, and they are unlikely to be changed.

MYSTIFICATION THROUGH THE LANGUAGE OF PROTECTION AND PHYSICAL STRENGTH

While psychologists theorized about the nature of gender identity for the individual, the law was required to make concrete decisions about the importance of gender in employment and other social relation-ships. Early legal decisions purported to want to protect women from the strains of the industrialized workplace by limiting hours (*Muller v. Oregon*, 1908). Making assumptions about the physical character-istics of women, these early decisions also helped promote stereotypes. It was now a legal fact that women were not as strong as men, and it was a legal value to protect women. More specifically, this was a value to protect women's bodies.

Consider the comments of Gloria Steinem (1994) about the his-tory of the treatment of women's bodies:

Though cultural differences were many, there were political similari-ties in the way women's bodies were treated that went as deep as patri-archy itself. Whether achieved through law and social policy, as in this and other industrialized countries, or by way of tribal practice and re-ligious ritual, as in older cultures, an individual woman's body was far more subject to other people's rules than was that of her male coun-terpart. Women always seemed to be owned to some degree as the means of reproduction. And as possessions, women's bodies then be-came symbols of men's status, with a value that was often determined by what was rare. Thus, rich cultures valued thin women, and poor cul-tures valued fat women. Yet all patriarchal cultures valued weakness in women. How else could male dominance survive? In my own country, for example, women who "belong" to rich white men are often thinner (as in "You can never be too rich or too thin") than those who "belong" to poor men of color; yet those very different groups of males tend to come together in their belief that women are supposed to be weaker than men; that muscles and strength aren't "feminine."...

If I had any doubts about the psychological importance of cultural emphasis on male/female strength difference, listening to arguments about equality put them to rest. Sooner or later, even the most intel-lectual discussion came down to men's supposed superior strength as a justification for inequality, whether the person arguing regretted or cel-ebrated it. What no one seemed to explore, however, was the inadequacy of physical strength as a way of explaining oppression in other cases. Men of European origin hadn't ruled in South Africa because they were stronger than African men, and blacks hadn't been kept in slavery or bad jobs in the United States because whites had more muscles. On the con-trary, males of the "wrong" class or color were often confined to laboring positions precisely because of their supposedly greater strength, just as the lower pay females received was often rationalized by their suppos-edly lesser strength. Oppression has no logic—just a self-fulfilling prophecy, justified by a self-perpetuating system....

The more I learned, the more I realized that belief in great strength differences between women and men was itself part of the gender mind-game. In fact, we can't really know what those differences might be, be-cause they are so enshrined, perpetuated, and exaggerated by culture. They seem to be greatest during the childbearing years (when men as a group have more speed and upper-body strength, and women have better balance, endurance, and flexibility) but only marginal during early childhood and old age (when females and males seem to have about the same degree of physical strength). Even during those middle years, the range of difference among men and among women is far greater than the generalized difference between males and females as groups. In multiracial societies like ours, where males of some races are smaller than females of others, judgments based on sex make even less sense. Yet we go right on assuming and praising female weakness and male strength....

But there is a problem about keeping women weak, even in a pa-triarchy. Women are workers, as well as the means of reproduction. Lower-class women are especially likely to do hard physical labor. So the problem becomes: How to make sure female strength is used for work but not for rebellion. The answer is: make women ashamed of it. Tough hard work requires lower-class women to be stronger than their upper-class sisters, for example, those strong women are made to envy and imitate the weakness of women who "belong" to, and are the means of reproduction for, upper-class men—and so must be kept even more physically restricted if the lines of race and inheritance are to be kept "pure." That's why restrictive dress, from the chadors, or full-body veils, of the Middle East to metal ankle and neck rings in Africa, from nineteenth-century hoop skirts in Europe to corsets and high heels here, started among upper-class women and then sifted down-ward as poor women were encouraged to envy or imitate them. So did such bodily restrictions as bound feet in China, or clitoridectomies and infibulations in much of the Middle East and Africa, both of which practices began with women whose bodies were the means of repro-duction for the powerful and gradually became generalized symbols of femininity. In this country, the self-starvation known as anorexia nervosa is mostly a white, upper-middle-class, young-female phe-nomenon, but all women are encouraged to envy a white and impos-sibly thin ideal [Steinem, 1994, pp. 94-96].

MYSTIFICATION OF POWER AND DOMINANCE

Jean Baker Miller (2003) reminds us that gender definitions have served as a means of domination and control, with this control often achieved through violence. To change the definitions of gender "appropriate-ness" is revolutionary and dangerous. Women have been killed for their difference (the witchcraft trials in Salem, Massachusetts, in the late seventeenth century). Women have been killed for their confor-mity (funeral pyres for the wives of deceased men). Women are killed for the behavior of others (honor killings of rape victims). Women are still routinely mutilated in Africa, and they are routinely beaten in America (domestic violence).

Gender equality is not an academic or philosophical issue. It has life-and-death implications for women, whether it involves access to safe abortions in Western culture, access to medications needed to treat HIV in Africa, or protection from murder (as an adult female in rural India or as a newborn female infant in China).

In recent news stories, we have seen rape trials treated as "he said-she said" relational disputes. We have discovered numerous police departments that have hundreds of "rape kits" in storage that were never sent off for DNA analysis. The explanations were consistent: it was too expensive to an-alyze this evidence of a crime. The results were also consistent: alleged rapists went free or never went to trial in the first place. This is vio-lence by omission.

MYSTIFICATION THROUGH INVISIBILITY

Law professor Leslie Espinoza (1997) describes the way in which even informed and well-intentioned professionals can disregard the per-spectives and feelings of women:

After a while, try as we might, domestic attorneys, whether we are clin-ical law professors or representing for-pay clients, become inured to the most shocking of social taboos. Abuse becomes normalized for us.

Rape of a child is awful, but it happens. Family law attorneys have routine ways of redressing the situation. This is the standard response: tempo-rary protective orders in district court, divorce action filed in the pro-bate court, and temporary orders during the pendency of the divorce providing for support, custody, and protection. The temporary probate court orders become permanent upon the final adjudication of the case.

The standard response is comforting to the attorney—you get to feel like the knight in white armor. It allows you not to think of the re-ality of what this family is going through.... A contextual under-standing of what happened does not really matter. Only enough of the background to support the outcome is relevant.

... We do not wrestle with the impact of gender-related trauma. Likewise we do not recognize that race matters.... Our legal distance validates the dysfunctional normalization of abuse that usually occurs in abusive families.

...The stories of women who are traumatized by abuse are sup-pressed by the normalization of violence toward women and children. Subordination of women—treating them like objects of property—is our cultural legacy. Historically, this violence has been acknowledged as the private right of men ruling families. Violence and rape of wom-en are now tacitly allowed by the suppression of knowledge about abuse and the failure of the society to redress abuse. When women and children do speak, their stories are distorted to make them willing vic-tims, liars, provocateurs, and crazies.

... Who is listening and how they listen affect the ability of the speaker to talk. There is an interaction between speaker and listener. In a symbiotic way they can work together for deeper levels of under-standing [pp. 904, 905, 908, 915, and 923].

PSYCHOLOGY AND THE LAW

The courts must make decisions about cases before them in a timely manner. The U.S. Constitution guarantees a "fair and speedy trial" to criminal defendants. The courts do not have to rely on the most cur-rent research on gender, but they do have to provide decisions that are consistent with past legal decisions (that is, precedent). Court deci-sions tend to reflect well-established social norms and conservative interpretations of the law, because the obligation to follow precedent tends to prevent dramatic changes in legal decision making. In exam-ining legal cases related to women, we can see how the judges are view-ing women and their role in society, and we can see how that role is then expanded or constricted as a result of their decisions. The courts give power to enforce gender roles when they define what is accept-able and not acceptable (not constitutional) treatment of women by employers, insurers, or the government itself. Scholars analyzing legal cases must spend as much time reading between the lines as they do reading the words of Supreme Court justices, since much of what af-fects women is in the unspoken assumptions made by those in power.

2

Psychological Gender Differences

Psychology has played a key role in the policy and le-gal arenas pertaining to the rights and protections of women. Sweep-ing changes have occurred for women in society since the mid-1990s. Women's rights, protections, and roles have been transformed in vir-tually all aspects of American society, most notably in the family, higher education, and the workplace. Psychology has both contributed to and benefited from these changes. The field itself has undergone major shifts during the past few decades that have involved both the inclusion of women in the profession and the inclusion of research and theory in areas that pertain to the lives of women.

Although gender has been a topic of research, theory, and specu-lation throughout the history of the field of psychology, the psychol-ogy of women developed as a formal field only in the 1970s. The focus on women in psychology came about with the rise of the feminist movement in the broader society, paralleling the relationship between cultural and social movements and psychology that has existed through-out the history of psychology (Furumoto, 1998; Minton, 2000). Research in gender, sex differences and stereotypes, the workplace and work-place discrimination, sexual harassment, reproductive rights, family violence, sexual assault, and childhood sexual abuse has burgeoned over the past few decades as women have become researchers and clin-icians and as the experiences of women have become legitimate top-ics of inquiry.

Questions about sex differences in attitudes, traits, behaviors, and abilities are central to both psychological inquiry and mainstream cul-ture. It would be difficult to find another area of psychology that has received an equivalent amount of attention yet where the results and interpretations are as hotly contested and as murky. Controversy exists about whether the research on sex differences substantiates the exis-tence of differences, whether the magnitude of the differences is suffi-cient to be regarded as important or relevant, whether the intragroup differences so outweigh the intergroup differences as to render the topic unimportant, and whether the differences are so context dependent that they reflect little about men's and women's actual behaviors in so-ciety. The etiology of sex differences, whether artifact, social construc-tion, social status, social structure and role, or evolution, is also an area of disagreement, with research providing support for multiple per-spectives. This chapter lays out the current research and perspectives about sex differences, beginning with quantitative research methods and conclusions and progressing to qualitative, discursive, and episte-mological positions and methodologies.

HISTORICAL CONTEXT OF CURRENT RESEARCH

The Psychology of Sex Differences by Maccoby and Jacklin (1974) is generally viewed as the first major contemporary review of the topic, but the study of sex differences in American psychology is as old as the discipline itself. Much of the early research was based on evolu-tionary theory interpreted to support a social structure that equated women's roles with procreation and child rearing and men's roles with work and authority over the family. Jeanne Marecek (2002) quotes a tract written in the late 1800s that embodies this perspective: "All that is distinctly human is man; all that is truly woman is reproductive" (p. 255). The writings on sex differences by the renowned early psy-chologist G. Stanley Hall used evolutionary theory to promote sex seg-regation in education because of the presumed necessity to maintain the sex differences inherent in the nature of boys and girls (Minton, 2000). Although Hall supported the education of several early women psychologists when he was president of Clark University (1888-1920), he also served as a leader in an anticoeducation movement, because he believed that girls and boys required segregated socialization in order to fulfill their distinct social roles. Girls were to be prepared for motherhood and the perpetuation of society through child rearing. Boys were to be prepared for the roles that created, led, improved, or otherwise contributed to civilization. Their socialization required that they not be unduly influenced and feminized by their teachers and mothers during adolescence (Diehl, 1986).

Helen Thompson Woolley was one of the first psychologists to sys-tematically investigate sex differences, to some extent in reaction to the types of assertions and conclusions about sex differences that her colleagues had drawn. She published a body of empirical work per-taining to sex differences in cognitive, motor, and sensory abilities as well as a critique of the work of her colleagues (Thompson, 1903; Woolley, 1910,1914). She argued that differences in abilities between males and females were relatively small and did not justify the inter-pretations of her male colleagues. She was one of the first to counter the prevailing biological explanations for sex differences with social and structural theories.

Sex comparisons in research continued mostly in a piecemeal fash-ion over the next sixty years, culminating with *The Psychology of Sex Differences* (1974), in which Maccoby and Jacklin reviewed nearly fif-teen hundred empirical studies that had reported sex differences in some form, evaluating their methods, instruments, results, and con-clusions. Like Woolley (1910,1914), they concluded that the literature documented relatively few or relatively small sex differences, given the level of professional and popular attention devoted to the topic. Their conclusion was that the research supported that differences existed in four areas—verbal, quantitative, and spatial cognitive abilities and the trait of aggression—with women scoring higher on verbal abilities and men higher on the other variables.

CONTEMPORARY RESEARCH FINDINGS

Research on sex differences has only increased since Maccoby and Jacklin's book. Marecek (2002) estimated that by 1985, over sixteen thou-sand studies of sex differences were reported in the literature. A major change that has occurred since the publication of *The Psychology of Sex Differences* in 1974 is the shift in the method of reviewing results across studies from cataloging those with significant results (*p* value) in order to locate trends or themes to using quantitative methods of meta-analysis. In the latter process, effect sizes (*d*value), derived from the standard deviation of the sex comparison for each study, are averaged (Cooper, 1979). This method is considered an improvement over ear-lier, more informal techniques of analysis because it evaluates effect size rather than statistical significance, which is tied to sample size, and because it involves establishing and complying with criteria-based rules for inclusion and aggregation that are uniformly applied throughout an analysis (Eagly, 1995a). This technique of aggregating and evaluat-ing the effect sizes of studies in a particular research literature along a continuum has been applied to many areas of psychology, including sex differences, where meta-analyses of comparisons of men's and women's emotions, attitudes, traits, and behaviors across research stud-ies have been conducted over the past two decades.

These meta-analytic techniques have not quelled the controversy about the existence or importance of sex differences. There is still little agreement on or clear direction about what traits, abilities, and attrib-utes differ between men and women and about the size of these differ-ences, their relevance to functioning in contemporary society, or their etiology. Critics of this approach counter that it does not solve the "file drawer phenomenon," meaning that only studies with some positive findings are published and available for another researcher's meta-analysis, while the studies with no results are filed in researchers' draw-ers. Meta-analysis attends only to those that have seen the light of day. A second critique is that studies may employ very different measures to evaluate the same disposition, and these measures may be lumped to-gether in meta-analysis without truly knowing whether they are mea-suring similar or different qualities (Marecek, 2002).

Cognitive Abilities

Meta-analytic techniques have been used to evaluate hundreds of stud-ies measuring cognitive and intellectual sex differences and have resulted in a range of interpretations of the results. Hyde (1981,1994) has ar-gued that sex differences in verbal, quantitative, and spatial cognitive abilities are small and diminish in late adolescence and adulthood. Halpern (1992) has interpreted the data as demonstrating that stable and significant sex differences exist for particular cognitive abilities even when the overall levels of quantitative and verbal sex differences appear to diminish over time (for example, in adolescence and adulthood). She and others cite research that has been focused on the specific dimen-sions of verbal, spatial, and quantitative abilities that seem to account for stable sex differences, such as visuospatial ability involving the men-tal rotation of three-dimensional objects, where males score higher than females (Masters & Sanders, 1993), verbal fluency (Halpern, 1992), and quantitative problem solving (Halpern, 1992).

Personality and Social Attitudes, Traits and Behaviors

Social and personality researchers have analyzed sex differences using quantitative techniques on synthesized databases from a vast array of databases in social, personality, clinical, organizational, and sports psy-chology. Eagly (1995a) has made the case for their analyses confirm-ing sex differences: "The psychologists who have conducted most of these syntheses of sex-related differences in social behavior and per-sonality are in general agreement that their meta-analytic findings yield evidence of differences. A major theme of much of the interpre-tive writing based on these new syntheses is that empirical research has provided evidence for numerous nontrivial differences in many aspects of behavior" (p. 148). Eagly asserts that these researchers have provided evidence of sex differences in many more areas than claimed by Maccoby and Jacklin in 1974.

Costa, Terracciano, and McCrae (2001) analyzed synthesized data-bases of the Revised NEO Personality Inventory (Costa and McCrae, 1992) from twenty-six cultures made up of 23,031 adults and college-age participants. The authors concluded that modest-sized but cross-culturally consistent gender differences were found that were similar to stereotypes held about gender differences. Women tended to score higher on agreeableness, warmth, openness to feelings, and neuroti-cism, whereas men scored higher on openness to ideas and asser-tiveness. This review supports earlier work by Fiengold (1994) and Nolen-Hoeksema (1987). Fiengold (1994) had previously used meta-analysis to review sex differences on nine of the thirty personality traits of the Revised NEO Personality Inventory (Costa & McCrae, 1992). He found that men scored higher in assertiveness, whereas women scored higher on gregariousness, trust, and tender-mindedness. Nolen-Hoeksema (1987) found that women score higher in symptoms of depression cross-culturally Nevertheless, Costa et al. (2001) interpreted their findings as showing that individual variation within sexes is greater than the differences between the sexes on these personality traits.

Eagly (1995a) summarizes the vast array of sex difference research in the areas of social and personality psychology: "Thematic analysis of demonstrated sex differences in social behavior suggests that they con-form to stereotypic expectations that women are communal and men are agentic. In general, women tend to manifest behaviors that can be described as socially sensitive, friendly, and concerned with others' welfare, whereas men tend to manifest behaviors that can be described as dominant, controlling, and independent" (p. 154). For example, quantitative syntheses of nonverbal and vocal behaviors by Hall and her colleagues have concluded that women are better at decoding non-verbal expressions and smile more, whereas men touch women more than women touch men, use more dominant eye gaze patterns, and interrupt and hold the floor in conversation more than women (Hall, 1978; Hall & Halberstadt, 1986; McClure, 2000; Stier & Hall, 1984).

In a vein similar to Eagly's statement already quoted, Cross and Madson (1997) consider the majority of social and personality sex dif-ferences to reflect differences in traits of independence and interde-pendence. They use the definitions proposed by Markus and Kitayama (1991) based on whether one views oneself as separated from (inde-pendence) or connected to others (interdependence). A person who val-ues independence focuses on self-fulfillment, whereas one with an interdependent perspective emphasizes the fulfillment of one's place in the broader social context. Cross and Madson (1997) provide exam-ples from the existing literature in social sex differences as support for their position. They note research findings showing that women cite interpersonal problems as sources of distress more than men do (Pratt, Golding, Hunter, & Sampson, 1988; Walker, de Vries, & Trevethan, 1987); that women are more likely to talk about interpersonal sub-jects, whereas men talk about sports and politics (Heatherington et al., 1993; McFarland & Miller, 1990); that women pay more attention to information related to relationships than men do (Josephs, Markus, & Tafarodi, 1992; Ross & Holmberg, 1992); and that men attend to in-formation pertaining to themes of social dominance (Maccoby, 1990).

Gabriel and Gardner (1999) suggest that both men and women are interdependent, but that their type of interdependence differs. They define *interdependence* as relational or collective and hypothesize that men demonstrate more collective (group-oriented and agentic) interdependence and women more relational (dyadic and intimate) interdependence. Their results across five studies investigating cogni-tive, emotional, and behavioral differences did not find sex differences in participants' tendencies toward independence versus interdepen-dence. However, they did demonstrate sex differences in whether the type of interdependence manifested was relational or collective. Wom-en described themselves in more relational terms, scored higher on a measure of relational "self-construal," reported more emotional ex-periences linked to relationships, appeared more attuned to informa-tion pertaining to the relationships of others, and were motivated to behave in ways that maintained close relationships. The male partici-pants described themselves in more collective terms, scored higher on a measure of collective self-construal, reported more emotional ex-periences linked to groups, appeared attuned to information pertain-ing to group memberships of others, and were motivated to behave in ways that supported their groups (Gabriel & Gardner, 1999).

ARE SEX DIFFERENCES OF SUFFICIENT MAGNITUDE TO MATTER?

Not surprising, central to the controversy about the existence of sex differences is the disagreement among researchers about the consis-tency across studies and the magnitude of the differences that have been reported. Eagly (1995a) contends that many feminist researchers want to ignore or minimize sex differences for fear that they perpet-uate social inequities. She summarizes the arguments put forth by the critics of the sex differences research: that differences are small and often inconsistent, results frequently are artifacts due to improper methods, and findings often conflict with stereotypes about sex dif-ferences, creating a second source of inconsistency (Eagly, 1995a, 1995b). Eagly (1995a) counters each of these arguments; she asserts that the meta-analyses of traits, abilities, and behaviors have demon-strated a range of consistent findings with effect sizes comparable to those in most accepted areas of psychology. She estimates that most effects in psychology for well-known research are in the moderate range of around "one half of a standard deviation or less; consider-ably larger effect sizes are relatively unusual" (p. 151). Compared to this standard, she points out that several aggregated findings of par-ticular sex differences show large effect sizes (examples include a test of visuospatial abilities, nurturance, and facial expressiveness), with most differences falling in the small-to-moderate range of effect sizes. Eagly points out that even small effect sizes can have significant cu-mulative real-world consequences and impact. To provide a context for the relevance of these effect sizes, Eagly (1995a) cites Cohen's ex-planation (1977) of the benchmarks pertaining to each effect size category: small effect sizes represent group distributions that are 85 percent overlapping and are more common in studies lacking good experimental or measurement control, such as new areas of research; moderate effects are 33 percent nonoverlapping and 67 percent over-lapping and represent group differences that are noticeable in daily life; and large differences are highly visible (47 percent nonoverlap-ping and 53 percent overlapping). Thus, Eagly's assertion is that most of the sex difference literature has findings that at least are noticeable in ordinary life. With regard to the other critiques of sex difference re-search, Eagly (1995a) asserts that researchers have increasingly taken into account and controlled for experimental artifacts.

Hyde and Plant (1995) take issue with Eagly's assertions, first, that feminist researchers have one perspective about the value of identify-ing or minimizing the existence of sex differences, and second, that the effect sizes of aggregated research in sex difference research are equivalent to those in other major areas of psychology. Hyde and Plant (1995) maintain that feminist empiricists have existed along a con-tinuum; in addition to those who argue that sex differences do not exist or that this research promotes inequity for women, there have been many feminist empiricists who have taken the position that clear differences between men and women exist, and still others who have taken a more mixed position—that some sex differences are in fact large, while others are quite insignificant. The authors use Gilligan's work on moral reasoning (1982) as one example of a feminist researcher concluding that men and women fundamentally differ in moral rea-soning, with men assuming a justice (agentic) perspective and women a care (communal) perspective. Hyde and Plant (1995) also cite the research in sex differences in nonverbal behavior as another widely ac-cepted area of research by feminist scholars in spite of large sex dif-ferences. Examples include sex differences in touching behavior (Hall, 1978), smiling, verbal interruptions (McMillan, Clifton, McGrath, & Gale, 1977; Porter, Geis, Cooper, & Newman, 1985), and other dif-ferences in conversational style and meaning (Tannen, 1990). In ad-dition, feminist psychologists disagree about whether differences in some abilities, such as cognitive abilities, represent substantial (Hal-pern, 1992) or insignificant differences (Hyde et al., 1990; Hyde & Linn, 1988).

Hyde and Plant (1995) reviewed the aggregated sex differences studies that had been conducted previously. They concluded that the effect sizes for the many sex differences reviewed in these meta-analyses were smaller than the figures given by Eagly (1995a) and smaller than the findings of meta-analyses of other psychological phe-nomena. They found that the magnitude of gender differences varied substantially from one variable to another, with one-fourth of the sex differences studies revealing effect sizes close to zero, 35 percent show-ing small effects, 27 percent moderate effects, and 13 percent large and very large effects. They compared these results with the aggregated analyses of other established areas of psychology, where only 6 per-cent of the research fell into the close-to-zero category, 29 percent in the small effects category, 38 percent in the moderate category, and 27 percent in the large and very large group. They argue that these com-parisons support their contentions that sex differences are generally not of the same magnitude as other psychological findings and the impact of these differences needs to be questioned. However, these re-searchers still advocate for the understanding of the differences that fall into large effect sizes. "An important direction for research will be to sort out the larger from the smaller gender differences to give spe-cial attention to understanding the processes that create the larger dif-ferences" (Hyde & Plant, 1995, p. 161).

It is important to note that even in areas of sex difference research showing robust effect sizes, men and women overlap in abilities, traits, attitudes, and behaviors more than they fall into two separate groups. It is this overlap that is the source of controversy. In some ways, the controversy about effect size boils down to the question of whether the glass is half empty or half full. On the one hand are researchers making the case that research on sex differences is an area worthy of study, with findings that will lead to our understanding of important phenomena. For example, is it not important to know that men are responsible for most of the violent crime in the United States if one is developing interventions or policies? Doesn't knowing that most sex offenders are male lead not only to better-targeted intervention and research efforts but to more informed legal and social policies as well? Wouldn't recognizing that women suffer more from depression aid in prevention and treatment efforts? Wouldn't awareness of sex differences in quantitative problem solving and visuospatial abilities lead to more effective teaching techniques for women? Aren't sex differences in cognitive abilities as important to understand as social class differences? Researchers who see the glass as half full line up on the side of these arguments, asserting that the differences found in re-search cumulatively "make a difference" in society (Martell, Lane, & Emrich, 1995).

Other researchers question why psychologists would attend to sex differences rather than individual differences given that men and women overlap so substantially on every trait studied. They remind us that for 60 percent of the psychological variables that show signif-icant sex differences, the group distributions for men and women overlap between 85 percent and almost completely. For the large effect sizes found only for 13 percent of the attributes studied, a 50 percent overlap between men and women still exists. Thus, these re-searchers argue that knowing that a person is male or female provides very little predictive value on where he or she would fall on any par-ticular trait. The "half-empty group" argues that the continued focus on sex differences in the light of their insignificance contributes to the unequal status of women because the justification of sex discrimina-tion and even unequal treatment under the law has been based pri-marily on sex differences. Hyde and Plant (1995) make this point: "Any possible bias that may have been introduced by minimalist psychol-ogists [that is, those who minimize differences] is more than balanced by the effects of the popular media, which glamorize and magnify findings of gender differences and are bored to tears with findings of no difference".

THE ORIGINS OF SEX DIFFERENCES

Psychological theories pertaining to the causes of sex differences pri-marily fall into the biological (essentialist) and social psychological (constructionist) domains. Wood and Eagly (2002) broadly summa-rize these positions: "Essentialist perspectives emphasize the basic, stable sex differences that arise from causes that are inherent in the human species such as biologically-based evolved psychological dispositions.... Social constructionist perspectives emphasize the vari-ation in sex differences across social contexts that emerges from the means of male and female within particular contexts" (p. 700). Al-though essentialist theories have been proposed from other perspectives, pertaining to parenting (Chodorow, 1978), moral development (Gilligan, 1982), and "ways of knowing" (Belenky, Clinchy, Goldberger, & Tarule, 1986), biological and evolutionary theories are the predom-inant ones.

Evolutionary theories postulate that basic sex differences are the re-sult of the adaptations of ancient men and women to distinct survival problems. In brief, sex differences in psychological attributes stem from different reproductive pressures and levels of parental investment, and mate selection (Buss, 1995; Buss & Kenrick, 1998; Geary, 2000). Nur-turance and relational qualities were adaptive for women as they ex-perienced pregnancy, childbirth, and child rearing. Women needed to be more selective about mates because they invested more in the off-spring and preferred males who could provide and protect successfully. Long-term mates were in their best interest and that of their offspring; thus, women historically have competed for more socially dominant, competitive, and aggressive men (Kenrick & Li, 2000). As men com-peted for sexual access to women, aggressiveness, competitiveness, and risk taking evolved because these traits increased their chances of being selected.

Men's control over women's sexual behavior and their sexual jealousy came about to ensure their paternity. Evolutionary psycholo-gists recognize that environmental conditions can influence the pat-tern of evolved traits but continue to attend more to demonstrating the universality of sex differences (Eagly & Wood, 1999). Wood and Eagly (2000) dispute that cross-cultural data support the evolutionary per-spective, showing instead greater flexibility in mate selection and so-cial organizations than that argued by the evolutionary perspective. They contend that the conclusions of evolutionary psychologists far outstrip their findings. Others maintain that the evolutionary per-spective becomes a way to rationalize male domination and aggression toward women (see Marecek, 2002).

Social structural and constructivist theories emphasize contextual and social psychological principles over biological determinism. So-cial role theorists posit that sex differences emerge from men and women assuming different family and occupational roles (Eagly, 1987). The sex differences found in these family and occupational roles may occur for a number of reasons: from the greater status and power as-sociated with men's roles (Geis, 1993), from sex-specific divisions of labor based on differing physical abilities (Eagly, 1987), and from dif-ferent economic and ecological contexts (Wood & Eagly, 2000). Because these factors will vary across cultures and periods, the organization of the social structure and, thus, sex roles will differ as well. Structural theories argue that sex differences and roles are not universal but re-lated to these contextual conditions.

Wood and Eagly (2000) have developed a biosocial model that in-tegrates the essentialist perspective with a social psychological per-spective. Their theory focuses on the "interactive elements between the physical attributes of men and women and the social contexts in which they live" (p. 701). This interactionist perspective is one in "which psychological and physical sex-linked attributes are repeatedly constructed or emergent in response to the evolved attributes of the species, the developmental experiences of each sex, and the situated activity of men and women in society" (Wood & Eagly, 2000, p. 1062).

The theory has the following elements:

1. Men and women are distributed differentially into societal roles, resulting in differences in social behavior.
2. These differences in social behavior occur through many pro-cesses, such as the formation of gender roles, where each sex is expected to have psychological dispositions congruent with the tasks usually performed by that sex.
3. These gender roles become stereotypical of women and men and guide social behavior, shaped by various processes of socializa-tion, expectancy confirmation, and self-regulation.
4. Biological processes such as hormonal regulation and changes work in unison with psychological processes to

direct the sexes toward specific social roles and to improve their functioning in these roles.

5. These causes of psychological sex differences arise from other determinants that have defined the positions of men and women in the social structure: sex differences in physical attributes and the behaviors associated with these differences (such as women's child rearing and men's greater size and upper-body strength) and the contextual factors within a society. These determinants have influenced social roles because of the ability of one sex or the other to perform particular tasks more efficiently in a society that is based on complementary relationships.

Although the biosocial model includes biological components, it differs significantly from the evolutionary theories. Wood and Eagly (2000) dispute that the types of sexual selection pressures that con-tributed to physical sex differences are related to sex differences in dis-positions. In their review of a considerable literature, they show that psychological sex differences in humans have not consistently covaried with physical ones or shared antecedents.

EPISTEMOLOGICAL, SOCIAL CONSTRUCTIVIST, AND POSTMODERN PERSPECTIVES

This chapter so far has focused on the quantitative research pertain-ing to psychological sex differences. Many contemporary theorists question whether quantitative research is the only way, or even a valid way, to approach these issues. They argue that women can be under-stood only in a context that includes the intersection of structural vari-ables such as social, economic, cultural, and ecological contexts. Any human can be understood only as a function of the interaction of race, ethnicity, gender, class, sexual orientation, disability, and age.

Many psychologists also dispute the objectivity theoretically in-herent in quantitative research methodologies, arguing that one's so-cial identity, values, and own social "location" shape all aspects of one's research and conclusions (Harding, 1986). For example, Minton (2000) has made the compelling argument that as North American psychol-ogy was emerging and searching for an identity, it adopted the androcentric biases emerging in early twentieth-century American culture. Leading psychologists of the time such as G. Stanley Hall and James McKeen Cattell were proponents of a cultural shift in the view of masculinity from the turn-of-the-century ideal of gentle intro-spection to a rawer, instinctually based ideal characterized by inde-pendence, aggressiveness, and competitiveness (epitomized by Teddy Roosevelt and the Rough Riders). One manifestation of this shift in psychology was its move away from its roots in philosophy to an em-pirical science where control and "objectivity" replaced introspection and qualitative methods. However, the shift itself occurred in the con-text of particular social identities and values and the power and sta-tus of individual men to define the field of psychology.

Marecek (2002) compares the efficacy of qualitative with quanti-tative research methods in truly understanding women. She describes qualitative inquiry as embedding "psychology in rich contexts of his-tory, society, and culture. It not only re-situates people in their life worlds, but also regards them as reflexive, meaning-making, and in-tentional actors" (p. 259). She contends that qualitative research fre-quently provides more accurate and meaningful information about people's lives because it captures psychological reality through the use of more natural language, allows more depth and input by partici-pants, resulting in a more active collaboration, and dispels false no-tions of objectivity that often pervade one's methods, findings, and interpretations.

Kaschak (1992) has concentrated on feminist epistemology and the deconstruction of patriarchal social structures. She uses an epistemo-logical approach, or making known the rules or meaning of "mean-ing," to illuminate the rules behind the relationships between the sexes. She questions whether sex differences can even be discovered, because in a patriarchal society, "the masculine always defines the feminine by naming it, containing it, engulfing, invading, and evaluating it. The feminine is never permitted to stand alone or to subsume the mascu-line" (p. 5).

By taking the noun *gender* and transforming it into a verb form, Kaschak reveals the epistemology of gender. In a gendered, or "engen-dered," world, gender is not static. Gendering is an active, interactive, and continuous process that is embedded in all aspects of our exis-tence, our relationships, and our meanings. To truly understand the embeddedness of gender throughout our social structures means to recognize that changes in these relationships and structures cannot occur within the context of the same rules. Regarding sex differences, Kaschak (1992) points out that women are penalized for being too feminine as well as too masculine. They are presented with the para-dox that to follow the rules is to be confronted with negative conse-quences for being female, and not to follow the rules is to be confronted with negative consequences for not being female enough. As women walk this tightrope between expressing too little or too much femi-ninity, there are few payoffs for doing what is expected.

Kaschak (1992) offers the Antigone myth as the embodiment of women's roles and sex differences within patriarchal family and cul-tural structures. It is emblematic of the realization that men exist always with the expectation that they are entitled to the love and care-taking of women, just as Oedipus expected his daughter Antigone to sacrifice her life to care for him. In a patriarchal, gendered society, wom-en's development is tantamount to preparation to serve men. Attach-ment to one's mother or other women or even conscious attempts to raise children in nonsexist ways cannot change these relationships or alter the course of gender in the broader context. In fact, in an Oedipal/Antigone world, women are separated from each other, as the role of mothers is to prepare their daughters for the same servitude.

Kaschak (1992) provides examples of the pervasiveness of the embeddedness of gender. Self-concept is "embodied" for women, meaning that it exists only within the context of the female body. For women, esteem is the result of the internalization of a social, rather than an individual, construct that revolves around the attributions given to women by men about women's bodies. *Relational*, according to Kaschak, is defined as being responsible for the success of relation-ships with others or for being sensitive to the needs of others, even when these needs go unexpressed or even unrecognized by men who assert their independence and separateness while expecting nurtu-rance and support.

Other feminist psychologists have considered language, or dis-course, as the primary source of shaping gender relations (and sex dif-ferences) and subsequently of understanding them (Hare-Mustin & Marecek, 1990). From this theoretical perspective, language creates re-ality. Through language, men and women negotiate their relationships and are either enabled or restricted in what they perceive about them-selves and their social relationships. In a patriarchal society, men de-fine the roles of both men and women through discourse, determining when women will manifest feminine behavior and when they are "per-mitted" to venture from strictly sex-typed roles.

Brown and Ballou have provided a feminist critique of sex differ-ences in both personality theories and psychopathological constructs. In *Personality and Psychopathology: Feminist Reappraisals* (1992) and *Rethinking Mental Health and Disorder* (2002), they have exposed the inadequacy of traditional quantitative approaches for understanding women's distress, their psychological development, or the static con-struct called "personality" as it pertains to women. They have pointed out that no psychological theories or constructs that fail to account for oppression in the lives of women can ever effectively be used to understand or treat women.

Worell and Remer (1992) elaborated on the ways in which assumed sex differences in psychopathology have resulted in bias in the psy-chological assessment and diagnosis of women. They have described the process as similar to a self-fulfilling prophecy where the outcomes are determined by initial assumptions. Assumptions of sex differences have had an impact on our understanding of psychopathology be-cause of researchers' "(a) disregarding or minimizing the effect of the environmental context on individual's behaviors; (b) giving different diagnoses to women and men displaying similar symptoms; (c) mis-judgments in selection of diagnostic labels due to sex-role stereotyped beliefs; and (d) using a sex-biased theoretical orientation" (p. 151).

Although the themes of these contemporary feminist theorists are wide ranging, there are common themes in the topics they have pur-sued. Attention to context, the diversity of women's lives, and the im-pact of multiple oppressions, such as race, ethnicity, class, or sexual orientation, on women are central to the work of these theorists. These authors have struggled to move beyond sex or gender as a dichoto-mous category to describe women's development, growth, and dilem-mas in all of their complexity and depth.

3

Women, Work and Discrimination

The context of work for women in the United States was radically altered in 1964. In that year, the U.S. Congress passed a historic civil rights act outlawing discrimination on the basis of race, sex, religion, and national origin. Title VII of that act is the basis for virtually all legal action against sex discrimination in the workplace, including sexual harassment, in the United States today. Interestingly, despite the history of women's rights activism in the United States, insertion of the term *sex* into Title VII of the Civil Rights Act was ac-tually the cynical attempt of some southern lawmakers to block the passage of this legislation, which would protect the rights of black Americans and outlaw the system of segregation that codified dis-crimination against black Americans in many southern states. Before exploring the ongoing effect, however unintended, of that important legislation on working women and women's work in the United States, it is useful to examine the history of women's role in the workplace, especially in the United States, and the psychological issues involved in our understanding of sex and gender.

HISTORY

For as long as there has been work, women have worked. (The issue of at what point in the history of humanity meaningful or productive human activity became "work" is well outside the scope of this chap-ter.) However, the devaluing of women and women's work also has a long history. For example, Mednick (1982), quoting an article from the *Washington Post*, notes that "in the book of Leviticus, the Lord tells Moses what women are worth: three fifths as much as men" (p. 48). This tradition of counting women as less than men found its way into early American law handed down from English common law

Although women have always worked, which women worked and the types of work that women have performed have changed over the ages. Furthermore, within a given historical period, the form of wom-en's work has varied from location to location. Labor economist Fran-cine Blau (1984) tells us that in colonial America, women and children were largely responsible for the making of thread, cloth, lace, clothing, soap, shoes, and candles. All of those activities, generally the province of craft guilds in Europe, were among the typical home work performed by women and children in the British colonies. By contrast, European women during the same time frame were more involved than coloni-al women in fieldwork and less involved in the production activities performed by European craft guilds. In addition, Blau reports that co-lonial women also worked as "tavern keepers, store managers, traders, speculators, printers, and publishers," in addition to the common roles of domestic servant, seamstress, and tailor (p. 298). Among colonial women, it is likely that only the wealthiest of women, with significant servant assistance, did not perform at least some productive labor. Fur-thermore, even those women were often the managers of the home, di-recting the productive activity of their domestic staff.

Later, during the industrialization of America, when production moved from the home into the factories, women continued to engage in productive work. Women were especially involved in the textile in-dustries. The spinning, weaving, and clothing making that women had been performing in their homes was now conducted in the factory. By this time, work was increasingly the task of younger and less well-to-do women, especially black and immigrant women. By the late nine-teenth century, as the frontier closed, the only groups of married women significantly participating in work outside the home were black and immigrant women. However, even in 1890, women still constituted 17 percent of the labor force, and 18.2 percent of women worked outside the home.

The appropriate tasks for women also decreased dramatically. By the end of the nineteenth century, black women typically performed the domestic work and fieldwork that black women had performed un-der slavery. Immigrant women and their children worked in the tex-tile mills. This concentration of women in "traditional" domestic and "women's work" factory jobs continued with little interruption for many years. As late as 1960, the small percentages of women working in pro-fessional or technical jobs were concentrated in the roles of elemen-tary school teacher, nurse, and social worker. Blau (1984) reports that in the 1975 census, half of all working women were employed in only seventeen of the four hundred job occupations listed by the Bureau of the Census, and a quarter of all working women were concentrated in only five occupations.

In 1960, four years before the Civil Rights Act of 1964 was passed, only 37.7 percent of women worked outside the home (Fullerton, 1999). There was no age group in which over 50 percent of women were employed outside the home. Furthermore, most women worked in a limited number of occupations and were seriously underrepre-sented in the ranks of upper management. Jobs were strongly sex and ethnicity segregated. Employment advertisements listed relatively few jobs as open to all candidates, with most being separated into men's or women's openings and often further split by ethnicity. When wom-en worked in jobs that were primarily male occupations, they faced a wide range of discriminatory practices and policies. In addition, so-called protective legislation limited the times and the number of hours women could work as well as the weight they could lift. In other words, women's work participation was constricted by closed doors, narrow hallways, and glass ceilings.

The first effects of Title VII of the Civil Rights Act of 1964 on wom-en's rights were in the reduction of the formal barriers to women's participation and equality in the workplace. The sex segregation of job advertisements was eliminated. So-called protective laws prevent-ing women from working longer hours or lifting heavier weights were eliminated, in some cases because of legal challenges.

In the years since the Civil Rights Act of 1964, a variety of social and economic factors have greatly increased women's participation in the workforce. By 1998, the only age group of women over age sixteen with less than 50 percent participation in the workforce was the group of women over age sixty-five, with a participation rate below 10 per-cent at both time periods.

The shift has been most dramatic for wom-en in the child-rearing years, from ages twenty-five through sixty-four. By 1998, women's workforce participation in this age range had in-creased by roughly 40 percent over 1950 levels. However, the sex seg-regation of work, the underrepresentation of women in the upper ranks of businesses and professions, and the inequity of income be-tween men and women have not disappeared.

This pattern of inequity is the context for claims of sex discrimi-nation, including sexual harassment, in the workplace. Psychology's involvement in these issues developed from the psychological study of stereotyping, prejudice, and gender hostility and the manner in which those phenomena operate in the workplace. These issues are enmeshed in the individual and group claims of sex discrimination, including sexual harassment. In addition, psychologists address the psychological consequences, primarily at the individual level, of ex-periencing discriminatory acts in the workplace.

BASIS OF DISCRIMINATION

Underpinning discrimination against women in the workplace is a set of attitudes and beliefs about gender and work. People have stereotyped views about both the characteristics of women and the characteristics of particular jobs or job duties. They often have difficulty accepting that women can do work that requires the attributes normally ascribed to men, such as intelligence, decisiveness, strength, or aggressiveness. In addition, at least some people respond with hostility when individ-uals fail to conform to the standards expected for their gender. Finally, in many instances, the work environment does not eliminate, and may enhance, the general social power men have over women.

In an extensive review of the literature on stereotyping, prejudice, and discrimination, psychologist Susan Fiske (1998) describes a num-ber of ways in which the cognitive properties of stereotyping create problems for women and other devalued groups. Psychological re-search has demonstrated that stereotypes, or preconceived expecta-tions, affect the information that is sought (Kruger & Clement, 1994; Rusher & Fiske, 1990; Snyder 1984) and the degree to which it is re-membered (Sekaquaptewa & von Hippel, 1994). Thus, an evaluator, supervisor, or hiring manager may fail to identify the stereotype-inconsistent abilities of women to perform "male" tasks and may forget about the evidence of effective performance that women demon-strate. Furthermore, the filtering effects of prejudice also affect the in-terpretation of information. For example, on "masculine tasks," men's successful performance tends to be attributed to ability, while women's positive performance is attributed to effort or luck (Swim & Sanna, 1996; Deaux, 1998).

Stereotyping and prejudice also constrain the way that behavior is interpreted. The finding that the same conduct, especially involving traditionally masculine characteristics such as strength, assertiveness, decisiveness, or goal rather than process orientation, is interpreted pos-itively when performed by men and negatively when performed by women has been confirmed by multiple studies (Eagly, Makhinijani, & Klonsky, 1992). Thus, when women perform their workplace duties in the same manner that men perform them, the women tend to be negatively evaluated, creating quite a double-bind for women per-forming tasks where those "male" behaviors are necessary or desirable.

What makes the actions of stereotyping and prejudice even more problematic is that they can operate without conscious awareness (Dovidio & Gaertner, 1993). Furthermore, social psychologists have re-peatedly demonstrated that stereotypes and prejudices become self-fulfilling prophecies, with the beliefs of the perceiver influencing the behavior of the actor in a manner consistent with the perceiver's orig-inal bias (Snyder, 1984,1992; Word, Zanna, & Cooper, 1974). Finally, calling attention to the stereotype or prejudice does not necessarily inhibit the effect and can make matters worse (Macrae, Bodenhausen, Milne, & Jetten, 1994; Bodenhausen & Macrae, 1996).

Discrimination toward women in the workplace is and has been manifested in a wide variety of actions. Some of those manifestations involve direct discriminatory action, like being denied positions, op-portunities, or training. Other manifestations include gender-based hostility and unwanted sexual attention. Many of the instances of dis-criminatory conduct that women, or members of other devalued and stigmatized groups, experience are not dramatic like the "men only" job signs of earlier years. They are instead what have been called micro-inequities and micro-aggressions (Pierce, 1970), seemingly minor slights, insults, and hostilities that form what has been labeled the mi-nutia of sexism (Rowe, 1981). Because these events are, each by itself, almost trivial, it is difficult for an individual to protest them without seeming thin-skinned or petty. Yet in their cumulative weight, these small acts of omission and commission provide the fabric of a hostile or unwelcoming environment, creating barriers to women's participa-tion and success in the workplace (Rowe, 1990).

One common manifestation of discrimination, whether based on unconscious stereotype or conscious plan, is the perpetuation of the gender segregation of work. Davison and Burke (2000), in a meta-analysis of studies that examined sex discrimination in employment over a thirty-year period, generally found that applicants applying for "opposite-sex" jobs received discriminatory evaluations. Although women now participate in many more than the seventeen job cate-gories that accounted for most of women's work in 1960, numerous studies have found systematic differences in the work assignments of men and women even when their formal job titles were the same (Deaux & Ullman, 1983; Epstein, 1993; Reskin & Padavic, 1994; Res-kin & Ross, 1992). As many have pointed out, one frequent pattern is for men rather than women to be assigned to the tasks and duties that improve their skills and prepare them for career advancement. This pattern of discrimination can be particularly difficult to address because the actual discriminatory effect can take years to accumulate. Furthermore, job assignment within a job classification is generally considered the purview of management rights, protected from inter-vention by union grievance or court scrutiny. Thus, all women and minority men are unable to effectively challenge the discriminatory practice until it has resulted in real differences of skills and experience, differences that can then be offered as a justification for differential rates of promotion or pay.

Some theorists (Glick & Fiske, 1996) have attempted to separate the discriminatory conduct by whether it is based on an overt en-dorsement of male superiority and female inferiority or on a more su-perficially benign endorsement of male and female difference. They label as hostile sexism the attitudes based on an endorsement of male superiority. A second set of attitudes, based on an endorsement of fe-male superiority in such stereotypical female attributes as nurturance, congeniality, and patience, are labeled benevolent sexism. One prob-lem with such distinctions is that although it is possible to develop scales that distinguish between the two attitudes, both are rooted in acceptance of categorical difference between males and females. All such beliefs overemphasize the stereotypical differences between males and females while ignoring the degree to which individual men or women frequently do not differ in the stereotyped direction on any particular attribute.

Other scholars have attempted to distinguish between behavior based on gender hostility and behavior based on sexual desire. Un-fortunately, this is not as easy or clear a distinction as it might initially appear because of the intertwining of sex and sexuality with power, dominance, and hostility. As psychologist Kay Deaux (1998) notes, "Sexual harassment can be primarily sexual or primarily hostile, that is, its goal could be to secure a sexual liaison or to make life uncom-fortable for a woman" (p. 812). Furthermore, as those working in the area of sexual assault frequently report (Koss et al., 1994), even acts that are designed to obtain sexual liaisons can be as much about pow-er, dominance, and submission as about genital stimulation.

LEGAL ISSUES: LEGAL CONTEXT

The psychological processes described above, operating in the histor-ical context of women's limited and devalued role in the work world, provide the context for the various complaints of discrimination that find their way into the legal system. As was noted previously, Title VII of the Civil Rights Act of 1964 is the principal foundation for most claims of sex discrimination in the United States. Prior to the passage of the Civil Rights Act, it was not unlawful to discriminate in employment on the basis of sex. Although some of the actions that can fall under the rubric of workplace sexual harassment, for example, sexual assault, were (and remain) crimes, they were not civil rights violations. Simi-larly, while pervasive or severe harassment may have been (and re-mains) the basis for common law tort claims of negligent or intentional infliction of emotional distress, assault and battery, false imprisonment, or invasion of privacy (Lindemann & Kadue, 1999), these did not fall under the banner of federal civil rights or employment law.

In the years since the passage of the Civil Rights Act of 1964, a num-ber of changes have occurred. States and many local governments have passed employment rights laws that parallel and, in many cases, ex-pand the federal protections against discrimination in the workplace. Legal actions have resulted in the abolition of various discriminatory practices such as sex-segregated employment advertisements, which provided formal barriers to women's full and equal participation in the workplace (Bergmann, 1986).

The legal actions brought under Title VII of the Civil Rights Act of 1964, as amended by the Civil Rights Act of 1991, can provide injunc-tive relief, forcing employers to rectify the discriminatory conduct. In addition, in some cases, monetary damages for lost wages and bene-fits, or even punitive damages, can also be awarded. However, mone-tary damages are generally awarded only when the discrimination has been intentional. Punitive damages are justified only when an employ-er acts with "malice or reckless indifference to the federally protected rights of an aggrieved individual" (Lindemann & Kadue, 1999, p. 317; for further discussion of damages, see EEOC Policy Guidance on Com-pensatory and Punitive Damages under the Civil Rights Act of 1991).

One of the many legal controversies developing from Title VII has involved the issue of "mixed motives," that is, situations where an em-ployer takes an action in part because of "legitimate" reasons and in part because of discriminatory reasons. This issue is critical for legal actions concerning discrimination in the workplace because employ-ment decisions are rarely justified purely on the basis of discrimina-tory factors. Instead, it is the discriminatory results of the psychological processes, like stereotyping and prejudice, that cause employers to dis-cipline women more or more harshly for certain actions than they would men. One could describe the cognitive effects of prejudice as the mental equivalents of flypaper and nonstick coatings. Thus, there is generally some legitimate basis for the employer's action: the woman did make a mistake, use a curse word, or behave rudely, even though the same behavior has not received the same punishment when per-formed by a male employee because all of the woman's past transgres-sions were both noticed and remembered.

This mixed-motive issue was addressed by the U.S. Supreme Court in *Price Waterhousev. Hopkins* (1989). In that case, evidence provided by psychologist Susan Fiske on sex stereotyping was cited by the Court in its decision supporting plaintiff Hopkins, who had been denied partnership because she was overly abrasive and advised by her em-ployer to wear makeup and attend charm school. The Court recently affirmed and extended this decision in *Desert Palace, Inc.* v. *Costa* (2003). In that decision, the Court noted that the Congress, when it amended the Civil Rights Act in 1991, made it clear that it is unlaw-ful for a company to use sex as a motivating factor in employment decisions even though other factors are also involved. This decision resolves almost twelve years of confusing case law concerning the proof a plaintiff must provide to establish that sex was a motivating factor. In *Desert Palace,* the Court stated that the plaintiff must estab-lish only by a preponderance of evidence that sex was a factor in the decision. This was important because some courts had suggested that plaintiffs must present direct "smoking gun" proof in order to claim sex discrimination.

SEXUAL HARASSMENT: A SPECIAL CASE

Sexual harassment is a somewhat complex issue, with discussion made more difficult by the fact that while the phenomenon is quite old, the term itself did not exist when the Civil Rights Act of 1964 was passed (Bularzik, 1978; Farley, 1978; Baker, 1989). From the fictional stories of female servants to the documented reports by female slaves and wage workers, the narrative of women being pressured or forced into sexual acts in the context of work is an all-too-common report. What is newer is the social recognition that such conduct is wrong and the legal apparatus for complaints about it. As late as the 1980s, male man-agers and supervisors, when challenged by a government agency in California about demanding sex from women as a condition of em-ployment, were "surprised in many cases that such behavior was against the law" (Coles, 1986, p. 91).

The legal system, even after the passage of the Civil Rights Act, took some time to recognize sexual harassment as an unlawful act. Quite early in the legal interpretations of the Civil Rights Act, the Equal Em-ployment Opportunity Commission (EEOC) recognized that Title VII prohibits harassment. The courts supported the EEOC position that Title VII creates an affirmative duty for employers to provide a work environment free from harassment. Court decisions, initially on race issues, recognized that harassment created a climate of discrimination *(Anderson v. Methodist Evangelical Hospital,* 1972). The prohibited conduct includes, but is certainly not limited to, berating employees for mistakes, imposing extra duties, restricting privileges, or suggest-ing that a woman does not belong in the job when these actions are based on the employees' sex/gender (or any other of the categories protected under Title VII). In other words, Title VII requires employ-ers to create an atmosphere where employees are not insulted or de-meaned because of their "race, sex, color, religion, or national origin" (Equal Employment Opportunity Commission, 1992, sec. 615).

Although there was an early recognition that Title VII prohibited harassment, initially the courts did not view demands for sexual fa-vors or other forms of sexual conduct as harassment. It was not until 1976 that a federal appellate court opined that a woman who had been fired because she refused the sexual advances of her male boss was the victim of sex discrimination *(Williams v. Saxbe,* 1976). The lower court had ruled that such conduct was the private and arguably natural be-havior of a man toward a woman rather than an issue covered by em-ployment law. However, the appellate court accepted the argument, developed largely by feminist legal scholars (MacKinnon, 1979), that this conduct was unlawful sex discrimination. The rationale is that the conduct is sex discrimination not because it involves sex but because it is conduct that is directed at a target because of her sex. In 1980, the EEOC developed and published guidelines on sexual ha-rassment that continue to be in use. The EEOC guidance on sexual harassment states:

Harassment on the basis of sex is a violation of Sec. 703 of Title VII (of the U.S. Civil Rights Act of 1964). Unwelcome advances, requests for sexual favors, and other verbal or physical conduct of a sexual na-ture constitute sexual harassment when:

1. submission to such conduct is made either explicitly or implicitly a term or condition of the individual's employment;
2. submission to or rejection of such conduct by an individual is used as the basis for employment decisions affecting such individual; or

3. such conduct has the purpose or effect of unreasonably interfering with an individual's work performance or creating an intimidating, hostile, or offensive work environment. [p. 74676].

In 1986, the U.S. Supreme Court, in *Meritor Savings Bankv. Vinson*, upheld the EEOC guidelines on sexual harassment. This case was particularly important because the Court upheld the concept of a hos-tile environment. In *Meritor*, the Court affirmed that the supervisor's demands for sexual favors created a hostile environment even though there was no direct threat of adverse job action.

Several important psychological issues are presented by the Court decision in *Meritor*. First, the standard for what constitutes a legally actionable situation was articulated as when the discriminatory con-duct is severe enough to alter the conditions of employment. Second, the Court asserted that what matters is not whether compliance with the sexual demands was voluntary but whether it was welcomed. The issue of what distinguishes "welcome" from "unwelcome" conduct continues to evolve through case law and interpretation.

In addition, the Court addressed the question of when an employer is liable for the action of a supervisor. One position on this issue, the strict liability position, is that the employer is always liable for the ac-tions of supervisors. The other position is that the employer should be held liable for the action of the supervisor only if the employer was negligent, meaning the employer knew about the supervisor's conduct or should have known about it and failed to take appropriate action.

For over a decade following the *Meritor* decision, the lower courts struggled with this issue. Finally, in 1998, the U.S. Supreme Court is-sued two opinions on the same day establishing clearer guidance on the issue of employer liability (*Burlington Industries, Inc.* v. *Ellerth*, 1998; *Fagherv. City of Boca Raton*, 1998). In these cases, the Court distinguished between situations where a tangible job action occurred and those where the issue was purely about the work environment or atmosphere. The Court stated:

An employer is subject to vicarious liability to a victimized employee for an actionable hostile environment created by a supervisor with im-mediate (or successively higher) authority over the employee. When no tangible employment action is taken, a defendant employer may raise an affirmative defense to liability or damages, subject to proof by a preponderance of evidence.... The defense comprises two necessary elements: (a) that the employer exercised reasonable care to prevent and correct promptly any sexually harassing behavior, and (b) that the plaintiff employee unreasonably failed to take advantage of any pre-ventive or corrective opportunities provided by the employer or to avoid harm otherwise.... No affirmative defense is available, however, when the supervisor's harassment culminates in a tangible employment ac-tion such as discharge, demotion, or undesirable reassignment [*Burl-ington Industries, Inc.* v. *Ellerth*, 1998, p. 765].

This decision appears to place employer liability for supervisors' ac-tions when no adverse job action occurs in roughly the same category as the actions of coworkers.

Since these rulings, the issue of an affirmative defense has become a focus of considerable attention. Although there appears to be a tendency to equate the mere existence of a complaint procedure not used by the complaining party as evidence of an "unreasonable failure," psycho-logical research may ultimately be important. In a recent article, psy-chologist Louise Fitzgerald and her colleagues (Bergman, Langhout, Palmieri, Cortina, & Fitzgerald, 2002) present data that suggest report-ing is often harmful to the complaining party. Their data also suggest that the likelihood of reporting is influenced by the way in which the complaint will be handled. Furthermore, other research suggests that the response of management to issues around sexual harassment affects the likelihood that victims will complain, with positive efforts to stop or eradicate harassment leading to more reporting and negative re-sponses leading to less reporting (Offermann & Malamut, 2002). Unless this issue is adequately addressed, the actual effect of the "un-reasonable failure" provision may be to reward employers for dealing with complaints so badly that victims do not complain.

The legal issues surrounding sex discrimination and including sex-ual harassment will continue to evolve, as they have since 1964. Both congressional action and case law will undoubtedly mold the landscape in new ways. The hope is that these changes will incorporate and reflect the information that psychological research can provide. Without that inclusion, victims will be penalized. For example, it has been important for case law to acknowledge the ubiquitous psychological research find-ing that experience is not gender neutral. Men and women experience and interpret behaviors relating to social interactions differently (Deaux, 1998; Rotundo, Nguyen, & Sackett, 2001). By emphasizing that the law's hypothetical "reasonable person" must be similarly situated (for exam-ple, of the same gender) as the actual victim, case law can incorporate the understandings that psychological research can provide.

SEXUAL HARASSMENT: WHAT ARE WE TALKING ABOUT?

One problem that occurs when discussing sexual harassment is that the experience is trivialized. Some have suggested that the prohibition against sexual harassment is like a code of civility for the workplace and complaints a matter of litigating bad manners. These suggestions miss two critical aspects of both the legal definition of sexual harass-ment and women's actual experience of it. To be legally actionable sex-ual harassment must be severe or pervasive (*Harris* v. *Forklift Systems,* 1993). For many women, it is both severe and pervasive.

Sexual harassment can include instances of rape, forced oral cop-ulation, and other sexual assaults. Some of the most egregious cases reported by those working with women complaining of sexual ha-rassment involve women who "consented" to have sex with supervisors as a condition of employment. While it may seem absurd that a woman would feel compelled to have sex just to hold on to a job, the women targeted by some of the more predatory harassers are extreme-ly vulnerable. Consider, for example, the case of a young woman in a position with insurance benefits, whose husband did not have insur-ance through his job, who had recently given birth to a child with a chronic and severe medical condition that was expensive to treat. Even the less dramatic case of a single mother with limited skills in "the best-paying job I've ever had" faces a difficult dilemma.

Documentation of sexual assault as part of sexual harassment is not limited to anecdotal report. Large surveys of women's experiences in a variety of workplaces have included reports of both demands for sex-ual favors and attempted or successful sexual assaults (Fitzgerald et al., 1988; Fitzgerald & Ormerod,

1993). A 1995 survey of women in the military found that 6 percent reported rapes or rape attempts as part of their military experience (Hay & Elig, 1999). The psychological con-sequences of these assaults are significant. For example, one study of women veterans seeking treatment for stress-related disorders found that for 43 percent of them, rape or attempted rape during their mili-tary service was a significant factor in their need for treatment (Fon-tana & Rosenheck, 1998).

Other forms of harassment not directly involving sexual activity but directed at women violating gender norms either in their own personal appearance or by working in stereotypically male jobs can also be se-vere. Studies of blue-collar workers find between 20 and 40 percent of respondents in traditionally male occupations report attempts by their male coworkers to cause them physical harm (Baker, 1995). Anecdotal reports and individual cases of women in traditionally male occupa-tions such as neurosurgery and investment banking include attempts either to cause physical harm or to sabotage their work product—and thus their professional standing or employment.

Of course, some harassing behaviors are not particularly egregious in isolation. As Mary Rowe (1990) so eloquently describes, they are the micro-inequities and micro-aggressions that gain power, like water dripping on granite, through endless repetition. Much of the early research on sexual harassment focused on delineating the extensive contours of the harassment experience. The early surveys by the U.S. Merit Systems Protection Board (1981,1987) demonstrated that sex-ual harassment was a common and destructive phenomenon among federal employees.

In the late 1980s, Louise Fitzgerald and her colleagues introduced a measure that assessed almost thirty specific behaviors derived from theoretical constructs of sexual harassment (Fitzgerald et al., 1988). Their instrument, the Sexual Experiences Questionnaire (SEQ), with some modifications, is the most widely used and adapted instrument for the measurement of sexual harassment. Research using the SEQ and other instruments has established that the behaviors involved in sexual harassment occur with great frequency (Fitzgerald & Ormerod, 1993; Gelfand, Fitzgerald, & Drasgow, 1995) and that women gener-ally report multiple forms of harassing experiences. Although the fo-cus of sexual harassment research has shifted from documenting its existence to addressing antecedents and consequences, ongoing re-search continues to document the extensive nature of the experience (Schneider, Swan, & Fitzgerald, 1997).

In general, the behaviors comprising sexual harassment occur fre-quently. Some estimates suggest that as many as 50 percent of women will experience sexual harassment at some point in their life (Schneider et al., 1997). Furthermore, although there is a range of behaviors start-ing with offensive verbal behavior, sexual harassment includes physical and sexual assaults and pressure for sexual favors. Although there is some evidence that individual psychological factors are significant for perpetrators of sexual assaults and attempts to coerce sexual favors as a condition of employment (Bargh, Raymond, Pryor, & Strack, 1995), the work environment and the gender stereotype of the work are the criti-cal factors in determining the overall level of sexual harassment in a workplace (Baker, 1995; Gruber, 1998; Schneider et al., 1997).

Women working outside the traditional female occupations have experienced the highest levels of sexual harassment, in both form of harassment and frequency of harassment (Baker, 1995; Harned, Ormerod, Palmieri, Collinsworth, & Reed, 2002). Their experiences can include daily occurrences of multiple forms of offensive conduct. In addition, the experiences of women working in stereotypically male occupations are more likely to include severe forms of nonsexual gen-der-based harassment. However, the data do not indicate that women in traditionally male jobs experience a differential rate of pressure for sexual favors as a condition of employment.

Feminist scholars and even the courts have recognized that sexual harassment is about power, not just about normal heterosexual be-havior. At an almost axiomatic level, people cannot persist in un-wanted behavior when those toward whom the behavior is directed have the power to make them stop. Conversely, research has found that structural changes that increase power inequities, such as the long-term use of temporary workers who lack standing as employees of the company, increase the likelihood that the less powerful workers will experience harassment (Rogers & Henson, 1997). Other factors that have been shown to influence the amount of harassment that occurs in a particular work setting are the number of men in the setting, the gender stereotype of the job, the gender ratio of the job, and the tol-erance of harassment by the organization (Fitzgerald, Hulin, & Dras-gow, 1994; Yoder & Aniakudo, 1996).

PSYCHOLOGICAL CONSEQUENCES OF SEX DISCRIMINATION

The issue of the psychological consequences of sex discrimination is complex because the variety of experiences that can occur as part of sex discrimination is vast. Sex discrimination can include everything from the experience of being not hired, not promoted, or not retained to the experiences of being insulted, assaulted, or physically injured. These experiences can occur individually but are often combined in a multifaceted pattern of discrimination. Furthermore, the experience of sex discrimination at work is compounded by both the general so-cial devaluation of women and specific social issues such as vulnera-bility to sexual assault, domestic abuse, and poverty (Vasquez, Baker, & Shullman, 2003). Finally, many women also experience racism, an-other powerful source of discriminatory treatment.

There has been relatively little research on the specific psychologi-cal consequences of experiencing sex discrimination in the workplace. Perhaps this reflects the invisibility that accompanies a pervasive social phenomenon, the absence being more noticeable than the presence. Perhaps this reflects the difficulty of studying the effect of something so ubiquitous. Or perhaps the focus of attention has been on the ex-tensive direct economic consequences rather than the psychological. Nonetheless, although it may have become fashionable to think of sex discrimination as something outlawed nearly forty years ago, it con-tinues to exist.

It has been widely suggested that the violence associated with dis-crimination against women is a significant factor in women's depres-sion, a position supported by the research on battered women and rape victims (Koss et al., 1994). One recent study that examined the psychological effects of discriminatory treatment based on sex found that women were more negatively affected by such experiences than were men (Schmitt, Branscombe, Kobrynowicz, & Owen 2002). One suggestion for this finding is that women experience the negative treat-ment as a confirmation of the pervasive discrimination against wom-en rather than a random act. Each negative experience may serve as a warning of more to come. It may also be that current experiences of discriminatory conduct based on sex trigger memories of prior mis-treatment based on sex, memories that women are immensely more likely to have than are men.

The negative consequences of sexual harassment have received somewhat greater research attention than sex discrimination in gen-eral. This may reflect the greater ease of studying a phenomenon that is more specifically focused. Or it may be that the legal attention to sexual harassment and the need to document damages caused by it has spurred research interest. Regardless, a number of studies docu-ment negative occupational and psychological outcomes as a result of experiencing sexual harassment (Glomb, Munson, Hulin, Bergman, & Drasgow, 1999). It is evident that the experience of sexual harass-ment decreases job satisfaction and increases the intent or desire to leave the job not just in the United States but in other countries and cultures where the effects of sexual harassment have been studied (Shaffer, Joplin, Bell, Lau, & Oguz, 2000; Wasti, Bergman, Glomb, & Drasgow, 2002).

Studies have found a variety of negative psychological and health outcomes as a result of sexual harassment. Women who have experi-enced sexual harassment involving sexual pressure are more likely than other women to be suffering from depression or posttraumatic stress disorder, even as long as eleven years after their harassment experi-ence (Dansky & Kilpatrick, 1997). Other research has linked sexual harassment to a variety of psychological and health outcomes (Koss, 1990; Schneider et al., 1997), including increased nausea and headaches (Goldenhar, Swanson, Hurrell, Ruder, & Deddens, 1998) and eating disorders (Harned & Fitzgerald, 2002). More subtle psychological effects of harassment are also found, including reduction in self-confidence (Satterfield & Muehlenhard, 1997). Obviously, the experi-ence of sexual harassment can be a significant stressor.

When the effects of race and ethnicity on the experience of sexual harassment have been examined, the picture has been somewhat un-clear as to whether levels of sexual harassment increase, decrease, or remain the same across ethnic or racial groups. There is some indica-tion that this may reflect the availability of multiple causal expla-nations for the harassing or discriminatory experiences of women in ethnic groups for whom racism is a common experience (Buchanan & Ormerod, 2002; Yoder & Aniakudo, 1996). Even when the behavior directed at a woman of color is explicitly sexual, it may be experienced as an outgrowth of racial prejudice or privilege, especially if the per-petrator is from the majority culture. Others have suggested that the instruments used to assess sexual harassment have not been cultur-ally sensitive, thus failing to capture important information about the experiences of women not from the majority culture (Cortina, 2001). It is quite likely that both factors are important.

WHAT HAPPENS WHEN WOMEN COMPLAIN?

In a perfect or just world, sexual harassment would not occur. But if it did, it would certainly disappear when the targets of the harassment confronted it or complained about it. Unfortunately, both data and the anecdotal experiences of those who have experienced harassment provide painful evidence that we do not live in a perfect or even just world. The research to date suggests that the failure of most women to confront harassers or seek organizational relief may well reflect wis-dom and a lack of real power rather than complicity or a lack of as-sertiveness (Bergman et al., 2002; Fitzgerald, Swan, & Fischer, 1995; Cortina & Magley, 2003). While some early self-report data, from a time when there was less general awareness of the inappropriateness of making sexual remarks and advances in the workplace, suggested that telling the harasser to stop the behavior was generally associated with positive outcomes (U.S. Merit Systems Protection Board, 1987), more recent data sug-gest the opposite (Hesson-McInnis & Fitzgerald, 1997; Stockdale, 1998). Those who confront the harasser do not report improved out-comes and often experience worse outcomes. This may reflect prob-lems with the original methodology, or it may reflect the effects of changing awareness. While an individual might have innocently be-lieved that sexual remarks, innuendo, and requests for sexual favors were appropriate in the workplace of the 1980s, such behavior today represents a more conscious decision to ignore prohibitions against sexual harassment.

In a recent examination of the factors associated with better and worse outcomes, Fitzgerald and her colleagues found that it was not reporting itself that resulted in negative outcomes but the response of the organization to a report of harassment (Bergman et al., 2002). In organizations that are tolerant of sexual harassment, the outcome for those who report is likely to be worse. This quite probably reflects both the failure of the organization to take adequate steps to stop future ha-rassment and a tolerance for retaliation against a complaining party. Working in a traditionally male job was also associated with a greater likelihood of negative consequences for reporting.

These findings are particularly important because the conventional wisdom is that women should confront harassers and complain if the initial confrontation is unsuccessful. The popular perception has been that the finding that most women do not confront their harasser and even fewer make formal complaints is a reflection of a failure or weak-ness. Organizational training generally encourages women to com-plain, and many organizational policies stress the importance of victims' making complaints. Even the courts, with the previously dis-cussed standard allowing an affirmative defense for employers against harassment charges if women have not used complaint procedures, appear to be endorsing the expectation that women should confront and complain. Fortunately, the language of the court in requiring that women not unreasonably fail to make use of complaint procedures leaves the court with the opportunity to respond to the reality of the consequences for reporting in an organization where harassment is tolerated and retaliation condoned.

A HYPOTHETICAL CASE: STEP BY STEP

To understand some of the reasons and ways that reporting can make life more difficult for the targets of discrimination and harassment, it may be useful to follow the process step-by-step. Taking as a hypothet-ical example a woman in a blue-collar environment, let us follow her steps in confronting and complaining about harassment. Although this example is hypothetical, all of the facts are similar to actual situations. First, our hypothetical victim may decide to tell her coworker that she is offended by his crude behavior. If, as is often the case, one rea-son for his conduct was his animosity toward the presence of women in his workplace, the information that she is upset by his conduct will increase it, not reduce it. Having failed to resolve the problem through direct confrontation, our victim now goes to the supervisor. If he takes no action or is dismissive of her complaint, she will feel more victim-ized, and her harasser may feel free to step up the harassment. If the supervisor takes disciplinary action but the work culture does not view harassment as a violation of the culture's code of conduct, the harasser and his coworkers may now view the victim as both a "wimp" and a "snitch." Harassment may not decrease, and retaliation, in the form of either hostile actions or social hostility and isolation, may occur. If there is hostility between the work group and management, both the likelihood and level of retaliation may be significant. Our victim is also in trouble if she is in one of the work cultures, like law enforce-ment, where complaining about a coworker is a serious violation of the informal work group ethic, that is, a code-of-silence culture.

Our victim now may find her situation becoming increasingly in-tolerable. The harassment may not have stopped, but retaliation is oc-curring. The supervisor may view her as a problem, since the turmoil may be interfering with the normal operation of his crew. This is es-pecially likely if the supervisor does not view harassment as an im-portant issue. Furthermore, since the supervisor failed to notice and stop the harassment before our victim found it necessary to complain, it is likely that he (or she) is tolerant of harassment.

Our victim now moves up the chain, complaining to human re-sources (HR). The pattern repeats, now at a higher level. If the HR rep-resentatives take no action or inadequate action, this again signals the supervisor and the work group that harassment is acceptable behav-ior. If HR takes action, then the potential for retaliation again in-creases. Unless the workplace culture really endorses the belief that what the harasser has done is not only wrong but a greater wrong than being a "snitch," then negative social consequences are the minimum reaction our victim can expect. Since most actions by HR will require an investigation to substantiate the victim's complaint, it is quite prob-able that the work group will close ranks to protect the harasser.

Our victim may now find her life becoming unbearable. Even if the original conduct has ceased to occur, she may find herself operating in an increasingly hostile environment. Her coworkers may ignore or insult her. Her every error and failing may be noticed, and the pres-sure of the social hostility may lead to an increase in her absenteeism and a reduction in the quality of her work performance. If this is a workplace where harassment is generally tolerated, she will be viewed as a problem. Her supervisor, now convinced that she is trouble, may begin to discipline her, perhaps even with the encouragement of upper management.

At this point, our victim may seek outside counsel and file a com-plaint. The organization, fearing large monetary damages, may now attempt to defend itself rather than step up its own efforts to correct the problem. Thus, efforts to end the harassment will stop, and efforts to prove that the company has done nothing wrong will begin or in-tensify. In many organizations, these attempts to prove that the orga-nization has done nothing wrong will also include attempts to paint or portray the victim negatively. Her work performance may be de-graded. There may be an effort to prove that she behaved in ways that show she welcomed any and all of the offensive conduct. Finally, es-pecially if her legal claim includes any suggestion of psychological damages or if she has quit the job because of the harassment or retal-iation, the employer may try to prove that she was emotionally un-stable before the harassment began.

A review of this hypothetical example identifies several critical is-sues. First, and arguably most important, what is the organization's ethic about sexual harassment? This ethic is probably closely related to the organization's general view about women and about how people are to be treated. In an environment where women are viewed nega-tively and racism or other forms of prejudice and intolerance are con-doned, the complaint, not the offensive conduct, is likely to be viewed as the problem. In such an environment, complaining is not likely to make the situation better. Second, and somewhat related, is the ques-tion of the relationship between the various levels and groups within the organization. In an organization where there is considerable hos-tility between front-line workers and management, or between the pro-duction and performance groups and HR (or, in police work, internal affairs), there is an increased probability that a complaint may get en-meshed in that conflict, with predictable negative consequences to the complaining party. Given the all-too-possible consequences, it is easy to understand why some harassment victims have described the deci-sion of whether to complain as like trying to decide what to do on the sixteenth floor of a burning building, with the fire escapes already in-flamed: Jump or burn?

CONCLUSION

The long history of discrimination at work has not been ended by the Civil Rights Act of 1964. Although blatant discrimination is less com-mon than in the past, many subtle and not-so-subtle forms of discrimination against women continue. The segregation of work remains a problem, with some evidence that occupations become feminized, with men leaving, rather than gender neutralized once women enter those fields in significant numbers. Women continue to earn less than men do even when controlling for occupation and experience.

Yet the picture is not entirely gloomy. Certainly the situation for women in the workplace has improved in the forty years since the Civil Rights Act of 1964 was passed. There are many women alive today who do not realize that their mothers or grandmothers grew up in a world where they were not allowed to hold certain jobs—a world where women could be refused any job simply because the company wanted to hire a man. And there are companies and workplaces where sexual harassment is not condoned and where respecting the dignity of all is expected. However, as long as the categories of male and female are viewed as significant determinants of who should do what work, the problems of discrimination in the workplace are likely to persist.

4

Sexual Harassment: Organizational Perspective

Human resource (HR) management has two con-stituencies and a dual agenda when it comes to responding to sexual harassment allegations: it must protect employees from harassment and protect management from the potential liability associated with harassment. Although there is the inherent potential of a conflict, that should not preclude a professional HR department from adequately protecting the rights of all parties, including those of the alleged ha-rasser. In fact, "doing the right thing" by the HR department is the best protection for everyone involved.

Following generally accepted HR management practices should en-sure that any harassment is promptly stopped and precluded from re-curring (as much as is reasonably possible), and that the accused harasser is warned against retaliation. It also should trigger an inves-tigation designed to determine what, if anything, actually happened and who is responsible. Nothing can be assumed or taken at face value. False accusations are as dangerous as lack of action. A professionally conducted investigation serves the interests of all of the participants: the organization, the alleged victim, and the alleged harasser.

An investigation is the best management defense and the best of-fense against both actual sexual harassment and false accusations of sexual harassment. For all these reasons, triggering a rapid neutral in-vestigation of any alleged sexual harassment has become a significant management priority. An effective investigation is a critically impor-tant weapon in responding to allegations of sexual harassment.

THE DEFINITION OF SEXUAL HARASSMENT

Both the federal and state governments create and enforce laws cover-ing workplace behavior such as harassment. For example, according to the Fair Employment and Housing Act in California, harassment be-cause of sex includes sexual harassment, gender harassment, and ha-rassment based on pregnancy, childbirth, or related medical conditions. The Fair Employment and Housing Commission regulations define sexual harassment as unwanted sexual advances, or visual, verbal, or physical conduct of a sexual nature. The Department of Fair Employ-ment and Housing goes on to explain that the definition includes many forms of offensive behavior as well as gender-based harassment of a person of the same sex as the harasser.

CONDUCT PROHIBITED ON THE JOB

By way of example, the Department of Fair Employment and Hous-ing in California is committed to preventing the following activities at work:

- Unwanted sexual advances
- Offers of employment benefits in exchange of sexual favors
- Reprisals made or threatened after a negative response to sexual advances
- Visual conduct such as leering, sexual gestures, display of sexu-ally suggestive objects or pictures, cartoons, or posters
- Verbal sexual advances or propositions
- Verbal abuse of a sexual nature, graphic verbal commentaries about an individual's body, sexually degrading words used to describe an individual, suggestive or obscene letters, notes, or invitations
- Physical conduct such as touching, assault, impeding, or block-ing movements

This is a rather comprehensive overview of some of the issues with which HR management professionals and experts must be prepared to respond to the challenges of sexual harassment allegations and the en-suing investigations. Although these are the specifics of the Depart-ment of Fair Employment and Housing in California, many of these concepts are more universal and generally reflected in equal employ-ment opportunity commission guidelines as well.

WHAT DOES MANAGEMENT REALLY THINK?

Management believes that most allegations of sexual harassment are either bogus or the result of a misunderstanding between the parties, often emanating from consensual relationships "gone bad." It is rare that an executive today would knowingly tolerate actual sexual ha-rassment. Yet managers tend to lose objectivity when they become in-volved in situations and relationships that may result in allegations of sexual harassment. From a corporate perspective, the situation is often compounded by the "strict liability" typically associated with sexual harassment by managers. The employer will be held legally responsi-ble for the harassing behavior of managers, and the corporation will be required to pay any court-ordered compensation to the victim.

Given the prerogative, management would probably prefer that employees not engage in romantic (read sexual) relationships. But the reality is that they will, and nobody gets too excited about it until some-one alleges sexual harassment or files an administrative complaint or lawsuit. The work environment constitutes the bulk of most people's lives, so it is not surprising that personal relationships do occur there. Also, most management efforts to preclude such activity are perceived as violating personal privacy, and they end in failure.

In general, these relationships are not a huge problem except when managers and subordinates are involved. That is why most organiza-tions prohibit romantic relationships only between direct reports, although they often miss the point that strict liability might apply to anyone in a management capacity. However, a lot of effort may be expended in defining who is actually a manager from a legal perspec-tive. At the very least, organizations should put these policies in writ-ing and follow up and reinforce them through training.

WHO IS EXPLOITING WHOM?

The question of which party in a relationship is exploiting the other is tricky, and there is no consistently correct answer. Perhaps "it de-pends" is the right response. Certainly in the past, there was less am-biguity. While management may have preferred not to deal with sexual harassment, when it emerged as an issue, the accuser (then typically a woman) was generally honest and motivated primarily to end the harassment. Today things are less clear. Sexual harassment remains all too prevalent, but frivolous accusations are common as well.

Frivolous accusations encompass the continuum from misunder-standings and misinterpretation of conduct and motives to outright disingenuous charges designed to blackmail an organization for mon-ey or to avoid confronting genuine performance deficiencies. As an investigator, I believe that I have encountered each of these variations, along with instances of genuine harassment, of course.

From a management perspective (and not simply an HR manage-ment perspective) there is usually a strong desire to discourage sexual harassment because of the obvious consequences to the organization. But there is also a level of skepticism as to the legitimacy of many claims, often as a function of the prior experience of management in what ap-pear to be similar situations. (This is how we all make judgments, in-cluding juries.)

When management is involved in the harassment, everything changes and the motivation to "do the right thing" becomes less clear. But en-lightened management is even more vigilant in such circumstances be-cause of strict liability as well as the obvious appearance issues.

ORGANIZATIONAL CLIMATE AND TRAINING

Industrial-organizational psychologists and most managers recognize that company culture has a significant role in determining how various policies will be perceived, interpreted, and followed. Most companies truly want and expect that their HR management policies will be ad-hered to. However, there is a difference in the nonverbal communi-cation that may be perceived as supporting—or undermining—the official policies.

It is rare that an organization deliberately sabotages its HR policies by its actions. But it is a common observation that companies may in-advertently shift the salience of their policies by the way that their man-agers conduct themselves in the presence of other employees and managers. That is why it is important for management (especially se-nior management) to be careful about its own behavior and vigilant about the behavior of others. An inappropriate casual remark by an influential manager may begin to subvert an entire program of for-mal training.

Training is usually an effective vehicle to reinforce the fundamen-tals of antiharassment and antidiscrimination policies. It is also an op-portunity to influence organizational climate in a desired direction. To have maximum impact, it is useful to establish periodic reference points as to a company's culture and values. A dynamic, interactive, and per-ceptive trainer is a wonderful asset in shaping organizational climate.

It is still the informal culture of an organization that has the great-est impact on how women are regarded and treated in most organiza-tions, and informal cultures are unfortunately quite resistant to change. That is why it is essential that management be committed to do the right thing over the long haul and not to accept compromise, even at an in-formal level.

DISCLOSURE AND "EQUAL OPPORTUNITY" HARASSMENT

Just as in the movie *Disclosure*, where the character played by Demi Moore harassed the character played by Michael Douglas, a female ha-rassing a male does occur, though not with great frequency. Never-theless, it is increasing as women gain organizational power and the perverse "perks" that are associated with that power.

In my own recent experience as an expert witness and HR man-agement consultant, I note that same-sex sexual harassment is in-creasing even more rapidly in organizations today, typically, but not exclusively, male on male. Perhaps it is simply a function of greater re-porting frequency, but that usually tracks the frequency of occurrence. Sometimes it appears as though it is confined to gay employees and sometimes appears to be triggered by the unilateral perception of the other party's being gay when in fact he is not. Not surprisingly, that misinterpretation is likely to trigger a sexual harassment complaint.

An even more troublesome issue from a management perspective is the use of a cross-complaint of sexual harassment as a proactive, though deceptive, defense against the original complaint. And in real organizational life, sexual harassment victims, such as that played by Michael Douglas in the movie, rarely get the fortuitous break that un-covers the truth that he received. Making life even more complicated, there often is ambiguity as to who may have initiated the contact or a proposed relationship.

Disclosure alludes to but does not fully address the situation in which a relationship is initiated consensually and then either party decides to end it unilaterally. Anyone has a right to do that, but it may have some unintended consequences in a corporate environment. Re-sentment by the spurned party may trigger a bogus sexual harassment complaint. Or the spurned party may not get the message and may continue to pursue the failed relationship, thus triggering a good-faith sexual harassment complaint, though perhaps one that was due to a legitimate misunderstanding.

What is the correct thing for management to do under these cir-cumstances? It is not always clear other than the need to investigate any and all reported complaints of sexual harassment, to stop harass-ment that is determined to be occurring, and to attempt to preclude retaliation following a complaint.

THE RECKLESS MANAGER

Reckless managers—those that act rashly, impulsively, or irresponsibly— pose a serious risk to a company. It is too easy to ignore their behavior as immature and brush aside their comments as not to be taken serious-ly. But their colleagues and subordinates (and the courts) may not view it that way.

Most companies understand that they bear some level of respon-sibility for the conduct of their managers and supervisors. Depend-ing on the circumstances, adequacy of responses, and jurisdiction, this may range from strict liability to no liability.

Reckless managers are often regarded and treated as "the life of the party." Sometimes they are respected for what is viewed as their "candor and directness"; that is, they say what they think. Unfortunately, this level of candor and lack of understanding is a double-edged sword. No one, especially the reckless manager, can correctly anticipate how in-dividuals will react to others' language, gestures, and contact.

Reckless managers need to be exposed to the potential consequences of their behavior, which they may regard as innocent. And the orga-nization may wish to document the exposure. Such sensitization can be accomplished in a variety of ways:

- Senior management must set a good example. Nothing under-mines desired management behavior as much as senior manage-ment's violating it, even in jest.
- Establish and publish guidelines. Do not make anyone guess (or assume) how they are expected to behave.
- Train all staff in their responsibilities regarding appropriate behavior. Do not assume that good behavior is obvious. It is not. Encourage everyone to confront and report violations.
- Reinforce the training. Do not assume that training needs to take place only once. That may be adequate, but it may not be.
- Document the training and the participants. This obvious step can prevent having to scramble to respond to future claims that the company was negligent by not providing adequate training.
- Employ a multimodality approach to sensitization. Use training tapes, professional training, written antiharassment and anti-discrimination guidelines, management reinforcement, and appropriate discipline to support the message.
- Use management by walking around frequently and randomly. Never permit managers or supervisors to control access to those who report to them. Doing so could inadvertently encourage misbehavior.
- Practice a true open-door policy. This has tremendous utility in shaping good management behavior and constraining reckless behavior if practiced judiciously.
- Investigate alleged infractions. A professionally conducted inves-tigation continues to be among the best defenses against sex and race discrimination and harassment claims.
- Confront violators immediately, and take appropriate action. Permitting misconduct to go unchallenged sends an inappropri-ate message to everyone.
- Protect employees against retaliation. All organizations are ob-ligated to do whatever is reasonable to protect accusers and wit-nesses from the possibility of retaliation. The consequences of not guarding against foreseeable and

demonstrated retaliation may be more serious than for the initial alleged harassment.

Reckless Managers and Egocentricity

The *Dictionary of Psychological and Psychoanalytical Terms* (English & English, 1966) defines egocentric as "concerned with oneself; preoc-cupied with one's own concerns and relatively insensitive to the con-cerns of others, though not necessarily selfish" (pp. 171-172).

Reckless managers tend to focus on themselves, not on how their behavior affects others. That is why they need coaching, mentoring, and perhaps discipline. They may have the leadership qualities needed to be effective, but they often come with considerable baggage. This situation must be dealt with in such a manner as not to intrude on these individuals' rights and privacy.

The risk problem is that egocentric managers are not likely to un-derstand how their behavior is perceived by subordinates. Whether this is due to selective perception, selective listening, or simply arro-gance and insensitivity as to how others react to their words and con-duct, reckless managers proceed as though only they matter. It is management's task to try to control the destructive interpersonal con-sequences of someone's reckless conduct in order to mitigate liability in the workplace.

The 80/20 Rule

While reckless managers may constitute no more than 20 percent of all managers, they account for more than 80 percent of all HR liability and exposure in the workplace. (In fact, the ratio may be more like 90/10.) This means that a very small proportion of management and supervi-sory staff (typically only one person in a smaller company) will account for the overwhelming majority of interpersonal conflict, employee dis-satisfaction, employee grievances, government agency complaints, legal and insurance costs, liability exposure, and senior management re-sources (a cost that is frequently overlooked).

It is ironic that the 20 percent of managers who are reckless may also be among the most productive managers (though they probably do not account for as much as 80 percent of overall managerial productivity and effectiveness). Even so, the corporate risk that they impose is cer-tainly not worth retaining them in their reckless mode. However, their high-performance potential creates a strong reason to do everything possible to try to coach, correct, and, when possible, retain them.

Dealing with Risky Behavior

There are few absolute thresholds for reckless managerial behavior that automatically trigger the need for immediate termination. The rights of all parties need to be protected and balanced, but this should not be used as an excuse to retain reckless managers who engage in unacceptable behavior, especially after they have been warned.

A pattern of warnings followed by repetitive risky conduct may substantially increase the vulnerability to later litigation—frivolous or legitimate. It is almost always a professional HR management/ legal judgment call. Managers should guide themselves accordingly. It is part of the challenge and responsibility of being in charge.

Examples of Reckless Management Behavior

A staffing manager did not pick up on a number of cues that his staff did not appreci-ate his interest in their personal affairs. He also had an unfortunate habit of making what he thought were innocuous comments about the attire of his female staff, despite being cautioned about the practice.

He also was a "touchy-feely" sort of manager, and despite being repeatedly warned to avoid all physical contact, he was eventually ter-minated for touching the hair of one of his employees after she initiated a complaint against him. He truly believed that his conduct was innocuous.

A corporate manager repeatedly took advantage of his powerful position—and effec-tive performance—to encourage women who reported to him to "entertain him" when he visited them during field trips. His misconduct was conveniently overlooked by other management because his operation was quite profitable. He had a history of sim-ilar difficulty with prior employers. He was eventually terminated after investigation of a documented complaint. He knew his conduct was inappropriate, but he probably thought he was too powerful and important to be held accountable.

SEXUAL HARASSMENT INVESTIGATIONS AND THE ROLE OF HR EXPERTS

The universal issue that appears on both sides of sexual harassment lawsuits is the timeliness and quality of the sexual harassment inves-tigation that should have been triggered by the sexual harassment complaint. My experience is that the quality and timeliness of the in-vestigation are among the most pivotal issues that courts consider in assessing the conduct of the company accused of sexual harassment. A professionally executed sexual harassment investigation is the most effective deterrent against frivolous litigation and the best defense against liability when harassment has actually occurred.

Preparation for the Investigation

In preparing for the investigation, management should review the writ-ten sexual harassment complaint, which should have been solicited at the beginning of an investigation. This will avoid accusations of con-veniently evolving stories and circumstances in addition to obtrusive measurement error. (Obtrusive measurement occurs when an inves-tigator changes the facts and circumstances by the very process of the investigation—obviously not a desirable outcome.)

Management should also determine whether the sexual harassment investigator has reasonably assessed the individuals privy to informa-tion about the alleged harassment before the actual investigation. They must be prepared to explain why any individual so identified might not have been interviewed for corroboration. Management may also need to comment about the nature of the investigation and interview team. A two-person team is ideal, though certainly not essential, for an internal investigation. If two interviewers are engaged, a male-female team is preferable.

Parties to the Investigation

Management should try to determine whether witnesses were told that there would be no retaliation for telling the truth or that their confi-dentiality could not be guaranteed. The experts should also be sen-sitive as to whether the complainant and witness information was shared only on a need-to-know basis. There is an obligation in an ef-fective sexual harassment investigation to avoid defaming the accused harasser and unnecessarily embarrassing the complainant. It is always important to be aware that both parties have rights in a sexual harass-ment investigation.

Those conducting a sexual harassment investigation also have an obligation to protect the interests and reputations of all parties and should make no a priori assumptions as to motivation and fault. An HR management expert can be particularly effective in examining the facts and circumstances surrounding a sexual harassment investigation to make a determination as to whether the guidelines were followed. At trial, the expert may also be asked to comment about the wisdom of allowing the complainant to confront the accused harasser directly during the course of the investigation. In most circumstances, it is nei-ther advisable nor necessary for the complainant to do this, although ideally, confrontation should have occurred prior to the initiation of a complaint.

The circumstances of any specific complaint may necessitate that the investigators interview other past or current employees who might have been exposed to harassment (if in fact it actually occurred). At trial, an HR management expert may be asked to second-guess the wisdom of those determinations (and the repercussions of the failure to do so).

Requirements of the Investigation

It is important that management understand that there is no single procedure that absolutely must be followed in conducting a profes-sionally appropriate sexual harassment investigation. If, for example, a consultant has produced a guidebook outlining suggested steps for an investigation, it is unlikely that each step is an absolute requirement exactly as articulated. There is leeway in conducting appropriate sex-ual harassment investigations. Investigators must also consider whether an alleged incident is isolated or part of a pattern of harassment in-volving the complainant and possibly others. This may also be a legit-imate area for expert inquiry in making a determination as to whether a pattern and practice exists.

Adverse Impact on Job Performance

A crucial issue in any employment situation is whether the conduct of the employer or its representatives had an adverse impact on job performance. That is a fundamental dimension of any assessment of harassment in the workplace. It is also understood to be an important motivating factor in the passage of antiharassment legislation. An ex-pert should be prepared to comment about that issue and critique the measures used to make that determination.

Issues in the Investigation

An effective HR management expert needs to able to differentiate and explain to a jury the differences among insensitivity, tastelessness, and rudeness, which do not automatically reach the standard for determin-ing that sexual harassment has occurred, unless other circumstances and conditions apply. An effective defense expert should be able to ex-plain these differences to a jury.

The basic issues in most sexual harassment investigations boil down to whether the conduct in question was sexual in nature and whether the conduct was unwelcome in the sense that the complainant neither solicited nor incited it and also found it undesirable or offensive. These sensitive issues require care and finesse in understanding and inter-preting. An expert may also be called on to determine whether the com-plainant or someone representing the complainant properly advised an alleged harasser in a hostile work environment situation that the be-havior was unwelcome.

After a finding that sexual harassment has occurred, there are final issues in determining the appropriate discipline:

- Whether the complainant properly notified the alleged harasser
- The severity of harassment (obviously a judgment call, appro-priate for expert testimony)
- The frequency of harassment
- Previous or concurrent harassment complaints

The conclusion of the investigation is also a subject for possible ex-pert commentary, specifically with regard to sharing the response of the accused harasser as well as the outcome of the investigation with the complainant. An expert will be able to explain to the court that while the claimant should not be permitted to dictate disciplinary pro-cedure or corrective action, if the claim is valid, the claimant's com-fort with a particular outcome could be taken into consideration.

With regard to a sexual harassment complaint that is found to have merit, an expert may need to evaluate whether follow-up mechanisms were required or effective in ensuring that the harassment cease, with little or no probability of recurrence. Furthermore, an expert may be asked to assess whether corrective action was proper in order to stop the harassment, discipline the harasser, and reinforce that sexual ha-rassment is neither acceptable nor tolerable.

Often the outcome of a sexual harassment investigation is incon-clusive or disputed by one or another party. Management should be prepared to determine whether the investigation was concluded with any unresolved material inconsistencies between the parties. An expert may be asked to comment on whether actions taken within that inves-tigation, such as separating the parties and minimizing their inter-action, were appropriate. The expert may also be asked to provide an opinion as to whether such actions could have been accomplished with less detrimental impact on either party's position or reputation.

Liability in the Investigation

An expert's comments can be vital when reviewing the requirement of good faith and fair dealing that is entailed within a sexual harass-ment investigation, especially as it relates to the speed of such an in-vestigation. When there is an attempt to achieve rapid resolution, an expert can determine whether greater speed might have compromised the integrity of the investigation, which is obviously not an acceptable outcome.

Retaliation

There is great sensitivity in HR to issues of retaliation or alleged re-taliation. If that is part of the complaint, an expert may be asked to assess the behavior of the parties before and after the complaint to determine whether there was a change in conduct that might be rea-sonably determined to be retaliation or have the effect of retaliation. Management must assess who initiated the change in conduct (the complainant or the accused harasser) and then determine whether the change was in response to objective performance-related issues in the workplace. Nothing is more critical than precluding the possibility of retaliation after a sexual harassment complaint has been lodged. The HR management expert must be prepared to address any lapses at trial.

PROACTIVE MANAGEMENT AND THE NEED TO CONFRONT WRONGDOING

There are few, if any, areas within HR management that are less toler-ant of procrastination and delay than confronting implications—or certainly allegations—of sexual harassment. Although such encoun-ters are awkward and unpleasant to deal with, it is nonetheless neces-sary to intervene quickly and aggressively to determine if harassment has taken place and to stop it if it has. This is the best possible approach to mitigating any ensuing liability and organizational damage. It should also be obvious.

What may be less obvious is the need to be proactive and confront wrongdoing—but with the utmost sensitivity to the feelings and vul-nerabilities of all the parties in an alleged harassment situation. It is remarkable how everyone loses their composure and their perspective when there is an accusation of sexual harassment. This is not to min-imize the seriousness of a sexual harassment complaint. But no one is immune to overreacting under these circumstances.

The alleged harasser typically encounters a range of strong emo-tions, only slightly as a function of whether this person is, in fact, guilty or innocent of wrongdoing. This apparent enigma is better un-derstood when it is recognized that many harassers do not believe that they are guilty of harassment. If the accused harasser is innocent (or believes that he or she is innocent), the anticipated reaction is anger (at the accuser), embarrassment, and defensiveness. If the accused harasser is guilty, the anticipated reaction is still anger (at the accuser), embar-rassment, and defensiveness.

The accuser also typically encounters a range of strong emotions. It often entails anger (at the harasser or the perceived harasser), embar-rassment, and defensiveness (at possibly having invited or encouraged the harassment).

Witnesses may be initially reluctant to provide damaging infor-mation, especially if management is accused. And unless they are mo-tivated to hurt someone, the typical reaction is annoyance at being asked or occasional indifference. Not surprisingly, it is almost always accompanied by embarrassment.

HR may appear excessively eager to assert its authority and con-front the alleged harasser—or defensive about not having prevented the harassment in the first place. A weak HR manager may appear re-luctant to confront senior management. Finally, HR may be conflicted about its dual responsibility (and loyalty) to protect employees as well as to protect management.

SETTING THE TONE

Management has the (negative) financial incentive to do the right thing when it comes to reining in sexually harassing conduct. It took a while to get there, but the financial consequences of failing to con-trol inappropriate behavior were ultimately most persuasive. Organi-zations did not systematically condone harassment in the past, but it was not a high priority to be proactive and—perhaps intrusive—about confronting it.

A more laudable reason for confronting sexual harassment early is slowly emerging, and it probably reverts to the original rationale be-hind Congress's prohibiting it. Sexual harassment is a form of sex dis-crimination, and sex discrimination was correctly viewed as interfering with anyone's ability to be productive in the workplace. The real in-centive may still be largely economic, and that is probably all right. Rather than interpret this as a condemnation of the capitalist system, it may be more accurate to view it as a serendipitous, self-regulating, and self-corrective feature of a surprisingly wise and enduring system.

Beyond crass motivation, management has an extraordinary abil-ity to influence the behavior of subordinates by their own conduct and example. It is a subtle power but an awesome one. It has the abil-ity to set the tone for future generations of effective and enlightened managers and productive employees. Senior managers should guide themselves accordingly.

5

A Feminist Reconstruction of Work

It is recognized with increasing frequency that organi-zations—in theory, practice, and general discourse—are gendered, ex-emplifying, and in many cases reifying, stereotypically masculine traits (Acker, 1992; Collinson & Hearn, 1994; Ferguson, 1984; Mills & Tan-cred, 1992; P. Martin, 1995). Traditionally, this masculine bias, where noted, has been cast as problematic for women, inhibiting their career progress in organizational settings and contributing to what is com-monly called the glass ceiling (Morrison, White, & Van Velsor, 1987). Re-cent organizational analysis from a feminist poststructuralist perspective, however, is beginning to broaden the implications of studying the gen-dered nature of organizing. Feminist poststructuralist critiques and rereadings of mainstream organizational theories, such as Mumby and Putnam's rereading of bounded rationality (1992), Martin and Knop-off's feminist critique of Weber (1995), and Barbara Townley's reread-ing of human resource management practices (1993), have begun to suggest that the gendered nature of these theories—the way they im-plicitly privilege stereotypically masculine attributes and devalue or ig-nore stereotypically feminine—is problematic in a more general sense.

That is, exploring the gendered nature of these mainstream theories has highlighted the way in which gendered assumptions are potentially problematic not only for women but also for men *and* for organizational effectiveness because they have resulted in narrow, conscripted under-standings of organizational phenomena. Reworking these mainstream theories to include previously ignored or discounted perspectives is serv-ing to challenge many of the organizational "realities" long accepted in the academy and to offer new ways of thinking about organizing.

The research summarized here is offered in this same spirit. It is feminist poststructuralist inquiry that seeks to expand the gendered definition of work by giving voice to a way of working—relational practice—that springs from a relational, or stereotypically feminine, belief system. Like other feminist poststructuralist rereadings of or-ganizational phenomena, it argues that the current, commonsense de-finition of work in organizational discourse is not a passive concept; it is instead an active, although unobtrusive, *exercise of power* that si-lences and suppresses alternative definitions that might challenge the status quo (Clegg, 1989; Flax, 1990; Foucault, 1980; McNay, 1992; Weedon, 1987). Furthermore, it argues that this silencing results not only in certain elements of the experience of work being marginal-ized, but also in an undertheorized representation of these activities— and their impact on organizational output and effectiveness—in the organizational literature.

The study summarized here explores this phenomenon in two steps. First, it gives voice to an undertheorized aspect of the nature of work by making visible, giving language to, and building theory about relational activity as practice in organizations. Then, it explores the gender-power dynamic of the silencing process itself. That is, in addi-tion to expanding the definition of work by detailing a way of working that springs from a relational belief system, this study explores the mechanisms—and the gender and organizational implications of the process—through which this way of working currently "gets disap-peared" from commonsense definitions of real work.

THEORETICAL CONTEXT

The theoretical framing of this inquiry occurs at the intersection of three streams of thought. The first is poststructuralism, a form of post-modern philosophy that, with its emphasis on the relationship between knowledge, discourse, and power, establishes the context of the study and positions it as a challenge to commonsense definitions of work. The second is a feminist reading of the literature on the nature of work that suggests that these commonsense definitions are gendered be-cause they are rooted in the social construction of the public-private dichotomy along gender lines. And the third is a particular type of fem-inist standpoint research, relational theory, that suggests what is likely to be invisible in these gendered definitions. The interplay of these three streams of thought as they relate to the research questions will be explored briefly.

Poststructuralism

Poststructuralism provides the theoretical context for this study. Of the many traits characteristic of poststructuralist thought, three dis-tinguishing features are key to understanding this study, its design and methodology, and the way in which it positions itself as a challenge to commonsense definitions of work, competence, and skill. The first of these three features is that poststructuralist inquiry problematizes the process of knowledge production and conceptualizes it as an exercise of power where only some voices are heard and only some experience is counted as knowledge. That is, poststructuralist perspectives chal-lenge the notion of transcendent or universalizing truth and assert that the very set of rules used to determine if something is "true" or "false" is ideologically determined and is itself an exercise of power intended to maintain the status quo and silence any serious challenge to it (Alvesson & Deetz, 1996; Clegg, 1989; Flax, 1990; Foucault, 1980; McNay, 1992; Weedon, 1987).

A second key feature of poststructuralist inquiry is that it empha-sizes the role language plays in mediating the relationship between power and knowledge. It asserts that it is in discursive practice that social reality and its patterns of dominance are constructed. Indeed, there is no experience, there is no "knowing" self except that which is an effect of discursive practice (Collinson, 1994; Diamond & Quinby, 1989; Fairclough, 1989; Mumby, 1988; Weedon, 1987). From a post-structuralist perspective, then, textual representation is never neutral; instead, it is a powerful means of constructing an ideological world-view that furthers the interest of dominant groups.

This emphasis on textual representation is related to the third dis-tinguishing feature of a poststructuralist perspective: the notion of resistance (Collinson, 1994; Clegg, 1989; Flax, 1990). The exercise of power in textual representation is not absolute but is "contingent, pro-visional, achieved not given" (Clegg, 1989, p. 151). Therefore, it can be resisted using destabilizing strategies, the most familiar of which is deconstruction (Jacobsen & Jacques, 1997). In other words, just as tex-tual representation is used to construct social reality, it can be used to deconstruct this reality. Deconstruction entails challenging unexam-ined dichotomies in the text, revealing suppressed contradictions, and calling attention to what has been hidden, obscured, or invisible (Fair-clough, 1989; Flax, 1990; J. Martin, 1990). Although this type of dis-course analysis typically refers to written text, the same techniques have been applied to the spoken word (J. Martin, 1990) and to ana-lyzing what Jacques (1992) calls "enacted text," that is, the practices and meaningful actions that precede and determine the printed text. Another destabilizing method is to focus on "subversive stories" that challenge the status quo. These usually take the form of personal ac-counts, emotional experience, or life stories of members of a margin-alized group whose voice has been silenced or whose experience has not been counted as knowledge (Alvesson & Deetz, 1996; Ewick & Sil-bey, 1995; Harris, Bridger, Sachs, & Tallichet, 1995).

It is important to note that whatever method is used, this type of inquiry is not intended to replace one social reality with another or to claim one truth is preferable over another, but rather to disrupt taken-for-granted notions and make discussable what has been uncontested and assumed (Flax, 1990; Jacobsen & Jacques, 1997). The goal is to cre-ate what poststructuralists call discursive space, where new ways of thinking might surface. Creating discursive space means offering an alternative interpretation of reality that relaxes taken-for-granted as-sumptions, thereby creating—theoretically—a place where new things can be said and new social structures envisioned (Calas & Smircich, 1989; Clegg, 1989; Mumby, 1988).

These three features of poststructuralist inquiry outline the research terrain of this study. Its goal was to destabilize the definition of work in organizational discourse from a feminist perspective: it sought to problematize the masculine nature of the meta-narrative of knowl-edge production about work in organizational discourse by calling at-tention to the feminine as a voice that has been silenced or obscured. It sought to add this voice to the discourse, thereby momentarily re-laxing taken-for-granted assumptions about the nature of work. And finally, by relaxing these assumptions, it sought to create discursive space in which new, less masculine ways of thinking about work, skill, and competence might be considered.

There are several methodological challenges in designing a field study covering this research terrain. These will be addressed in more depth in the methods section. But first, there are two additional the-oretical positions that need to be established. The first is a rationale to support the claim that the current definition of work is gendered. The second is an identification of the marginalized voice that will be used to destabilize the definition of work and an explanation of how that voice can claim to represent the feminine.

The Definition of Work

Those studying the gendered nature of organizations, the social con-struction of skill, and notions of comparable worth (Acker, 1989,1992; Bradley, 1989; Harding, 1986; Mills & Tancred, 1992; Smircich, 1985) suggest that the current definition of work in organizational discourse is a social construction premised on a gendered dichotomy between the public and private spheres of life. This dichotomy divides the world into two separate, gendered domains: a public work sphere where the dominant actor is assumed to be male and a private family sphere where the dominant actor is assumed to be female. While traditional conceptualizations of this public-private split posit the two spheres as complementary—separate but equal domains that function together for the good of society (Bellah, Madsen, Sullivan, Swidler, & Tipton, 1985; Parsons & Bales, 1955; Perrow, 1986)—these more recent con-ceptualizations problematize the split along two dimensions. The first has to do with the separateness of the two spheres and the second with the way in which they are gendered.

The problem in the separation of the two spheres is that knowledge production in each sphere proceeds independently, resulting in two separate discourses, each with certain "truth rules" and global criteria characterizing activity in its domain (Bailyn, 1993; Ferguson, 1984; Game & Pringle, 1983; Harding, 1986; Nicholson, 1990; Wadel, 1979).

From a poststructuralist perspective, the problem with the sepa-ration of the two spheres is that it is a social construction. Although subject positions operate in both spheres, often simultaneously, the discourse (social practice, structures and language) continues to cre-ate, reinforce, and textually represent them as separate and dichoto-mous (Bailyn, 1993; Bailyn, Rapaport, Kolb, & Fletcher, 1996; Bradley, 1993; Fletcher & Bailyn, 1996; Friedlander, 1994; Parkin, 1993). This sets up a situation in which knowledge from one sphere is likely to be considered inappropriate to the other and thus unlikely to challenge its underlying narrative. As a result, public sphere attributes such as rationality, cognitive complexity, and abstract thinking are often ab-sent from commonsense definitions of work in the private sphere (De-Vault, 1990; Reverby, 1987; Roberts, 1990; Ruddick, 1989). By the same token, private sphere attributes, such as emotionality, caring, and community, are often invisible in commonsense definitions of work and competence in the public sphere (Fineman, 1993: Hall & Mirvis, 1996; Mumby & Putnam, 1992).

This brings us to the second dimension of the problem. If this sep-aration is a social construction, how did it come to be, and what pur-pose is it serving? More to the poststructuralist point, what particular systems of power and inequity is it maintaining? Many feminists sug-gest that at least part of the answer to these questions lies in the gen-dered nature of the split and the way it reinforces patriarchal systems of power. For example, Harding (1986) suggests that the public-pri-vate dichotomy is rooted in the acceptance in Western thought of a more general gender dichotomy between culture and nature where men and masculinity are strongly associated with the public, cultural role and women and femininity with the private, natural role. The re-sult is a gender split in which the notion of growth, effectiveness, and an ideal worker in the public work sphere is conflated with idealized masculinity and where, in the private sphere, these same notions are conflated with idealized femininity (Acker, 1990; Bradley, 1993; Collinson & Hearn, 1994; Gherardi, 1995; Lorber, 1991; P. Martin, 1995; Parkin, 1993). This suggests that assumptions about what is ap-propriate and inappropriate in each sphere are held in place not only by notions of separation but also, and perhaps more firmly, by deeply held images of masculinity and femininity that function to keep pa-triarchal systems of power in place (Acker, 1990; Cockburn, 1991; Con-nell, 1995).

This discussion of the public-private sphere split frames several important features of the study: it not only posits that the feminine is likely to be absent from organizational definitions of work, but also hints at the deeply interior power of a silencing process in which as-pects of work that can be textually represented as congruent with ide-alized masculinity will be considered "real" work and those that are associated with idealized femininity will not (Bradley, 1993; Fletcher, 1994a; P. Martin, 1995). It also begins to give a sense of the way in which giving voice to private sphere, feminine knowledge could momentar-ily disrupt the gender-power dynamic inherent in the current defini-tion of work in organizational discourse.

This brings us to the issue of what voice can be used to bring pri-vate sphere knowledge and its association with the feminine into or-ganizational discourse and how this knowledge can be brought in as a destabilizing story, that is, with its inherent challenge to the discourse intact. To answer these questions, we move to a discussion of relational theory and its positioning as a feminine alternative to masculine the-ories of growth and development.

Relational Models of Growth, Development, and Achievement

First proposed by psychologists and psychiatrists at the Stone Center at Wellesley College (Miller, 1976; Jordan, Surrey, & Kaplan, 1991) and supported by the work of Carol Gilligan (1982), Sara Ruddick (1989), and others (Belenky, Clinchy, Goldberger, & Tarule, 1986; Brown & Gil-ligan, 1992), relational theory and its correlates were developed by listening for and to the experience of women. Although it draws on Chodorow's extension of object relations theory and gender differ-ences in early life experience (1974), it makes no claim to speak for all women or to claim that only women subscribe to it. Nonetheless, it is a theory that positions itself as an alternative to the masculine bias in mainstream theories of psychological, intellectual, and moral growth (Miller, 1976; Gilligan, 1982) that underlie many societal structures.

Relational theory suggests that although the prevailing models of adult growth and achievement are based on public sphere character-istics such as separation, individuation, and independence, there ex-ists an alternative model, called growth-in-connection, that is rooted in private sphere characteristics of connection, interdependence, and collectivity (Miller, 1986a; Jordan, Kaplan, Miller, Stiver, & Surrey, 1991). Unlike mainstream models that emphasize autonomy and the individuation process as central to personal growth and identity, growth-in-connection models emphasize the role of relational inter-actions in the development process. It is important to note that while both mainstream and relational theories of growth encompass both individual and relational processes, it is the preeminence of connec-tion over individuation in the developmental process that gives re-lational theory its potential as a destabilizing alternative voice in organizational discourse and marks it as feminine (Fletcher, 1994a; Hall & Mirvis, 1996; Hall, 1996; Kram, 1996; Liou & Aldrich, 1995).

The basic tenet of relational theory, that growth and development occur best in a context of connection, is further delineated by the iden-tification of specific characteristics of these growth-fostering connec-tions. In other words, growth is conceptualized as occurring not in any engagement or relationship but through a specific kind of rela-tional interaction. These growth-fostering interactions are character-ized by mutual empathy and mutual empowerment, where both parties recognize vulnerability as part of the human condition, approach the interaction expecting to grow from it, and feel a responsibility to con-tribute to the growth of the other. The ability to develop relationally requires certain strengths: empathy, vulnerability, an ability to expe-rience and express emotion, an ability to participate in the develop-ment of another, and an expectation that relational interactions will be sites of growth for both parties involved (Jordan, Kaplan et al., 1991; Miller, 1976). As Miller notes, however, the characterization of these attributes as "strengths" is itself a challenge to the dominant discourse, especially the psychological discourse in which giving preeminence to connection has traditionally been characterized as a weakness or psy-chological deficiency.

Although this model of growth does not presume to speak for all women, it does assert that there are strong forces operating simultaneously to discourage men and encourage women to enact it. These include internal forces based on early development (Chodorow, 1974) and external forces based on socialization and societal expectations of gender-appropriate behavior (Brown & Gilligan, 1992; Gilligan, 1982; West & Zimmerman, 1991). Indeed, Jean Baker Miller (1976) offers a radical view of these societal expectations, proposing that because men are socialized to deny in themselves the relational skills needed to sur-vive psychologically, they rely on women to be the carriers of these traits in society. Thus, society assigns relational activity to women and it be-comes "women's work," a phenomenon that has been noted in organi-zational settings (Huff, 1990; Kolb, 1992). These formulations suggest that enacting a relational model of growth is likely to be a site for the social construction of gender in the workplace, as it is one way of mark-ing oneself "feminine." In summary, this discussion provides the ratio-nale for using relational theory as a surrogate (one of many possible) for a feminist ideology from which to challenge the growth and effec-tiveness model underlying the organizational discourse on work.

RESEARCH PLAN

With this groundwork laid, it is now appropriate to detail the research plan of this poststructuralist field study. The first step in the plan was to collect a potentially destabilizing textual representation of work in an organizational setting. The ideal setting would gain its legitimacy from the extent to which it was an exemplar of public sphere charac-teristics and their underlying logic of growth and effectiveness. The ideal subject would be someone who stood at the "line of fault" (Smith, 1990) between the public and private spheres: that is, someone who was located in two particular and inherently contradictory subject po-sitions in organizational discourse—"woman" and "worker"—and who would embody the contradictory expectations and predispositions at-tending these two subject positions (Gherardi, 1995; Harding, 1987; Morrison et al., 1987). The second step in the plan was to analyze the textual representation of work gathered from these subjects to reveal those practices that were motivated by tenets underlying relational the-ory. Relational theory had been selected on the basis of its legitimacy as representative of feminine, private sphere characteristics and their underlying logic of growth and effectiveness. The third step in the plan was to compare this alternative reality to the mainstream, common-sense definition of work in that particular organizational culture. It was expected that this comparison would reveal the differences between the two and the mechanisms by which the alternative representation of work was suppressed, invisible, or silenced in the dominant discourse. The last step was to take advantage of the discursive space created by destabilizing the commonsense definition of work in order to envision not only new ways of working but also new organizational structures to support them.

The following research questions guided the inquiry:

- Is there evidence that relational practice exists in this organiza-tional setting? If so, what behaviors characterize it? What beliefs, assumptions, and values do these behaviors reflect?
- What are the mechanisms through which relational practice and the belief system underlying it are brought into the dominant discourse and subjected to the sense-making "truth rules" of that discourse?

METHOD

This study was an independent part of a larger action research project focused on gender equity that was conducted over a period of four years in a major high-technology company based in the northeastern United States. At the time the data analyzed in this study were collected, the research team had been on-site for two years, engaged in a process of cultural diagnosis that involved interviewing people at all levels of the organization, shadowing key employees, attending a wide range of technical and staff meetings, and analyzing company documents and policy statements (Bailyn et al., 1996).

The research questions for this portion of the study required three types of data. The first was a "potentially destabilizing textual repre-sentation of work" gathered by observing what Smith (1990) calls "line of fault" subjects; that is, people who live on the fault line between two competing subject positions, such as "worker" and "woman." These data were collected through a method of structured observation mod-eled on that used by Mintzberg (1973) in his study of managers and further refined by Jacques (1992) in his study of female knowledge workers. The design, as adapted for this study, entailed the intensive shadowing of six female design engineers. These six engineers were a sample of convenience, determined by organizational constraints. There were only seven female design engineers in the entire product development team who were available during the time frame. Six were shadowed and interviewed as planned. The shadowing of the seventh, who was in manufacturing design, was aborted after two hours be-cause my presence on the shop floor was so intrusive that note taking was impossible.

The day-long shadowing produced a systematic unselective record-ing of each engineer's interactions with the environment: all encounters with people, objects, data, and systems. Each interaction was recorded in a log detailing the time, location, participants, and dialogue accom-panying the event. At the end of the day, I taped my reactions, responses, and questions about the day's events. The following day, an intensive interview with the shadowee was held in which I walked her, minute by minute, through the previous day's events. This generated the sec-ond type of data—what is generally called contextualizing data—expected to yield the intentions, beliefs, assumptions, and values that comprise the participants' sense making around observed behavior (Alderfer & Brown, 1972; Spradley, 1979). In the interview, I asked an open-ended question for each interaction, such as, "What was this about?" or "What was going on here?" After the engineers got over their initial surprise at the level of detail in my notes, they grew quite com-fortable with this contextualizing procedure, and I would just have to mention an incident with an uplift indicating a question, such as, "Then Dave came by?" and they would fill in the details.

These data were transcribed, encoded, and sorted into categories using The Ethnograph, an ethnographic software program. A list of potential categories was generated based on the attributes of relational theory. This initial list changed as unused categories were discarded and new ones were added as they emerged from the data. The result-ing categories were refined using an iterative process described by Glaser and Strauss (1967, p. 101) as a "constant comparative" method of qualitative analysis. This method entails continually revisiting the underlying principle of each category as new incidents are added in order to refine the principles and allow theoretical precepts to emerge. When the categories had been integrated to the point where there was little overlap between them, a roundtable discussion with participants was held in which these still pıeliminary categories (now numbering six) were shared and reactions invited (Bougon, 1983). The format for the roundtable discussion was unstructured and straightforward. I simply listed the categories with examples of each and asked for reac-tions after all six were described. Data from the roundtable discussion, which had been recorded and transcribed, were used to integrate the categories further, resulting in the four described in the "Findings" section. A name for each category was selected to reflect what had emerged as its unifying property.

For the poststructuralist analysis, a third type of data was required: a representation of the current definition of work in that particular organizational setting. As a high-technology engineering firm, the set-ting met the criterion of being a potential exemplar of the gendered power-knowledge structures generally accepted as underlying orga-nizational discourse (Ferguson, 1984; McIlwee & Robinson, 1992). Three other members of the research team and I gathered data used to represent the manifestation of the definition of work in this setting, using the cultural diagnosis process described briefly above and in more detail in Bailyn et al. (1996) and Perlow (1997). Data-gathering techniques for this cultural diagnosis paralleled those suggested by Levinson, Spohn, and Molinari (1972) for collecting interpretative data for organizational diagnosis and were informed by Schein's de-scription of the elements of organizational culture (1985).

For exam-ple, interview questions focused on eliciting organizational narratives that would help us understand the sense-making frameworks people used to understand things such as the formal and informal reward sys-tems, the attributes of "ideal" workers, the commonsense definition of success, and the perception of the most pressing business problems facing the company. Along with the observational data noted earlier, these interview data were analyzed to reveal the assumptions and be-liefs driving the way work got done in this environment. When the findings from the diagnosis were fed back to the organization, there was widespread agreement that they were representative of the cur-rent work culture in that group.

Additional data representing the commonsense definition of work as understood by the line-of-fault subjects themselves were obtained by analyzing the interview and roundtable transcripts to reveal the inconsistencies, contradictions, and unexamined dichotomies between the hegemonic definition of work they embodied as members of the system and the subversive sto-ries their observed behavior told.

FINDINGS

The findings from these three sources of data are reported next. First, we examine the basic components of relational practice. Then we look at the way in which relational practice was brought into the dominant discourse, subjected to the truth rules of that discourse, and ultimately "got disappeared" as work and got constructed as something other than work.

Components of Relational Practice

Analysis of the data collected to answer the first research question re-vealed four categories of activities constituting relational practice:

Preserving: These are relational activities associated with *task*. This category includes activities intended to preserve the life and well-being of the project.

Mutual Empowering: These are relational activities associated with an *"other."* This category includes activities intended to en-able or empower others to achieve and contribute to the project.

Achieving: These are activities associated with *self*. This category includes relational activities intended to empower oneself to achieve goals and contribute to the program.

Creating Team: These are activities associated with building a *collective*. This category includes activities intended to construct the social reality of "team" by creating an environment in which positive outcomes of relational interactions can be realized.

Selected examples of each type of activity are used to capture the essence of relational practice in the engineers' own words.

PRESERVING

The first category, Preserving, had to do with maintain-ing the well-being of the project through activities intended to foster its growth or protect it from harm. It encompassed three types of be-havior: shouldering, connecting, and rescuing.

Shouldering refers to picking up on tasks that were outside the tech-nical definition of the job. Examples included things such as taking on lower-level tasks—for example, soldering a board themselves if the technician was busy on something else—as well as things like this en-gineer's description of coming in on a weekend to prevent what she considered substandard products from going out the door: "I just could not *believe* Marketing was going to let those prints go out the door— I mean, I showed them to Tony [the copy quality person] and he just shrugged like 'whatever' and I just said to myself'no way'... so Sara and I? We came in on Saturday and redid them, because, I mean, it had to be done."

Shouldering also included scanning the environment for informa-tion that needed to be passed on and then stepping out of a strict de-finition of the job and taking the initiative to pass it along. For those who did it, shouldering behavior was undertaken with an attitude of "if I don't do it nobody will." They appeared to consider it an essen-tial part of the job and were hard on others who refused to work this way. As one subject put it, "What's wrong with picking up a soldering iron? Nothing. Your hands aren't going to fall off."

Connecting activities were those meant to keep the project con-nected to the people and resources it needed. For example, this en-gineer describes how she took the initiative to make sure that people who suppiy valuable resources to the project but have no reporting relationship to their team feel appreciated and valuable: "It's just that because I was more sensitive to it than Ned [the manager]. Like, if someone didn't feel that it was their job? and I might have sensed that they were getting to the point that they were going to get hurt or feel that they were being taken advantage of? Then I've put myself in that role and I've just said to Ned, 'Maybe we should send so-and-so a thank you' or whatever."

Other examples included a manager who sent one of the team to talk with someone she thought had "ruffled feathers" and another who "translated" one coworker's technical jargon for the rest of the team so his input would be included and not dismissed by those who con-sidered him irrelevant and incomprehensible.

Another type of Preserving had to do with *rescuing*, or calling at-tention to problems. For example, one engineer, in describing the pur-pose of a meeting she had attended, explained that she had identified a problem she thought was serious. She had convinced her boss and her boss's boss that it was a problem and had arranged for a meeting with another division. She explained:

If I am just one person going over there to them saying, "Look, we've got this terrible problem,"... but if we've got someone at a higher level like Mike who can communicate to them that it's a problem [pause]. I mean if it was just me saying it... I mean, otherwise, they might not think it really is [pause], but I could tell. I thought it was a really good meeting because you don't see them that wound up about problems that often, you know? They would rather dust them under the rug and say, "Look, if it's just one occurrence..."

At the meeting she had taken a back seat, deferring to her boss and let-ting him explain her data. Her description of the meeting indicated that this taking a back seat was a conscious decision she made to give the problem visibility.

What differentiated Preserving from other categories of relation-al practice was the focus on task and the relational representation of this focus as one of protection, nurturing, and connecting. In this way, Preserving activities were similar to what Sara Ruddick (1989) calls "preservative love," one of the three practices underlying maternal thinking. The engineers who engaged in these activities replicated the dependency relationship of mother and child in their adoption of an attitude of selfless giving, motivated not by love but by an apparent sense of responsibility. Taking on this responsibility for the whole ap-peared to be part of what it meant to these engineers to be effective workers, and they clearly expected others to do the same, holding in disdain those who refused to care for the project in this way.

Another belief underlying Preserving activity and the notion that everyone should put the needs of the project ahead of individual is-sues such as status or hierarchy was that such action would be seen as a sign of competence and commitment. In other words, the indirect nature and apparent invisibility of these activities was assumed to be characteristic of their effectiveness. Thus, the engineer who sacrificed an opportunity for self-promotion and deferred to her boss in order to give a problem visibility described her action with pride, as evidence of her competence: because of her action, they were now "wound up" about the problem.

The final dimension of the belief system underlying this practice was evidenced by the engineers' willingness to put effort into maintaining relationships they deemed critical to the project's health and vitality. Whether it meant sending thank-you notes to show appreciation, send-ing a peacemaker to smooth ruffled feathers, or protecting the project from the consequences of severed relationships, these activities implied a belief that keeping relationships in good working order was an im-portant aspect of ensuring the life and well-being of the overall project.

Preserving required a certain set of skills, including the ability to think contextually, the ability to anticipate consequences, and the ability to sense the emotional context of situations in order to rec-ognize and take action when, for example, someone "might be feel-ing like they're getting taken advantage of."

Mutual Empowering

The second type of relational practice, Mutual Empowering, refers to behavior intended to enable others' achieve-ment and contribution to the project. Although the term *empower* is used to describe this category, the behaviors included are quite differ-ent from those typically associated with an empowered worker in the management literature. The organizational definition of an empow-ered worker is one who has the information and authority to make decisions, structure and prioritize tasks, or improve process (Senge, 1990). The relational practice described here has less to do with au-thority and decision making and more to do with the act of enabling, or contributing to, the development of another. Nonetheless, the term *empower* with the modifier *mutual* was chosen to reflect the fact that the behavior in this category was intended to enhance others' power and was mutual in that both parties were expected to benefit.

The first practice associated with this type of empowering was *em-pathic teaching*—a way of teaching that took the learner's intellectual or emotional reality into account and focused on the other (What does she or he need to hear?) rather than on self (What would I like to say?). As one engineer said when explaining why she always talks someone through the process while she is fixing a computer file: "Look, the whole point is so they can do it without you next time, right?" Some-times empathic teaching meant simplifying the information intellec-tually, like giving an everyday example of a statistical concept, and sometimes it meant modifying the emotional context of a teaching interaction. As one engineer put it, "Well, the way I work with Frank is a little different. You don't want to bruise any egos. I wanted Frank to feel comfortable, so that's why I sat down next to him and worked through stuff with him.... It's just a style thing."

This concern with minimizing the status difference inherent in a teaching interaction sometimes took the form of bracketing infor-mation with phrases like, "One of the things that might help..." or, "There may be lots of ways to do this but what I like to do is..." Often this collaborative language was marked by a self-deprecating tone that the engineers indicated they used intentionally because, as one noted, "you have to be careful not to intimidate." However, it appeared that making others feel comfortable was only part of the motivation to minimize the expert role. The other goal was to communicate an open-ness to learning and hearing other points of view. As another subject describes, "It sets my own learning and I always come away with some-thing new." Implicit in this approach was an expectation that they, as teachers, were colearners in these enabling interactions.

The second practice associated with empowering was *protective connecting*, a practice that insulated people from their own lack of re-lational skill. For example, when the boss asked a coworker a question and he replied "That's not our job anymore; go ask Katie," the engi-neer I was observing jumped in and answered the question. The next day when I asked her about this incident, she explained:

> Oh, that was part of the problem I was explaining before... that we wanted that project and we lost it? [Our boss] lost it to that other group. So that was Sam using a little sarcasm there saying, "Hey, you guys; you didn't fight enough for it, so now you go talk to Katie about it. She's in charge of it." So that was the little zinger. But I could tell by Carl's voice that he was getting upset and Sam sometimes, like, grrrr [grind-ing noise], twists the knife in harder and harder. So I just jumped in and answered the question. Sam does that... if he really doesn't want to help you, he won't help you, END OF STORY. So I'm the middle-man who goes, "Okay, this is the reason..." [pause] Sort of like a ten-sion breaker, solving two problems at once I guess.

In summary, Mutual Empowering activities were those that enabled others to produce, achieve, and accomplish work-related goals and objectives. They were characterized by a willingness to put effort into what Cato Wadel (1979) calls embedded outcomes:

outcomes em-bedded in other people, such as increased competence, increased self-confidence, or increased knowledge. What differentiated these activities from other types of relational practice was this focus on em-powering an "other." Unlike the previous theme of Preserving, which is analogous to the dependency relationship in a mother-child model, this theme of empowering draws on a model of relational interaction characterized by interdependence and more fluid power relations. Mu-tual Empowering behavior appeared to be rooted in the belief not only that outcomes embedded in others were worth working for, but that everyone needs and should be able to expect this kind of help. As one subject described, "But everyone should feel like that. Because if every-one knew everything, we all wouldn't be here, you know? We all know something other people don't know, so it shouldn't be a big deal.... People should realize that... but some people don't, though."

Thus, Mutual Empowering appears to be based on a concept of power and expertise that is fluid, where dependence on others is as-sumed to be a natural but temporary state. Implicit is an expectation that others should adopt this same attitude and be willing to both give and receive help and that there are benefits to be gained in each role. This notion of mutuality was evident in the way the engineers spoke of enabling activities not as altruism, but as something that enhanced their own self-esteem and self-efficacy. In fact, it was part of what it meant to be good at a job: "I know I'm doing a good job when people think of me when they have a problem. I've succeeded when people think of me as someone who is (1) competent and (2) someone who will help. Most people around here only care about the first thing—competence—they don't care if they are seen as approachable. I do."

The people who enacted Mutual Empowering evidenced an ability to operate in an environment of fluid expertise, where power or ex-pertise (or both) shifts from one party to the other, not only over time but in the course of one interaction. This required two sets of skills. One was a skill in empowering others: an ability to share—in some instances, even customizing—one's own reality, skill, knowledge, and other char-acteristics in ways that made it accessible to others. The other was skill in being empowered: an ability and willingness to step away from the ex-pert role and minimize status differences in order to learn from or be influenced by the other.

Achieving

The third type of relational practice, Achieving, refers to using relational skills to enhance one's own professional growth and effectiveness. It entailed three types of activities: reconnecting, re-flecting, and relational asking. *Reconnectinghad* to do with repairing potential or perceived breaks in working relationships. Those who en-gaged in this practice did things such as following up with someone they had disagreed with in a meeting or going out of their way to track someone down whose feelings they had hurt. What was striking about these activities was the distress and sense of urgency to "make things right" that accompanied many of these reconnections.

Reflecting, the second type of Achieving behavior, had to do with paying attention to the emotional overlay of situations in order to un-derstand what was happening and what the most effective response should be. Sometimes this meant accessing one's own feelings as a source of data. For example, one engineer used "feeling bad" to un-derstand the dynamics of getting recognized at meetings.

I have been thinking about this a lot lately. This isn't true confessions but I came to a realization that I was being rude in meetings... a LOT... and I didn't like it because I didn't feel good. And I was pondering, Why am I doing that? Because it doesn't feel good, but I am still doing it. So there is something else rewarding me.... And it was the getting noticed. It was the easiest, fastest, simplest way to get noticed. And once you are noticed, you get heard. But since it doesn't feel good, I really want to find a different way that is still effective.

Sometimes reflecting meant assessing others' emotional contexts and modifying one's own behavior in response. For example, as we were sitting in the lab, an engineer came in and demanded, in an angry voice, to know what was going on. The engineer I was shadowing gave him some information about the problem she was working on and he turned and left. The next day she talked about the incident this way:

Well, I told him about the problem because I think he feels a little ter-ritorial about it. He thinks of the lab as his area. Also, the meeting I have with him later is to get information from him that [our boss] wants me to document because she wants it documented in my style. Technically, this is his job, so I don't think he feels real comfortable with that, so he may be a little threatened and that may have some-thing to do with his coming in here now and wanting to know.

This explanation indicates that her ability to understand how he might be feeling motivated her to share the information rather than withhold it. The sharing of the information appears to have been an intentional strategy to enhance her own effectiveness by increasing the chance that the meeting they have later in the day will go smoothly.

The third type of Achieving had to do with asking for help in a way that made it likely one would get the help needed. This *relational ask-ing* called forth responsiveness in others. One engineer described it this way: "A lot of people around here will say something like: 'Katie, I'm in a position of leadership over you, and you have to do this for me. Make these files.' And I tend to like to say, 'Katie, can you show me how to do one of these?'"

It was not just the way of asking for help that was important; it was also the kind of help sought. As another subject said, "I know people don't mind helping me, because they know I'll share it with others in my group, so it's not like everyone will be coming to them." She con-trasted her type of "empowering asking" with people who asked for help in an exploitative way. In noting why she refused to help someone who asked her to do a mundane part of his job, she commented, "He always does this. This is not real work for me because it's something he *could* do. I'm not adding any expertise to doing that part of it."

In summary, Achieving activities were those in which engineers used relational skills to enhance their own achievement. It was this focus on self, and the use of relational skills to strategize their own ef-fectiveness, that differentiated Achieving from other categories of re-lational practice. Implicit in these activities was the belief that not just personal but professional growth is rooted in connection and that the long-term benefits of maintaining a relationship are worth the short-term costs. Relational theory suggests that the urgency to prevent or mend disruption is indicative of a belief that severed relationships have potentially negative effects that should be avoided (Brown & Gil-ligan, 1992; Jordan, Kaplan, et al., 1991).

Another belief had to do with the role of emotion. Spending time and effort reflecting on the emotional complexity of situations indi-cates a belief that emotions are an important source of information about oneself and about situations. Using these data enabled the en-gineers who engaged in this practice to develop what they perceived as more effective strategies in dealing with situations. Finally, the prac-tice of relational asking implies a belief in a particular definition of interdependence, where asking for help is not a sign of weakness but an invitation to empower. The ability to differentiate it from other forms of asking suggests that this practice was a conscious decision, a strat-egy designed to increase the likelihood they would get the empower-ing outcome they sought.

In terms of skills, Achieving behavior required an ability to access emotional data and skill in understanding the complexity of these data. In addition, it required an ability to stay with contradictory information—feeling good about getting recognized, feeling bad about how it was done—so that a new strategy might evolve. Thus, it required an ability to blend thinking, feeling, and action in a way that bridged the rational-emotional divide.

Creating Team

The relational practice of Creating Team had to do with working to create the background conditions in which group life can flourish. As differentiated from activities intended to create a par-ticular team, these activities had less to do with managing group pro-cess (such as setting boundaries and defining who is "in" or "out" of the group defining task) and more to do with creating the experience of team. In other words, the activities in this category were those intended not to enhance one's personal relationships or to enable oth-ers (although they might have those effects), but to create the back-ground conditions in which group life could flourish.

Creating Team entailed two types of activities: attending to the in-dividual and attending to the collective. The first, attending to the individual, was expressed through practices that acknowledged oth-ers' unique preferences, problems, feelings, and circumstances. This included sending verbal and nonverbal messages of affirmation such as maintaining eye contact when others were talking and nodding, smiling, or making encouraging comments like, "Right," "Good point," "Okay, good" or even just "Yeah" and "Uh-huh." Pamela Fishman (1978) notes that this type of response during conversation is the main-tenance work of conversational interaction and demonstrates an ap-preciation of and involvement with the speaker. Each of the engineers evidenced behavior of this sort in abundance.

Other ways of responding were associated with empathic responses to other's feelings, preferences, or particular circumstances. For ex-ample, this engineer, in explaining why she took time to listen to an older coworker "ramble about the good old days," goes on to say:

The other thing is, because men joke around so much with each other, when a man does have something he wants to talk about, he won't go to another man... they'll go to a woman. I've had men who I know don't even like me use me to vent about really personal things. Like this one guy—I know he doesn't like me and I don't like him much— started to talk about the fertility problems he and his wife were hav-ing. I mean that's heavy stuff. And I've talked to several women who say that men come in and sit down and talk to them. You don't really have to say anything, just listen. They just want someone who will lis-ten and not joke around about it. I feel bad when others are feeling bad or having a hard time, and I know it's not going to kill me to spend some time with them. And also, who else are they going to go to? It doesn't cost me anything, really, just to listen. But sometimes it just feels like a big responsibility because even if you are not really in the mood, you HAVE to do it. I mean, if they are coming to you, it must be pretty bad, and where else can they go?

Clearly, she felt that this type of response was indeed work. At times it "just feels like a big responsibility," and she responded empathically even though she was fully aware that "he doesn't like me and I don't like him much." Nonetheless, she took it on herself to respond to him in a way that would validate and acknowledge his feelings. Rather than simple knee-jerk reactions, empathic responses such as this appeared to be motivated by a desire to create a certain kind of environment in the workplace. As another said, "The more team-spirited people are more effective in what they're doing. And I equate being conscious of other people's feelings with working in a team spirit. I think people are much more effective this way."

Relational theory supports this view and suggests that individuals who feel understood, accepted, appreciated, or "heard" are more likely to extend that same acceptance to others, leading to a kind of group life characterized by what Miller (1986b) calls a "zest" for interaction and connection.

Attending to the collective, the second type of behavior in this cat-egory, entailed creating conditions among people in order to create an environment that would foster collaboration and cooperation. Sometimes this meant creating the reality of interdependence by in-venting structures that supported collaboration, such as one engineer who described creating a "liaison position" on her team. More com-monly, it meant smoothing relationships between people or using col-laborative rather than confrontational language in expressing ideas in a meeting—for example, saying things like, "What I like about Dave's idea is..." and then going on to add to it.

In summary, Creating Team appears to be characterized by a cer-tain set of beliefs and assumptions about group life. First is the belief that individuals have a right to be noticed and that part of what it means to be a good coworker is to do the noticing. Second is a belief that team spirit and achievement depend on paying attention to oth-ers' feelings and preferences and that the intangible outcomes that re-sult from these efforts—outcomes embedded in other people and in social relations—are things worth working for. Third, it was a prac-tice that appears to be rooted in the assumption that a collective understanding of problems or situations, where others' ideas are fully ex-plored and built on, is a good thing; that is, it is something that will enhance organizational effectiveness and lead to better decisions. It was this focus on creating a collective that distinguishes this category of activities from other types of Relational Practice.

In terms of skills, the behavior in this category required an ability to respond empathically to others and an ability to understand the emo-tional context in which they operated. In addition, it required a type of cognitive complexity not dependent on affect, one similar to what Irene Stiver (1991) calls "response/ ability": the capacity to freely and wholeheartedly engage with another's subjectivity (that is, drawing out others' ideas), being able to acknowledge and affirm that reality while maintaining and being in touch with one's own to the extent that one could add to those ideas and create something new.

Summary

It should be remembered that the goal of this first phase of the analysis was to tell a subversive story by reading organizational text to reveal those practices that met a particular set of truth rules, those re-siding in relational theory. Thus, the answer to the first research ques-tion is intentionally selective. It focuses only on behaviors motivated by a belief in the preeminence of connection and highlights the re-lational skills required to enact them, such as empathy, mutuality, reciprocity, and a sensitivity to emotional contexts. In addition, it pur-posefully highlights the strategic intentions of the behavior, that is, the way in which it was motivated by a belief that operating in a con-text of connection was more effective, better for the project, and bet-ter for getting the job done. In describing the behavior from this relational perspective, the first phase of the analysis tells the story of relational practice as if it is the only plausible interpretation of the behavior and as if no tension exists between it and the current defin-ition of work in organizational discourse.

Gender, Power, and "Getting Disappeared"

This brings us to the second part of the analysis. As noted earlier, a re-lational belief system—in which relational interactions are assumed to be sites of growth, achievement, and professional effectiveness—stands in sharp contrast to traditional organizational norms and beliefs about competence, effectiveness, and organizational success. The second stage of the analysis addresses the second research question of what happens to this relationally motivated behavior when it is practiced in an envi-ronment that is hostile to its basic assumptions. It explores the mech-anisms by which relational practice is brought into organizational discourse and subjected to the truth rules of that discourse.

The poststructuralist framing of this study argues that all public sphere activity is implicitly subjected to general truth rules about the characteristics of real work, rules that are a reflection of the instru-mental narrative underlying this sphere. Within this general frame-work in which all organizations reflect the instrumental values of rationality, abstraction, and linearity, a high-technology environment was intentionally selected as the research site (as opposed to, for ex-ample, a hospital, school, or social service agency) because it was assumed to be an exemplar of this power-knowledge structure.

The cultural diagnosis conducted prior to the shadowing indicated that this was indeed the case (Bailyn et al., 1996; Perlow, 1997). This work-place was found to be similar to other environments in which design engineering is highly valued (McIlwee & Robinson, 1992).

For exam-ple, an analysis of the organizational narratives gathered in the cul-tural diagnosis about the definition of success, the attributes of the ideal engineer, and the perception about what types of behaviors were likely to lead to promotions revealed that this was a work environment where autonomy, self-promotion, and individual heroics were highly prized, an environment where time was a surrogate for commitment and competence was measured by short-term results. Not only was technical competence highly valued and seen as the route to organi-zational power, but self-promotion was considered a display of com-petence. "Real" work was consistently defined as "solving problems," and engineers who moved on to supervisory positions even spoke of "no longer having a job" because all they did now was help other peo-ple do their work. It was a culture in which the definition of outcome was clear: outcomes were tangible, measurable, and concrete. In fact, in this environment, if something was not quantifiable, it was assumed to be of no consequence and often was eliminated as a variable.

When behavior motivated by a relational belief system (model of growth-in-connection) was brought into this organizational discourse, it "got disappeared" as work because by its very nature, it violated many of the truth rules mentioned above. By rereading the textual representation of work collected in the shadowing, interviewing, and roundtable discussion in order to surface inherent inconsistencies, contradictions, and dilemmas in the text, by observing and listening closely to how others responded to those who enacted relational prac-tice, and by noting my own reactions to observing these activities, it was possible to identify the process by which relational practice "got disappeared" in this organizational setting. The following sections de-tail the disappearing of each relational practice.

Disappearing Preserving

The practice of Preserving was rooted in a belief system that privileged context and connection. As such, it vi-olated many of the truth rules in this engineering culture based on in-dividualism and the hierarchical separation of specialization and connecting functions. For example, the engineer who attempted to pass information across functions by telling her manager that mar-keting would be sending out substandard prints was met with a shrug and a dismissive wave of the hand. The manager did not thank her for what she had done or give any verbal or nonverbal affirmation that this was an appreciated or expected piece of work. The nonverbal mes-sage appeared to be, "That's not your job; don't worry about it." In this culture of specialization, the willingness to put effort into taking responsibility for the whole seemed to mystify this manager, who ap-peared to be operating from a different belief system about what it means to be an effective worker. Another engineer who called her boss to warn of a possible duplication of effort was met with a similar re-sponse, one that seemed to suggest that such a warning was evidence of nitpicking or excessive devotion to detail.

Other types of Preserving were disappeared in a similar fashion. For example, being quietly competent or sacrificing an opportunity for self-promotion for the sake of the project violated some basic norms of be-havior in this work culture, where competence was measured by an ability to self-promote, talk technical, and associate oneself with high-visibility problems. In fact, I found that even I, as an observer who was making an effort to view the engineers' behavior through a relational lens, "disappeared" this type of competence and constructed it as a per-sonal aberration. When I observed the event described earlier of an en-gineer who took a back seat in a meeting and let her boss talk about her data, I at first coded this as evidence of her fear of power and suc-cess and wrote the word *meek* in the margins of my notes. I made sense of her behavior as some sort of personal aberration, assuming that she was uncomfortable with self-promotion or with being seen as an ex-pert. It was not until later, as she spoke of the incident with pride and explained to me that it was an intentional strategy on her part to give the problem increased visibility and make sure it was taken seriously, that I began to realize that her behavior at that meeting could be un-derstood differently and that I had been "disappearing" her work by la-beling the behavior not only as inappropriate to the workplace and but also as evidence of her personal inadequacy.

Disappearing mutual empowering

The practice of Mutual Empow-ering also violated some truth rules in the dominant discourse that got it "disappeared" as work and constructed as something other than work. In a culture of independence and self-promotion, where individual achievement is what is prized, and competition means beating the other person out so you finish on top, voluntarily helping others achieve was puzzling behavior. Enacting a relational belief system in which interdependence is a natural state and enabling others is a source of self-esteem so violated professional norms that it seemed that the only way to make sense of the behavior was to attribute it to either powerlessness or naiveté. As one of the subjects notes: "If you try to nur-ture around here, they just don't get it. They don't understand that is what you are doing. They see it as a weakness and they use it against you. They don't see that you are doing it consciously... they think you have missed something or that they've gotten something over on you. So if you try to be nice, you end up doing other people's work."

Her experience suggests that in this environment, anyone who puts effort into achieving outcomes that are embedded in others appar-ently gets constructed not as someone working in a way that has the potential to enhance organizational learning and effectiveness, but rath-er as weak, naive, or exploitable. In her attempt to find organization-ally strong language to represent what she is trying to do, she rejected the negative attribution of *weakness*. However, the more positive words she chose to describe the behavior—*nurture, being nice*—actually may have disappeared the work even more powerfully, as they tend to de-skill the practice, making it seem more like evidence of a personal at-tribute than conscious, intentional action.

She was not alone in trying to find organizationally strong language to describe enabling activity. Consider, for example, what this engi-neer said: "I've succeeded when people think of me as someone who is (1) competent and (2) someone who will help. Most people around here only care about the first thing—competence—they don't care if they are seen as approachable. I do."

It is clear that she is trying to describe an expanded definition of competence that includes a willingness and an ability to share and em-power others. Having no organizationally strong language readily available to her to describe this kind of outcome—an outcome that would be embedded in another person—as evidence of competence, she uses *approachability* and *help,* words that are not nearly as strong and leave the definition of competence unchallenged. Ironically, her struggle with language actually ends up reinforcing the notion that enabling others is not part of competence but something separate.

Another subject described how taking several hours from her day to help someone from another unit gave her conflicting feelings. On the one hand, she felt proud that she had helped him "not reinvent the wheel," something "we should do more of around here." On the other, she felt that maybe she was naive to have helped and had been "taken down the garden path." She recognized that in this culture of individ-ualism, the help she gave him was probably going to get disappeared from his achievement. As she said, "I don't have any trust that I am going to get anything back for that. He is going to look real good... and I don't think he should look as good as he is going to look!"

Interestingly, while many of the engineers struggled to enact and articulate a different definition of helping, they themselves often "dis-appeared" this work when it was done by others. For example, one subject spoke disparagingly of a contract employee in marketing as "O'Connor's little errand boy" because he did support work for that group. The implication was that as a contract employee, he had no power and therefore was reduced to being an errand boy. As if the message in that might not be clear enough, she added the adjective *lit-tle* to show what stature such a position confers.

Disappearing achieving

In this engineering culture, where models of growth and achievement were based on individuation, indepen-dence, and autonomy, those who violated these truth rules by seeking growth-in-connection stood outside the discourse on achievement. As the following quotation indicates, subjects who put effort into con-necting, reconnecting, and maintaining relationships in the service of their own achievement felt themselves to be understood as motivated by a need to be liked, that is, as seeking not growth but affection. As this subject indicates, it was difficult to articulate the possibility that achievement needs might be met through relational means. As she tries to transcend the achievement-affiliation dichotomy, she ends up going around in circles:

> So if I do get into a situation that is confrontational, not angry neces-sarily but even if we're just being very direct with each other and this person wants to do it one way and I want to do it another way, I'd be concentrating more on [pause, then little laugh] *winning* than on how they felt about it. I gave up a long time ago caring about how they felt about it, other than if how they feel about it is going to get in the way of getting it done. But if I don't perceive that their feelings are going to get in the way, then I kind of don't notice anymore [laugh]. So that's the only reason why I'm paying attention to their feelings. It isn't that I care that much about their feelings. It's because if they feel threatened enough, I won't make any progress and not because [pause]. If I thought I'd win in spite of that, it wouldn't bother me at all. So it isn't that I'm terribly worried about whether the guys that I work with like me. I worry a lot about whether they respect me. *I don't really care if they like me or not* [emphasis added]. [laugh; pause]... I happen to think that usually those kind of end up going together, though. If you respect someone, you usually end up liking them, too... at the end of it all.

The contradictions and inconsistencies in this quotation give a good sense of the disappearing dynamic that occurs when relational practice is brought into the organizational discourse on work. She struggles to find language to represent her experience and is careful to distance her-self from attributions of inappropriate motivation: she would be more concerned about winning, she wants me to know, than she would about someone's feelings. But then she gets entangled as she tries to describe her experience that these two things are not dichotomous. If feelings are going to get in the way of success, then of course she is concerned about them. If feelings were not real, that is, if she accepted the conventional wisdom that feelings are irrelevant to organizational phenomenon, she would not care about them at all because they would not stand in the way of winning. But she wants to make it clear that the reason she is concerned about feelings is not that she wants to be liked. She under-stands that this would be the "normal" attribution and wants to make sure I do not make it regarding her. So she falls back again into the di-chotomy: she does not care if they like her as long as they respect her.

Any language available to her to describe worrying about the effect of confrontation on the relationship, or to describe the possibility that be-havior that gets her liked might also make her more effective, would risk the attribution of "needing to be liked," an attribution that would taint her as incompetent. Not having the organizational language to describe such a possibility *and* still be considered competent, she chooses to rep-resent herself as competent.

This reinforces rather than challenges the dichotomy, but it serves the purpose of making it clear that she is savvy enough to understand the difference between being liked and being re-spected. However, after giving me the party line, she recognizes the in-adequacy of what she has said in trying to capture her experience so, after a slight pause and a little laugh, she undermines this dichotomous thinking: she happens to believe these two things go together—that being liked and being respected are not mutually exclusive.

Others went through similar verbal gymnastics to simultaneously reinforce and resist dominant sense-making schema about appropri-ate ways of working. For example, this engineer gives voice to the in-violate nature of the public-private split, carefully aligning herself with normative behavior: "I was talking to this guy the other day about it. And I said that you really have to be two totally different people: a businessperson who is really direct and then at home a different per-sonality. So at home, sometimes I just withdraw, and they don't un-derstand. And he said, 'Would you write that down and send it to my wife?' [laughs]."

Then, after a pause, she continued, subtly undermining this public-private dichotomy by offering an alternative that challenged it: "But really, I don't think... I think confrontation doesn't really work that well in the business place. Like all that women's lib stuff about de-manding what you need? It doesn't work that way."

Disappearing creating team

The practice of Creating Team "got dis-appeared" through a similar process. Despite some organizational rhetoric about teamwork and collaboration, this was an environment in which individual heroism was the valued currency. Thus, it was un-derstandably difficult to articulate or understand the motivation to en-gage in activity intended to create the conditions in which the benefits of group life could flourish. For example, this engineer has difficulty trying to describe her effort to use collaborative language to create an environment where ideas can be explored rather than attacked. She notes that if she uses this approach, rather than being seen as effective, she and her ideas disappear. In the roundtable discussion, she described this disappearing so vividly that the group laughs in recognition:

I think sometimes if you're in a meeting, and somebody states an idea. If I stand up and I say, "That's totally inappropriate, that's just plain stupid, this is what we should do" or if I stand up and say, "Well, that's a really good idea but another way of looking at it is this..." The per-son who stood up and was abusive about it is the person that people are going to remember as having come up with that idea later, when it's time to evaluate people. [This last sentence is said quite forcefully, and then after a slight pause and in a softer, more tentative voice she adds:] I think, lots of times [back to a more forceful tone, she contin-ues] because even though it's a bad impression, you've made an im-pression. The other person, in being polite and a little self-effacing, has sort of melted into the background.... Sometimes if you're nice you'll say [pause]. I might be in a meeting and somebody will come up with an idea and I'll say, "Well, that's a really good idea, but I looked at it this way and this is what I came up with." And then [after you give your idea], they'll say, "Well, anyways..." [general laughter]. And be-cause you haven't like stomped on them, *you're not even in the room* [emphasis in original].

What she recognizes is that if there is only one right way and dis-covering it makes her the winner, then building on others' ideas is likely to be considered inappropriate, or a sign that she has nothing new to add. Again, the private sphere language she uses to describe the behavior—*nice, polite, self-effacing*—tends to deskill and devalue it. This contributes to its near invisibility as a challenge to confronta-tional norms. Not having organizationally strong language readily available to describe it, she uses words that strongly associate it with femininity *(polite, nice)* and powerlessness *(self-effacing).* This belies her belief in it as a strategy that could make visible the reality of team, by, for example, creating a shared solution to a problem that transcends any one individual's ideas. This relational belief is buried in all the other sense-making schema vying for attention here:

> I see it as avoiding conflict. Because at least for me personally, I'm not somebody who feels very comfortable negotiating in an atmosphere of conflict. *I like to talk about things, explain why I think something, hear about what the other person thinks about something* [emphasis added]. But I know that there are some people that... they like to ne-gotiate in a state of conflict, with voices raised, "That's NOT a good idea" instead of, "Why do you think that's a good idea?" So if I can keep it from ever getting elevated to that, then I can be working in an at-mosphere that is more comfortable for me. I don't like yelling and screaming and accusations and the rest of that stuff.

Summary: disappearing dynamic

This description of the way in which the different types of relational practice were brought into the discourse suggests that there was a dynamic process in operation in which relational practice "got disappeared" as work and got con-structed as something other than work. There were three specific as-pects of this process evident in the data. The first had to do with the misattribution of the intention underlying relational practice, whereby it was seen as having been motivated not by a desire to work more effectively but by some sort of personal idiosyncrasy or trait. These included negative characteristics such as naiveté, powerlessness, weak-ness, and emotional need, as well as more positive attributions such as thoughtfulness, personal style, or being nice. What got disappeared in this construction of relational practice as personal aberration was the intentional strategy to enact a relational model of growth, achieve-ment, and effectiveness as an alternative way of working.

It should be noted again that no claim is being made here about which interpretation of the behavior is more "true." Was the engineer who alerted her manager to the substandard prints being responsible or a nitpicking busybody? Was the engineer who helped someone from another unit a hero or a chump? Was the strategic intention to enhance effectiveness through relational practice actually realized? This study did not gather data that could answer these questions. In-deed, from the poststructuralist perspective of the study, these ques-tions are beside the point. The interesting finding here is that the misattribution of motive tainted the behavior as inappropriate, there-by silencing the challenge that relational practice might have presented to organizational assumptions about achievement, success, and effec-tiveness. In poststructuralist terms, it filled in the discursive space that might have been created by acknowledging a different definition of work based on a model of growth-in-connection, thereby truncating the possibility of theorizing or envisioning alternative, relational strate-gies for success.

The second aspect of the disappearing dynamic had to do with the lack of organizationally strong language to represent this type of be-havior as work. Many of the words the engineers used to describe re-lational practice *(helping, nurturing, nice, polite)* tended to associate it with the private sphere and femininity. This association gendered the behavior, diminishing its organizational relevance. At the same time, organizationally acceptable words that would have captured the unique belief system underlying this behavior—words like *outcome* and *competence*—had already been defined in this organizational discourse in ways that implicitly excluded relational aspects of work. Thus, the engineers seemed to have no way of describing the output of some re-lational activity as an achievement in its own right because, for exam-ple, outcomes embedded in people did not fit the organization definition of outcome and could not be claimed as "real work." As one of the engineers noted, "I don't do a lot of real work now. I do a lot of helping people understand what the problem is, *helping people believe they can do something on their own* [emphasis added]." In the same vein, the word *competence* could be used to describe only half of what made another engineer feel good about herself as a worker. She had to describe the other half as "approachability" even though it was clear that helping others was part of what defined competence in her mind. The third aspect of the disappearing dynamic had to do with the so-cial construction of gender. It was different from the first two aspects of "getting disappeared" because it had to do with how this way of work-ing got conflated with images of femininity and motherhood. Thus, the first two mechanisms of disappearing—being labeled inappropriate and not having the language to describe these things as work—would per-haps operate on all who worked this way, regardless of gender. But when women enacted relational practice, something else happened. Because of gender roles, the female engineers felt they were expected to act rela-tionally, to be soft, feminine, helpful, good listeners. In fact they did not seem to believe they had the option of acting any other way. As one said, "I try swearing, but I feel so stupid!" Another described what happened when she tried using confrontation to make a point:

> People notice that you said it, and it definitely gets the point on the table. But it certainly isn't good for your long-term relationships with that person. Especially, I think, if it comes from a woman to a man. I think that another man could do that, could say the exact same words, the exact same tone, and after the meeting it would just be over [pause]. I don't think it would be over if one of those players was a woman, even if it was over for the woman. I don't think it would be over for the man.

The conflation of gender expectations with relational practice was a powerful way of disappearing the motivation behind the behavior. It was difficult to articulate a relational way of working as an inten-tional choice when they sensed that they did not have a choice. As a result, the engineers often contradicted themselves or got hopelessly confused as they tried to capture the experience that they simultane-ously resented being forced to use relational strategies *and* they be-lieved these strategies were more effective.

Even more problematic for these line-of-fault workers in female bod-ies was that when they tried to enact certain elements of relational prac-tice, such as Mutual Empowering, a practice characterized by mutuality and an expectation of reciprocity, they often were misinterpreted as en-acting mothering, a practice characterized by selfless giving and little expectation of reciprocity. That is, they got responded to as women, not as coworkers. While they might have been willing to "do whatever it takes" to preserve the life and well-being of an inanimate object such as the project (with no expectation of reciprocal attention), it was clear they were not willing to be cast in this role permanently in their rela-tionships with others. For example, several of the engineers described being asked rou-tinely to do support tasks by male engineers, things like copying, de-livering papers to another office, or packing boxes. When they began to feel the lack of reciprocity and recognized that they were being tak-en advantage of, they would try to set some boundary around how much or what kind of help they were willing to give. As one said, "I mean really... you can't always give somebody your work. It's okay to do it once in awhile; that is not a problem. But you can't *always* do that." When she tried to limit her helping, however, she described being (jokingly) called things like "Tarantula Lady" or "Queen Bee." Getting called names for not being willing to help limitlessly makes visible the expectation that she, as a woman, should embrace this kind of helping behavior and do it willingly and gladly, with no expectation of reciprocity. To set limits, qualify, or differentiate among different types of help one was willing to give was to be called not unhelpful, but unfeminine, poisonous, arrogant.

Negative experiences such as this appeared to overwhelm the en-gineers' belief in this as an alternative way of working. Because they recognized the career implications of being exploited or seen as naive, in the roundtable they ended up simultaneously touting the value of this way of working and cautioning themselves and others not to do too much of it. As one said, "Although it might be good for the project, if you do it, you'll end up being a gopher your whole life."

In summary, it appears that these three aspects of the disappearing dynamic operated in concert, such that activity springing from a rela-tional belief system "got disappeared" as relational practice (something new) and got constructed as something familiar (personal style, a nat-ural expression of gender, private sphere behavior inappropriate to the public sphere, or something else).

This set in motion a misunderstand-ing of the motivation underlying the behavior that silenced its poten-tial challenge to the dominant organizational discourse on work. Thus, the disappearing dynamic was a sort of self-reinforcing cycle in which the behavior and its potential benefits were absorbed by the system, but the system itself was not challenged. The female engineers them-selves were caught up in this cycle, wanting to work differently, unwit-tingly colluding in the "disappearing" of the behavior as work in the way they talked about it, cautioning each other about the negative ef-fects of working this way but yet apparently unwilling to give up try-ing to enact this different, more relational way of working.

BROADER IMPLICATIONS

Discussing these findings and their broader implications presents a challenge. Although this was not framed as a sex differences study, the findings have compelling gender implications that raise sex differences questions. Readers can be forgiven for wondering what the male ex-perience of these issues might be and wishing there were data to illu-minate it. However, all the customary cautions about sample size and composition and the limits of generalizability to other populations and work environments apply here. Certainly it should be noted that, although tempting, it would be unwise as well as unwarranted to draw essentialist conclusions about men and women based on these find-ings. Rather, conclusions and implications must be drawn within the theoretical context and goals of the study, which were twofold. The first goal was to document the existence of a way of working in the public sphere that springs from a relational model of growth and de-velopment, a model conceptualized as marginal to public sphere think-ing because of its association with the feminine. The second was to explore and explicate the power-knowledge forces acting to silence any challenge to the status quo that might be contained in this alternative way of working.

Within this theoretical context, there are a few interesting points for discussion. The first, which is related to the first goal of the study, has to do with the existence and detailing of relational practice as work. Although the findings cannot support a claim that relational practice exists and gets disappeared in all organizational settings, they certainly suggest that looking for relational practices—even in settings as un-likely as this engineering environment—is likely to yield expanded understandings of traditional organizational concepts. Thus, one con-tribution this study makes is that it identifies the extent of the gap in our knowledge about relational aspects of work and highlights the need to develop expanded models of organizational effectiveness and a new language of relational competence. It invites exploratory re-search that extends and further typologizes relational activity as work, making it an object of study rather than a taken-for-granted aspect of interpersonal relationships or process.

For example, the findings sug-gest that the notion of helping in organizational settings may be a more complex concept than is generally accepted. These engineers clearly differentiated among types of helping interactions and, in the same vein, were able to categorize ways of asking, ways of teaching, and ways of encouraging collaboration. The variety of relational ac-tivity apparent even in this limited study suggests that the one-sided models of relational interactions currently used to understand these phenomena in the workplace (see, for example, Cammock, Nilakant, & Dakin, 1995) need to be expanded.

Exploring organizational phenomena from a relational, two-sided, or interdependent perspective could yield not only theoretical but also practical results. Take, for example, the concept of organizational learning. Adopting a two-sided focus to this concept has the potential to expand our understanding of the conditions that promote organi-zational learning by calling attention to the largely invisible task of continuous teaching. Conceptualizing workers not only as continu-ous learners but also as continuous teachers might raise some inter-esting questions for organizations to consider—for example: What are the conditions that promote, encourage, or support routine, contin-uous knowledge transfer within and across functional boundaries? What are the conditions that discourage or disappear this behavior? How might formal and informal reward systems need to change to promote both sides of relational interactions that lead to organiza-tional learning? Expanding research on communities of practice (Seely-Brown & Duguid, 1991), knowledge workers (Nonaka, 1994), and multifunctional teams (Lipnack & Stamps, 1993; Slater, 1994) to include both sides of the relational interactions implicit in these con-cepts might yield more useful—and potentially more radical—sug-gestions for changes in organizational structures and systems to enhance organizational learning.

The second point for discussion has to do with the gender-power implications of the findings and their potential to challenge the or-ganizational status quo. Detailing relational practice as *intentional action to achieve goals of achievement, growth, and effectiveness* mo-mentarily reconstructs the definition of work by calling attention to the potential benefits to organizations of valuing relational practice and the variety of relational skills needed to enact it. This poststructuralist reconstruction is an act of resistance that challenges common-sense assumptions about work and competence, calls into question the hierarchical norms that support these narrow definitions, and creates discursive space in which new, perhaps radically different, practices, structures, and norms might surface.

It would appear that the organizational world would be eager to accept this particular challenge to the status quo. In the name of re-engineering, reinvention, and organizational learning, organizations are routinely being encouraged—even warned—to move from tradi-tional hierarchical structures to flatter, more collaborative entities in order to foster a new way of working. This way of working is remark-ably similar to relational practice. Workers in new "boundaryless" or-ganizations (Slater, 1994) are to be flexible and team oriented, not only continuous learners (Watkins & Marsick, 1993; Byham & Cox, 1994) but also emotionally intelligent (Goleman, 1995) systems thinkers, an-ticipating consequences, accepting ownership of problems, and work-ing to solve them (Senge, 1990; Hammer & Champy, 1993).

What the findings from this study suggest, however, is that chang-ing organizations in ways that might encourage the emergence of this kind of worker will not be so easy. Although the calls for radical change are real and the need may indeed be urgent, there appear to be powerful forces that silence and suppress just such challenges to orga-nizational norms. In other words, the findings suggest that behaviors such as relational practice are not merely overlooked in organizations; they are systematically disappeared through a process in which they are coded as private sphere (feminine) activities that stand outside the definition of work and competence. What this means for organiza-tions that are calling for team-oriented, less hierarchical, empowered workers is that they are unlikely to get them from current practice, re-gardless of calls for transformation. The inability to recognize the new behavior as evidence of competence, the lack of language to describe it as such, and the coding of such behavior as feminine are powerful dynamics undermining efforts to restructure work and the workplace in this way. Transformation will require far more than an exhortation to change organizational culture or reengineer the work process. Rath-er, it will require an acknowledgment of and an engagement with the complex gendered forces underlying current organizational norms. Without such an acknowledgment, efforts to disrupt these structures are likely to fail because, while calls for this radical change might appear benign, the way in which organizations would have to change in order to foster these changes are neither benign nor gender neutral.

Take, for example, the structural and practical implications of the suggestion that organizations value relational practice and encourage the development of relational skills in their workforce. The question of sex differences in relational competence aside, there is some evidence in the broader literature that many of the skills associated with this type of competence can be acquired in caretaking settings. The literature on the sociology of caring (Ruddick, 1989; Benner & Wrubel, 1989), for ex-ample, suggests that caring for others encourages a holistic approach to understanding and responding to events, an approach that develops an ability to integrate emotional, cognitive, and behavior data in forming a response. Interestingly, a recent study of service workers (Johansson, 1995) found that those who were able to assume this holistic approach, or what was called "total responsibility" for the work, were those who were involved in some sort of caretaking activity outside work, such as parenting, coaching, or being a team leader in a youth group.

This suggests that organizations intent on developing relational skills in their workers might do so through the systematic encour-agement of all individuals to be involved in some sort of caretaking experience. Taking this a step further, developmental programs in or-ganizations intent on transformation might even include some form of family or community involvement as a necessary condition of ad-vancement or continued employment. Suggestions for meeting these developmental needs could include the use of "outside consultants" (children, elderly parents, members of shelters, schools, hospitals, and others) to assist in relational skills acquisition. This, of course, is rad-ically different from the traditional view that employees who are in-volved in family or community are less committed or less valuable than those who focus only on work. Highlighting the organizational benefits of relaxing the boundary between work and family/community as a way of developing relational competence in workers has the potential to change the landscape of work-family interventions that organizations might consider.

The suggestion that organizations might want to relax the work-family boundary in order to develop relational skills in their workers may have been met with some form of skepticism or even amusement in the reader—a sense, perhaps, that the suggestion was naive or the connection far-fetched.

This response highlights the most powerful implication of the findings: the suggestion that it might be in an organization's best interest to relax the work-family boundary is im-plicitly a challenge to organizational assumptions about the necessity of keeping a strict boundary between the public and private spheres of life. These assumptions manifest themselves in organizational norms, structures, and practices that reify that gendered separation, a separation that implicitly assigns one set of tasks and associated behaviors to women and another to men. Challenging these norms, then, challenges not only the separation but also the deeply held gender-linked assumptions that maintain that separation and rein-force a patriarchal pattern of male dominance in the public sphere.

What this points out is that the poststructuralist "act of resistance" inherent in reconstructing the definition of work in order to value the relational is not simply an act of resistance to hierarchy or other as-pects of organizing.

It is also, at a deeper level, an act of resistance to the way in which these ways of organizing create, recreate, and main-tain a gendered dichotomy between the public and private spheres and to the power structure (patriarchy) that depends on this split. More specifically, it suggests that organizations intent on transforming will be unable to do so in any long-lasting way without engaging these pa-triarchal forces.

One way to engage them is to begin to expose the gen-dered nature of the structures, norms, and practices that reinforce the public-private dichotomy at every level of analysis—from the deeply interior processes that privilege one source of self-esteem and self-identify (public sphere accomplishments) over others; to the group level where structures, reward systems, and managerial practices sup-port gendered, public-private split definitions of commitment, suc-cess, competence, and achievement; to the organizational level where work and family are constructed as separate and distinct spheres of life; to the societal level where the dissolution would mean counting both the public and private costs of doing business.

Openly challeng-ing the gendered nature of the public-private dichotomy at each of these levels has the potential to transform work and organizations for the next century in ways that go beyond superficial suggestions and calls for transformation. Indeed, challenging this dichotomy openly has the potential to highlight the more general, societal-level assump-tions about gender that would need to change in order to respond to what are commonly represented as gender-neutral organizational calls to meet the challenges of this century.

6

Pregnancy Discrimination in the Workplace

There are over 58 million women in the American labor force, and 85 percent of those women are expected to become pregnant at some point while they are working (U.S. Census Bureau, 2003; Jacobson, 1988). Given that the workplace is still fairly tradition-al in structure, it is not surprising that problems and discrimination surrounding pregnancy exist. In fact, complaints of pregnancy dis-crimination with the Equal Employment Opportunity Commission (EEOC) increased by 39 percent between 1992 and 2002 (Equal Em-ployment Opportunity Commission, 2003).

Until 1978, discrimination against pregnant workers was widespread and usually legal. Employers could indulge in whatever stereotypes they had about pregnant women and act on their opinions as to what wom-en should do once they became pregnant and after the birth of the child. Since then, the Pregnancy Discrimination Act and the Family and Medical Leave Act, as well as state and local laws, have changed the workplace dramatically for pregnant women and eliminated the most blatant and egregious forms of discrimination. However, these laws do not apply to all employees, and even when they do, they leave gaps in protection. Problems remain, and stereotypes persist.

This chapter briefly lays out the trajectory and current status of the law regarding pregnant workers. It covers the history of the treatment of pregnant workers, how and why the law changed to remedy that discrimination, and the problems with those laws and proposals to ex-pand them. It also briefly reviews the efforts of states to supplement federal protections for pregnant workers and compares American poli-cies to those of other nations.

LIFE BEFORE THE PREGNANCY DISCRIMINATION ACT

The history of the treatment of pregnant women, or even women who may become pregnant, in the workplace is not a pleasant one. Based on the idea that women, especially mothers, did not belong in the work-place, as well as the desire to reserve jobs for men, protective legisla-tion for women was passed in the early part of the twentieth century (Strimling, 1989). This protective legislation is typified in the famous 1908 Supreme Court case of *Muller*'v. *Oregon.* The state of Oregon had limited the number of hours per day that women could work but had passed no such limitation for men. The Court upheld this law, reason-ing that it was women's "performance of maternal functions" (p. 421) that placed them at a natural disadvantage in life compared to men and that long working hours could injure women's fragile health, yet women needed to remain healthy in order to have healthy children. While a limitation of working hours today might be considered a rea-sonable and humane law, in the exploitative labor conditions at the turn of the twentieth century, legislation such as this deprived women of employment opportunities, which was its intended result.

This treatment was not just a phenomenon of the early twentieth century. Strikingly unequal treatment of pregnant women persisted into the 1970s, and during the 1950s and 1960s, some states even adopted new legislation that prohibited women from being hired for a specified period of time before and after childbirth (Caplan-Cotenoff, 1987). Em-ployers routinely denied women disability benefits for pregnancy while providing coverage for many other temporarily disabling conditions. In some cases, employers forced pregnant women to take leave without as-surance that their jobs would be there upon their return to work.

The women's movement of the 1970s aimed to change these prac-tices, as well as other forms of discrimination against women. To ad-dress pregnancy discrimination in employment, women's advocates thought they already had the necessary legal tools. In *Reed* v. *Reed* in 1971, the Supreme Court first adopted the view that the equal pro-tection clause of the Fourteenth Amendment prohibited differential treatment by the government based on sex. Feminists then argued that based on the clear connection between women's reproductive capa-bilities and societal discrimination, pregnancy discrimination was part and parcel of sex discrimination, and thus was covered by the equal protection clause. In 1974, the Court decided *Cleveland Board of Ed-ucation* v. *LaFleur*. In *LaFleur*, the Supreme Court addressed two pub-lic school district polices that required teachers to take mandatory maternity leave for four or five months before the expected childbirth, which is long before most pregnant women would prefer to stop working. The lower courts that had previously heard these cases based their decisions on the equal protection clause, but the Supreme Court held that these polices violated the due process clause of the Fourteenth Amendment due to the burden they imposed on the fundamental right to bear children. Although this case advanced the rights of preg-nant workers by invalidating these discriminatory policies, the ratio-nale for the case focused on women in relation to reproduction, not sex discrimination (Strimling, 1989). The Court also later used this due process rationale to invalidate a Utah unemployment compensation statute, which had provided that women would get no benefits during unemployment in the third trimester of pregnancy or six weeks after childbirth because the state presumed a woman could not work then *(Turnerv. Department of Employment Security*, 1975).

In addition, there was a federal statute protecting women in the workplace. Title VII of the Civil Rights Act of 1964, the foundation of modern employment antidiscrimination law, prohibited sex discrimi-nation in employment, and it provided simply that discrimination based on sex was forbidden. But Title VII itself did not provide a definition of the term *sex*, and due to the unusual way in which the word was in-cluded in the act, the legislative history behind the inclusion of this term or what Congress considered it to cover was scant. The EEOC stepped into this breach and began addressing to what extent the prohibition of discrimination based on sex applied to the treatment of pregnancy. Though it took eight years, the EEOC produced administrative guide-lines by 1972 that clearly stated that Title VII prohibited differential treatment of pregnancy, including in disability and other benefits poli-cies. This was at a time when the exclusion of pregnancy from such pol-icies was routine. Thus, when women challenged policies that denied disability benefits for disability from pregnancy but not from other sources, including ones that primarily affected men, they met with suc-cess. Many federal district courts and several courts of appeals agreed that differential treatment based on pregnancy violated Title VII.

However, this initial success was short-lived. The issue of whether pregnancy was included within the meaning of sex under the equal protection clause reached the Supreme Court in 1974 in *Geduldig v. Aiello.* At issue in *Geduldig* was the California State Disability Insur-ance Program, which provided disability payments to workers who were temporarily disabled by an illness but not eligible for workers' compensation funds. This plan specifically excluded disability based on pregnancy from coverage, while covering disability from almost every other cause. The Court examined this plan as it traditionally did other social insurance schemes, which meant it gave a wide berth to the policy choices of the state. The Court defined the policy of the state as excluding a benefit that would be expensive so as to keep employee contributions low and still keep the system solvent. The Court refused to see the exclusion of benefits for pregnancy as discrimination based on gender and stated in a line that later became famous (though it was relegated to a footnote in the opinion itself), "While it is true that only women can become pregnant... the program divides potential recip-ients into two groups—pregnant women and nonpregnant persons. While the first group is exclusively female, the second group includes members of both sexes. The fiscal and actuarial benefits of the program thus accrue to members of both sexes" (p. 497).

This seductively simple statement masks the reality of pregnancy dis-crimination, which feminists of the 1970s and today argue is that preg-nant women are discriminated against because they are engaging in the reproductive role of women and that women are discriminated against in large part because they are the gender that is capable of bearing chil-dren. Justice William Brennan wrote a strong dissent to the *Geduldig* de-cision in which he examined pregnancy discrimination in a more thorough manner and concluded, "Such dissimilar treatment of men and women, on the basis of physical characteristics inextricably linked to one's sex, inevitably constitutes sex discrimination" (p. 501). Today, the *Geduldig* decision remains much criticized but valid law.

Geduldig was a constitutional decision, but Title VII was statutory law that reached beyond the Constitution to regulate private employ-ment and was not necessarily subject to the same analysis. So even after *Geduldig,* women continued to challenge the exclusion of coverage of pregnancy from disability policies under Title VII against private em-ployers. And the lower courts hearing those cases found that the analy-sis in *Geduldig* did not necessarily apply in the context of Title VII and that pregnancy was included in the prohibition of sex discrimination in Title VII (*General Electric Co.* v. *Gilbert,* 1976).

The issue of whether pregnancy was included within the meaning of "sex" under Title VII reached the Supreme Court in 1976 in *Gen-eral Electric Co.* v. *Gilbert.* Gilbert challenged a disability plan that was almost identical to the one in *Geduldig,* though offered through her employer, and the Court proceeded to analyze her challenge almost identically as well. The Court found that its analysis under the equal protection clause was applicable to Title VII and this time emphasized the "nonpregnant persons" language to state that the reason *Geduldig* rejected the feminist argument about the nature of pregnancy discrim-ination, and the Court was doing so again, was that neither plan in it-self discriminated based on sex, since both men and women were the nonpregnant comparison group. However, Title VII also has a second avenue of liability that is not available under the equal protection clause: liability based on disparate impact. The theory of disparate im-pact liability is that a practice by an employer, even if neutral on its face, may be discriminatory if its negative effects fall disproportion-ately on a protected group. The Supreme Court in *Gilbert* recognized the possibility of applying this theory to the disability policy chal-lenged, but it found the disparate impact theory not applicable to the case, reasoning that overall, the plan did not discriminate against wom-en in that it covered them for many causes of disability. In so doing, the Court did not consider that the particular practice of excluding pregnancy, not the plan itself, was having the negative effect and that its sole effect was on women.

Justice Brennan also wrote a dissenting opinion in this case, and in that opinion he explored the context of sex discrimination at the com-pany that provided the challenged plan. The company sued had "a his-tory of... practices that have served to undercut the employment opportunities of women who become pregnant while employed" (p. 150), including scaling women's wages at two-thirds of men's and forcing employees to take maternity leave while not providing them with disability payments. That is, of course, the better way to see preg-nancy discrimination: as part of a larger pattern of discrimination.

The reaction to the *Gilbert* decision in the feminist, union, and civil rights communities can be fairly described as livid. Critical discussions of the case immediately surfaced in legal articles, and feminists and oth-ers began a campaign to have Congress overrule the Court's decision, which it could do, since the Court's decision was interpreting a statute, not the Constitution. It was called the Campaign to End Discrimina-tion Against Pregnant Workers, and it offered, among other strategies, the testimony of prominent feminists to Congress (Strimling, 1989).

A year later, however, the Supreme Court issued a ruling that ap-peared to back off its stand in *Geduldig* and *Gilbert*. In *Nashville Gas Co.* v. *Satty (1977)*, the Court found that a policy of forcing pregnant women to both take leave and forfeit their accrued seniority when they returned from leave, requiring them to compete with less senior peo-ple for their old jobs back, did violate Title VII. In distinguishing this situation from that in *Gilbert*, the Court used a benefit-versus-burden analysis to find that although employers did not have to extend ma-ternity disability benefits to women that were inapplicable to men, they could not punish a woman by imposing on her the "substantial burden" (p. 142) of losing her seniority. This benefit-versus-burden analysis was briefly the law under Title VII, and at least two courts ap-plied it to invalidate employer policies that did burden pregnant work-ers (*Zuniga* v. *Kleburg County Hospital*, 1982; *Mitchell* v. *Board of Trustees*, 1979).

THE PREGNANCY DISCRIMINATION ACT

Congress reacted quickly to the Supreme Court's decisions and the fem-inist campaign against them. After *Geduldig*, it amended the Internal Revenue Code to prevent the states from excluding pregnancy from their unemployment compensation programs. And in 1978, after *Gil-bert*, Congress passed the Pregnancy Discrimination Act (PDA; PL. 95-555) as an amendment to Title VII. Title VII already prohibited dis-crimination based on sex, and the PDA defined *sex* to include "preg-nancy, childbirth, or related medical conditions." This amendment was passed specifically to reject the Supreme Court's interpretation of *sex* in

Gilbert, and its legislative history makes this clear: "The Supreme Court's narrow interpretations of Title VII tend to erode our national policy of nondiscrimination in employment" (Prohibition of Sex Discrimination Based on Pregnancy, 1978).

With the PDA passed, the question for the courts (and advocates) was no longer whether the law covered pregnancy but the extent of that coverage. The PDA contains two clauses, the first of which is quoted above and the second of which states, "Women affected by pregnancy, childbirth, or related medical conditions shall be treated the same for all employment-related purposes, including receipt of benefits under fringe benefit plans, as other persons not so affected but similar in their ability or inability to work."

Under this law, it is clear that employers can no longer discrimi-nate based on pregnancy. They cannot fire or refuse to hire pregnant women because they are pregnant, and they must offer coverage of pregnancy in any health and disability plans they offer that provide coverage of similarly disabling conditions. Mandatory leave is a clear-cut violation of the PDA, and voluntary leave around the time of child-birth is required under the PDA if the employer would allow such a leave for other reasons.

But because the PDA did not provide an "affirmative definition of gender equality" (Strimling, 1989, p. 189), what treatment of pregnant workers was allowed under the PDA and how best to remedy preg-nancy discrimination became a defining issue in the "equal treatment" versus "special treatment" debate among feminists that was so promi-nent in the 1980s. Those who advocated equal treatment called for strict equality and neutrality in the law. They argued that laws explic-itly based on pregnancy would only reinforce stereotypes of women as childbearers. Advocates of special treatment, however, contended that absolutely identical treatment of men and women resulted in in-equality between the sexes where women's needs were different. Preg-nancy, then, became a central part of this debate, as the capability to bear children is the defining biological difference between the sexes. Equal treatment proponents asserted that the PDAs equality approach was preferable, as it did not demand any treatment different from that which was available for similarly disabling conditions. They argued that any particular maternity policies smacked of the paternalism and sexism of the early twentieth-century protective legislation and would make women workers less attractive to employers, thus disadvantag-ing them in the workplace. Special treatment advocates countered that there was no condition similar to pregnancy and that it is simply a fact that women and men are different in this regard. To hold women to the same benefits as men perpetuated a male norm in the workplace. Only by providing for this unique condition of women would women actually be able to achieve equality in the workplace.

The PDA creates equality of treatment only; it does not mandate any kind of treatment: time off, rehiring, or anything else. That is, an employer who offers no time off, no health insurance, or no disabil-ity insurance for its other employees need not offer those benefits just to pregnant employees. So while the mandate of equality in the PDA is essential, this bare requirement of equal treatment is also lacking: "Employers can treat pregnant women as badly as they treat similar-ly affected but non-pregnant employees" (*Troupe* v. *May Department Stores*, 1994, p. 738). Thus, while the PDA has been a great step for-ward for women in the workforce, it still leaves gaps in protection. Some states attempted to go further than the PDA and passed laws guaranteeing maternity leave or job reinstatement after a woman returns from maternity leave (or both). Such laws were seen as prob-lematic to supporters of a strict equal treatment view, but were ap-plauded by special treatment advocates.

The Supreme Court addressed the issue of whether these state laws were permitted under the PDA in *California Federal Savings and Loan Association* v. *Guerra* (1987). Although the case was decided on very narrow grounds of federal law preemption, as a practical matter it still answered the question of what states could and could not do to in-crease protections of pregnant workers. The Supreme Court upheld a California law that guaranteed new mothers four months of leave and reinstatement after the leave. The opponents of the California law, in-cluding some feminist organizations, argued this law was contrary to the PDAs second clause that mandated equal treatment only and would have the feared effect of making women stand out in the workplace as less desirable employees. The Court, however, agreed with proponents of the law, including other feminist groups (Strimling, 1989), that the PDA served only as a "floor" for the protection of pregnant workers. Since the California law and the PDA had the same goal—equality in the workplace for pregnant women—the state law was not preempted by the PDA. States are thus able, though not required, to provide greater protections for pregnant employees than are offered by the PDA, as some now do.

JOHNSON CONTROLS AND SPECIAL SUSCEPTIBILITIES DURING PREGNANCY

A particular quandary with regard to pregnant workers is the extent to which the physical changes during pregnancy make a woman more susceptible to any harm in the workplace. This can be a particular problem in industries in which workers are exposed to potentially harmful chemicals or other agents. There are two sides to this prob-lem: the extent to which employers are allowed to mandate different treatment for pregnant employees and the extent to which employees are entitled to request different treatment. Within the framework of the PDA, employers are limited in what they can mandate for their employees, but employees have limited ability to request changes in their working environment.

In *International Union* v. *Johnson Controls* (1991), the Supreme Court addressed the legality, under Title VII, of an employment policy that prohibited all women of reproductive age, unless they could dem-onstrate infertility, from jobs that involved exposure to lead, due to concern about health risks to the fetus of any women who may be-come pregnant.

The company's actual policy stated that women "ca-pable of bearing children" would be forbidden from the jobs with exposure to lead, whereas there was no such limitation on the jobs available to fertile men. The Court held that this policy was a facially discriminatory one as fertile men were treated differently from fertile women, the only difference being sex. The express language of the PDA supported the Court's holding because the use of the phrase "ca-pable of bearing children" thus "explicitly classifies on the basis of po-tential for pregnancy" (p. 199). The employer's fear of liability suits for injured babies did not justify this facial discrimination. Thus, since *Johnson Controls,* women may not be singled out for different treat-ment in the workplace solely due to their potential to become preg-nant, which was an increasingly common practice in industry until this ruling (Jason, 1990).

In *Johnson Controls,* the Court expressed approval of the approach of the Occupational Health and Safety Administration (OSHA) to reg-ulating lead. That approach considers that lead is a potential danger to all employees; it prescribes a program of medical surveillance for all employees exposed to certain levels of lead and temporary removal of an employee from a job with exposure if he or she has a high blood lead level or on the recommendation of a physician.

Physicians can rec-ommend employees for removal based on any medical condition, in-cluding pregnancy. Pregnant workers, then, are protected from potential harm to their fetuses without being singled out for treatment different from other employees. This is an example of equal treatment combined with just a little bit of special treatment, as pregnancy is specifically mentioned as a temporary condition that may justify temporary job removal.

Johnson Controls did not, however, address whether pregnant em-ployees have the right to request changes in their job conditions due to any increased level of danger to themselves or their fetuses. Again, under the PDA, employees are only guaranteed the same rights as others sim-ilarly able or unable to do their jobs.

That means that if an employer generally allows changes in job structure or duties, or specifically does when a worker faces a new inability to do certain tasks, then that option must be made available to pregnant employees. But if the employer al-lows no such job alterations, then they need not be made just for preg-nant employees.

A well-known example is the case of a nurse who asked not to treat an HIV-positive patient due to her compromised immune system during her pregnancy. Her request was denied because an alter-ation of job responsibilities was not usually allowed. Accordingly, her resulting claim for pregnancy discrimination failed as well (*Armstrong* v. *Flowers Hospital, Inc.,* 1994). In another case decided under the Dis-trict of Columbia Human Rights Act, which has language identical to the PDA, the court found a pregnant medical technician did not have the right to avoid work involving radiation exposure.

As is discussed below, there is no right to reasonable accommodation in the PDA (Weirich, 2003).

LIMITATIONS OF THE PREGNANCY DISCRIMINATION ACT

Although the Pregnancy Discrimination Act represents an important milestone in the protection of women's legal rights in the workplace, it is based on a model of equality that also creates obstacles for preg-nant women workers.

Limitations in What the PDA Covers

The PDA is the ultimate example of the equal treatment advocates' ar-gument: pregnant workers are to be treated exactly like other employ-ees who are similarly able or unable to perform their job duties—no better, no worse. However, that minimum of equality does not extend to behavior that is caused by or related to pregnancy, such as tardiness due to morning sickness or the need for frequent breaks to use the rest-room or have snacks (Greenberg, 1998). Courts view such effects of pregnancy as actions standing alone, without considering that they are directly caused by the pregnancy. Lateness due to morning sickness is treated as the inability to be at work on time, not as the temporary result of the pregnancy *(Troupev. May Department Stores,* 1994). There are even worse examples: employees have been laid off or fired while on maternity leave due to their absence. Courts nevertheless find that the reason for the dismissal was the absence from the workplace due to the leave, not that the pregnancy of the woman was the cause of the leave and thus the cause of the dismissal (*Crnokrak* v. *Evangelical Health Systems,* 1993). In addition to these limitations of coverage, not all em-ployees are even covered by Title VII, which applies only to employers with fifteen or more employees. However, much smaller employers are often covered by state and local antidiscrimination statutes.

The lack of consideration of the effects of pregnancy, which vary from woman to woman, has led commentators on the law to propose that a model of reasonable accommodation should be applied to preg-nancy. This model already applies to disabled workers under the Amer-icans with Disabilities Act (ADA) and also to religiously observant workers under Title VII itself. Both the ADA and Title VII with regard to religion mandate that employers make reasonable accommodations in the workplace on an individualized basis in consideration of the employee's disability or religious observance, as long as the accom-modation does not impose an undue burden on the employer. This model would provide coverage of many of the needs surrounding preg-nancy, such as morning sickness, while taking into account that each woman's experience with pregnancy is different. However, pregnant women are not normally covered under the provisions of the ADA (Greenberg, 1998; Millsap, 1996) and reasonable accommodation is not a part of the PDA. But at least one state, Minnesota, currently pro-vides reasonable accommodation of pregnancy in its state antidis-crimination laws (Greenberg, 1998).

The protection of the PDA does extend to the spouses of male em-ployees (*Newport News Shipbuilding and Dry Dock Co.* v. *EEOC*, 1983). And the PDA explicitly covers "related medical conditions," which has been held to include insurance coverage for birth control pills but not for infertility treatment (*Erickson* v. *Bartell Drug Co.*, 2001; *Krauelv. Iowa Methodist Medical Center*, 1996). The Eighth Circuit Court of Ap-peals held that infertility is not covered under the PDA because infer-tility, unlike pregnancy and childbirth, is not limited to women and is different from the latter two conditions, which are postconception. Other courts, however, have disagreed with that position on infertil-ity (Weirich, 2003). The PDA has also been held to prohibit discrimination based on whether a woman chooses to abort her pregnancy, though the language of the PDA itself specifically does not require em-ployers to pay for insurance coverage of abortion (*Turicv. Holland Hospitality, Inc.*, 1996).

Difficulties with Pursuing a Lawsuit Under the PDA

For all employees who feel they have been discriminated against, tak-ing a case to court is a difficult undertaking. Disparate treatment un-der Title VII must be intentional, and though the *McDonnell Douglas* burden-shifting procedure is designed to aid plaintiffs, such cases are still notoriously difficult, though of course not impossible, for plain-tiffs to win. In the case of pregnancy discrimination, the obstacles are, if anything, even greater. First, the prima facie case a plaintiff must prove to proceed with her case requires her to identify a similarly sit-uated man (since pregnancy discrimination is a subset of sex discrim-ination) who was treated more favorably than she was. However, as numerous commentators have pointed out, there really is no other con-dition like pregnancy. It is not an illness, though it may have effects similar to some illnesses. It is necessarily of a limited and predictable duration, and the woman was likely not ill before her pregnancy and will not be ill after it. She probably does not consider herself ill. But without such a similarly situated person to compare herself to, most pregnancy discrimination plaintiffs' cases fail (Greenberg, 1998).

Second, the power that stereotypes still play is evident in the deci-sions of judges regarding so-called direct evidence of discrimination. A plaintiff with direct evidence of discrimination, usually a statement by the employer, should have a stronger case than one with only in-direct proof. But some courts demand that for such a statement to be considered direct evidence, it must be close in time to and directly connected to the negative employment action, or the statement must be a bald one that the employer acted due to the employee's pregnancy (Greenberg, 1998; Magid, 2001; Millsap, 1996).

However, employers have had experience with Title VII for forty years and the PDA for over twenty-five, and seldom make such incriminating statements. Rather, such comments are likely to come at more casual moments (Green-berg, 1998). Courts are unlikely to consider casual comments as indi-cating any discriminatory motive. Also, courts are likely to judge any comments about pregnant women other than "you're fired because you're pregnant" as insufficient evidence of motive. Examples include statements that women should not return to work after having a child and that pregnant women do not perform well in the workplace (Greenberg, 1998). Furthermore, as Greenberg argues in her article on the limitations of the PDA, judges may not accept such statements as discriminatory because they play into deep stereotypes of pregnant women: that they are and should be preoccupied with their families and that they are lazy or hysterical (or both). When stereotypes and assumptions are so deeply held, they are often difficult to see. But the persistence of these stereotypes makes it even more difficult for preg-nancy discrimination plaintiffs to win lawsuits. Perhaps that fact is not unrelated to the increasing number of EEOC complaints of pregnancy discrimination (EEOC, 2003). However, one study found that verdicts for plaintiffs in pregnancy discrimination cases are substantially larger than those in other types of sex discrimination suits, such as sexual harassment and gender discrimination (Schultz, 2003). This suggests that although pregnancy discrimination is hard to prove, juries are es-pecially outraged when it is proven.

THE FAMILY AND MEDICAL LEAVE ACT

The Family and Medical Leave Act (FMLA) acts as a supplement to the PDA that provides a positive mandate of treatment: leave from work for pregnancy, childbirth, and medical complications of either. This law was signed into effect by President Clinton in 1993 after years of advocacy by women's rights groups. The FMLA is a very technical law, and its coverage is limited: it applies only to employees of com-panies with fifty or more employees, who have worked there for at least twelve months and have worked at least 1,250 hours over those twelve months. The fifty-employee threshold means the FMLA's cov-erage is limited to 58 percent of employees in the private sector (Can-tor et al., 2001). Covered employees are guaranteed up to twelve weeks of (unpaid) leave per year for qualifying events, including the birth of a child or a serious health condition of the worker. There is also guar-anteed reinstatement to the same position or an equivalent one after the leave. Significantly, this is a strict liability statute, meaning that some-one whose FMLA rights have been violated does not need to prove her employer violated her rights for any particular reason to prevail in a lawsuit, only that they were violated.

More important, this is a positive statute that creates a substantive entitlement to a particular amount of leave after the birth of a child or due to the health problems of the worker, which can include any pregnancy or childbirth-related problems if they are serious enough. This is a different type of remedy to the problems of pregnancy in the workplace, and one that is necessary for new mothers to avoid even more difficult choices than are inherent in both working and raising children. And it is an entitlement that many women are taking ad-vantage of: in 2000, a Labor Department-sponsored survey of em-ployees found that 7.9 percent of people taking FMLA leave, or 1.88 million women, had taken maternity-disability leave under the FMLA in the prior eighteen months and an additional 4.4 million people had taken leave to care for a new child (Cantor et al., 2001).

The women's rights community views the FMLA as a good start to meeting the needs of workers faced with conflicting demands between their jobs and their families. But it is only a start. Advocates would like to see leave allowed for more purposes, leave guaranteed for employ-ees of smaller employers, and especially paid leave (National Partner-ship for Women and Families, 2002b). Advocacy for paid leave is taking place at both the federal and state levels and is having the most effect in the states. Paid leave would expand the practical impact of the FMLA enormously: 2.73 million workers in the Department of Labor survey did not take leave they needed because they could not afford to do so (Cantor et al., 2001).

A portion of the FMLA was recently challenged under the Eleventh Amendment: whether the FMLA can provide monetary damages for employees of state governments if they win a lawsuit under that law (there was never any doubt that the FMLA applied to the states as em-ployers; the question was only about the type of enforcement).

In a ringing opinion in *Nevada Department of Human Resources* v. *Hibbs*, the Supreme Court in June 2003 held that the FMLA does properly au-thorize monetary damages against state governments, due to the fact that it addresses gender discrimination prohibited by the equal pro-tection clause. This decision is important for many reasons, many of which have nothing to do with pregnancy discrimination. But it is vitally important for preserving the rights of millions of women who are employed by state governments, and it buttresses the interpreta-tion of the equal protection clause that recognizes that stereotypes and expectations of women are a cause of discrimination and can be dis-criminatory themselves if applied to women.

STATE LAWS AND EMPLOYER POLICIES

Since the Supreme Court's ruling in *California Federal Savings and Loan Association* v. *Guerra* (1987), several states in addition to California have enacted legislative protection for pregnancy that exceeds that in the PDA. Many of those laws now are also state versions of the FMLA, which are often more generous than the federal law. State laws have the disadvantage of covering only workers in individual states, but they do expand protections for pregnant women in those states and can be "laboratories" *(New State Ice Co.* v. *Leibmann,* 1932) to provide posi-tive examples and proof to counter arguments about costs to business used to argue against expanded federal protections. Many states take the path that was affirmed in *California Federal Savings and Loan Association* v. *Guerra* and guarantee maternity dis-ability leave. This leave is either for a set period of time, often six to eight weeks, or for the time of physical disability caused by pregnancy and birth, which is usually a similar period (Jacobson, 1988). As of 2004, twenty-one states have such maternity disability laws (Zintl, 2004). Those laws usually have a minimum number of employees an employer must have to be covered by the law, but that number is al-ways lower than the high fifty-employee threshold in the FMLA. A few of the maternity disability laws (in Hawaii, New York, and Rhode Is-land) also give women a portion of their weekly wages while out on leave, a significant advantage over current federal law under both the PDA and FMLA. Several other states (some of which overlap with the maternity disability states) provide their own versions of the FMLA (U.S. Department of Labor, 2004). Like the FMLA, these state laws are broader than maternity disability laws in that they cover other reasons for leave as well, but they always provide leave for childbirth and the postpartum period.

The latest frontier in this area of protections for pregnant employ-ees is the idea of guaranteed paid leave. Although this idea is not new (Wilson, 1976-1977), it has only recently been seriously considered by state governments. California became one of the first states to provide paid FMLA-type leave for several reasons, including the birth of a child. Employees in California are guaranteed 55 to 60 percent of their wages for up to six weeks of leave per year. This program is an exten-sion of the employee-funded State Disability Insurance system, the same one challenged in *Geduldigv. Aiello*. Eligibility for paid benefits under this program began in June 2004, when leave became a reality for millions of lower-income workers in California who could not oth-erwise afford to take the leave they or their families may require. Four other states have similar temporary disability benefit programs that could also be extended to cover maternity leave (National Partnership for Women and Families, 2002a). And in other states, paid leave study commissions have been set up or legislation has been introduced (Na-tional Partnership for Women and Families, 2002b). However, a differ-ent option for funding paid leave, apart from the expansion of existing disability payment systems, was recently eliminated. The Department of Labor had ruled in June

2002 that states could create "Baby UI" plans, programs by which states could choose to use their unemployment compensation funds to pay for leave due to the birth or adoption of a child. This was a significant step that opened up a realistic source of funding for this leave. However, no state implemented a "Baby UI" plan, and in the fall of 2003, the Department of Labor rescinded the rule allowing such programs.

In addition to state laws, the *California Federal Savings and Loan As-sociation* decision also allows employers to offer maternity policies that are much more generous than those required by any law (Lindemann, Grossman, & Cane, 1996). And many do: 24 percent of employers offer more than twelve weeks of unpaid leave per year, and 34 percent of all employers continue pay during maternity-related leave (Cantor et al., 2001). However, an admittedly unscientific poll by *American Baby* mag-azine in 2001 found that three out of four women are dissatisfied with the maternity leave offered by their employers, and almost half of wom-en get no paid leave whatsoever from their employers ("Fifty Percent Increase in Women in the Workforce," 2001).

COMPARISON TO OTHER INDUSTRIALIZED COUNTRIES

The protection of pregnant workers in the United States, though in-creasing, is far less generous than international standards and the re-quired leave and benefits for pregnant women in other industrialized countries. The International Labor Organization, a United Nations agency, has created a set of minimum standards for maternity leave: twelve weeks of leave, payment during leave of at least two-thirds of a woman's income, with such payments coming from a social security or insurance plan, not employers. The United States meets only the first of those standards, through the FMLA, and even that presumes that a woman has not had any other reason to use any of her total al-lotment of twelve weeks of leave per year. In contrast, other industri-alized countries offer guaranteed maternity leave with some payment during that leave. And 140 countries around the world offer guaran-teed maternity leave, although it is often not enforced in developing countries ("A Break for New Moms," 1996).

The European Union has a policy directive on pregnant workers that is binding on member countries. It directs its member countries to provide workers with at least fourteen weeks of maternity leave, in-cluding at least two weeks of compulsory leave around the birth itself; time off for prenatal medical care; protection that workers will not lose their jobs due to pregnancy or leave taking; and special proce-dures to protect pregnant women from potentially harmful chemicals in the workplace. Member countries must implement these provisions and are free to offer more generous leave, benefits, or protections if they desire. And many countries do.

Some countries' policies origi-nally had the nonfeminist purposes of encouraging childbirth and thus population growth (Hunt, Hsia, Smith, Martin, and Rosenwein, 1995) or were based on ideas that pregnant women should not work, but they are now based more on equality and general ideas of social welfare. All nineteen Western European countries provide mater-nity leave job protection and paid parental leave, most of them offer-ing benefits and protections that are far more generous than, though different from, those in the United States.

For example, Germany guar-antees mothers 100 percent of their wages for up to six weeks of leave before childbirth and eight weeks after it, with an additional sixty-nine weeks of leave at a flat rate. In France, parents are guaranteed six-teen weeks of leave at 100 percent of their wages and up to three years of unpaid leave with job protection. Perhaps more typical is the Netherlands, which offers sixteen weeks of paid leave and job protec-tion for six months (Jordan, 1999).

Those kinds of protections are ob-viously much more generous to new parents than current U.S. laws, and also better recognize the demands that new babies place on their parents. They allow parents the time they may wish to have with their children by making it economically feasible to take the time off. And they create a norm that parents do take significant time off from work after a child is born. Other industrialized countries are also ahead of the United States when it comes to maternity leave. Canada guaran-tees maternity leave, with the amount of leave up to the individual provinces. In Quebec the leave is for eighteen weeks, and in Ontario it is for seventeen weeks. There are also maternity leave benefits paid by the Federal Unemployment Insurance system (Invest in Canada, 2003; Glavinovich, 1996). New Zealand offers fourteen weeks of ma-ternity leave and up to fifty-two weeks of extended parental leave, and in 2002 it initiated paid parental leave for twelve of those weeks (In-ternational Observatory of Labour Law, 2001; Thomas, 2002).

American policies, in contrast, have been described as "Third World" ("A Break for New Moms," 1996). But the policies of other nations in-spired American advocates to work toward the PDA and FMLA ini-tially, and they continue to inspire (and embarrass) advocates who want to continue to improve U.S. policies, especially toward paid leave (National Partnership for Women and Families, 2002b). European policies on maternity and parental leave differ in two other significant ways from American laws. First, seven countries restrict parental leave to women (Jordan, 1999). In the United States, though women do take more FMLA leave than men do (Cantor et al., 2001), the FMLA allows either parent to do so. As the Supreme Court recently recognized, open-ing parental leave to both men and women serves the simultaneous purposes of relieving gender discrimination against women and dis-couraging the stereotype that men are not involved in the care of chil-dren *(Nevada Department of Human Resourcesv. Hibbs,* 2003). Limiting leave to women may relieve overt discrimination, but it also may re-inforce the already prevalent stereotype and profound expectation of mothers that they are the primary caregivers for their children. While many women embrace that role, it is not always possible or even pre-ferred. Having achieved a gender-neutral leave law in this country, though, it is unlikely that the United States would then limit leave to women.

Nine European countries mandate that women take prenatal or postnatal leave (or both) from their jobs (Jordan, 1999), something that is not allowed under the PDA. There is an argument that com-pulsory paid leave, especially after the birth of a child, has the benefit of eliminating all pressure not to take the leave and stigma for tak-ing it. However, mandated leave also deprives women of the option to choose for themselves how they want to handle the demands of both work and motherhood. And compulsory prenatal leave, regardless of the health status of the woman, deprives the many healthy and active pregnant women the option of working if they choose and reinforces the stereotype that pregnant women cannot or should not work.

Although generally other industrial countries provide pregnancy and parental leave policies that are far more generous than American ones, they sometimes do so in ways that are different from American policies and are not likely to be adopted here. The central policies of other na-tions with regard to maternity leave (longer leave and some pay during the leave) are clearly policies that the United States is slowing moving toward and may someday reach.

CONCLUSION

Pregnancy discrimination is an ongoing problem facing working women. Although the legislative achievements and judicial decisions of the past thirty years have greatly reduced the severity of such discrimi-nation, it still exists and is difficult to prove. Advocates are pushing for, and many states are experimenting with providing, greater protections to pregnant workers, though a comparison to the law of other countries shows that it is possible to go much further.

7

Update on Abortion Law

In the United States, the intensity of the discourse over abortion is frightening and frequently beyond reasoned debate. When physicians are murdered as a result of their abortion-related activities and clinics providing abortions require security precautions reminis-cent of a prison system, it becomes difficult to imagine a middle ground. The goal of this chapter is not to revisit political and religious debates over whether abortion is right or wrong. Rather, it seeks to present a broader perspective. The reality of abortion has been acknowledged by the American legal system, with each Supreme Court decision redefin-ing the line between a woman's legal right to make decisions about her own body and its reproductive functioning, and the limitations on that right as a pregnancy progresses and the viability of an unborn child outside the womb is more likely.

The evolution of American case law reflects the ongoing debate over the control of a woman's reproductive life, and it is often only in ret-rospect that we can see how unnecessarily intrusive a law has been. For example, until the Supreme Court began to discuss reproductive pri-vacy in *Griswoldv. Connecticut* in 1964, it was illegal in Connecticut for even married women to use birth control. Since then, case law has extended privacy to include a right to abortion *(Roev. Wade,* 1973), but has continued to review the conditions under which this privacy can be exercised. It has examined the interests of a range of possible stakeholders in a woman's reproductive decisions (such as the spouse of an adult woman or the parents of a teenage girl), including the state and the unborn child. It has allowed constraints on access (funding, waiting periods) that make the right to abortion more theoretical than actual for many women. The politics of abortion have resulted in iso-lated rights for unborn children (twenty-six states have "fetal homicide" laws), while some legislators attempt to eliminate a pregnant woman's right to choose late-term abortion when her own life or health is at risk (the federal Partial Birth Abortion Act of 2003). The abortion debate has evolved to include moral judgments as well as moral loopholes: those who oppose abortion will generally allow it in the case of rape or incest; those who support abortion will tolerate Medicaid exclusions that make abortion effectively unavailable to poor women for finan-cial reasons. This chapter reviews the legal reasoning underlying case decisions about abortion, as well as the psychological research on women's experience with abortion. It looks at current efforts to set lim-its on women's reproductive lives in what some have called "the new civil war" (Beckman & Harvey, 1998). It also looks at the efforts of a group of women who sought, if not reconciliation, then at least a mu-tual understanding in this "war" in the aftermath of the 1994 Boston-area shooting at a Planned Parenthood clinic by John Salvi.

HISTORY

Legislation and case law continue to struggle with two central issues: When do other people, including the state, have the right to make de-cisions about any individual's body? To what extent does a woman have the freedom to control her own reproductive activities? The abortion debate is partly about a woman's control of her own body and whether she is able to choose when and if she will get pregnant, and partly about a woman's control of the course of her life generally. For women, re-productive rights are not simply about access to abortion, but also in-clude access to birth control and protections against discrimination once they become pregnant.

Historian Linda Gordon (1990) notes,

> Because of the different interest of men and women in the practice of birth control, differences in birth-control techniques have social significance. Some techniques are more amenable than others to being used independently and even secretly by women; some give full con-trol to men; others are more likely to be used cooperatively. Thus, it is important to be specific when considering birth control. For example, a list of the types of birth control might

look like this: infanticide; abortion; sterilizing surgery; withdrawal by the male (coitus in-terruptus); melting suppositories designed to form an impenetrable coating over the cervix; diaphragms, caps, or other devices which are inserted into the vagina over the cervix and withdrawn after inter-course; intrauterine devices; internal medicines—potions or pills; douching and other forms of action after intercourse designed to kill or drive out the sperm; condoms; and varieties of rhythm methods, based on calculating the woman's fertile period and abstaining from intercourse during it. All these techniques were practiced in the an-cient world and in modern preindustrial societies. Indeed, until the modern hormone-suppressing pill there were no essentially new birth-control devices, only improvements of the old [pp. 28-29].

In *Griswoldv. Connecticut* (1965), the Supreme Court first addressed the issue of reproductive privacy when it overruled a Connecticut law banning the distribution or use of contraceptives, even within mar-riage. In writing for the majority, Justice William Douglas noted:

The present case... concerns a relationship lying within the zone of privacy created by several fundamental constitutional guarantees. And it concerns a law which, in forbidding the use of contraceptives rather than regulating their manufacture or sale, seeks to achieve its goals by means having the maximum destructive impact upon that relation-ship.... Would we allow the police to search the sacred precincts of marital bedrooms for telltale signs of the use of contraceptives? The very idea is repulsive to the notions of privacy surrounding the mar-riage relationship.

We deal with a right of privacy older than the bill of rights—older than our political parties, older than our school system. Marriage is a coming together for better or for worse, hopefully enduring, and inti-mate to the degree of being sacred. It is an association that promotes a way of life, not causes; a harmony in living, not political faiths; a bi-lateral loyalty, not commercial or social projects. Yet it is an associa-tion for as noble a purpose as any involved in our prior decisions [pp. 485-486].

ABORTION

Until relatively recently, abortion was treated like one of many meth-ods of birth control and was not viewed as morally distinct from other methods. Law professors Sylvia Law, Jane E. Larson, and Clyde Spil-lenger reviewed the history of abortion in the United States in their amicus curiae brief submitted to the Supreme Court in *Planned Par-enthood of Southeastern Pennsylvaniav. Casey* (1992). They noted that at the time of the drafting of the federal constitution in the late eigh-teenth century, abortion was known and not illegal. In the nineteenth century, it became even more widely accepted.

Through the nineteenth century, American common law decisions uniformly reaffirmed that women committed no offense in seeking abortions. Both common law and popular American understanding drew distinctions depending upon whether the fetus was "quick," i.e. whether the woman perceived signs of independent life. There was some dispute whether a common law misdemeanor occurred when a third party destroyed a fetus, after quickening, without the woman's consent. But early common law recognition of this crime against a pregnant woman did not diminish the woman's liberty to end a preg-nancy herself in its early stages.

Abortion was not a pressing social issue in colonial America, but as a social practice, it was far from unknown. Herbal abortifacients were widely known, and cookbooks and women's diaries of the era con-tained recipes for such medicines. Recent studies of the work of mid-wives in the 1700s report cases in which the midwives appeared to have provided women abortifacient compounds. Such treatments do not appear to have been regarded as extraordinary or illicit by those ad-ministering them....

In the late eighteenth century, strictures on sexual behavior loos-ened considerably. The incidence of premarital pregnancy rose sharply; by the late eighteenth century, one third of all New England brides were pregnant when they married, compared to less than ten percent in the seventeenth century. Falling birth rates in the 1780s suggest that, at the time of the drafting of the Constitution, the use of birth control and abortion was increasing....

Through the nineteenth century and well into the twentieth, abor-tion remained a widely accepted practice, despite growing efforts after 1860 to prohibit it....

... The most common methods of abortion in the nineteenth cen-tury involved self administered herbs and devices available from phar-macists. Nonetheless, women also relied on professional abortionists: in 1871, New York City, with a population of less than one million, supported two hundred full-time abortionists, not including doctors who also sometimes performed abortions.

The late nineteenth century saw a movement toward professional-ization across disciplines. This was a time when industrial and scien-tific developments were rapid, and meaningful progress was being made in the understanding of the basic sciences and their applications to medicine. At the same time, many workers perceived economic com-petition from both increased immigration and the increased levels of education (including professional education) becoming available to blacks and to women. The late 1800s saw the opening of the first wom-en's colleges and the first black colleges, as well as some progress toward allowing these previously excluded groups to attend state uni-versities.

As occupations such as medicine and law developed professional associations, they also created standards of training and licensure that were narrowly drawn and inevitably excluded women, minorities, and recently arrived immigrants. Law et al. (1992) note that between 1850 and 1880, the American Medical Association became the "single most important factor in altering the legal policies toward abortion in the country":

> The doctors found an audience for their effort to restrict abortion be-cause they appealed to specific social concerns and anxieties: maternal health, consumer protection, discriminatory ideas about the properly subordinate status of women, and racist/ nativist fears generated by the fact the elite Protestant women often sought abortions. Some of these doctors also sought to attribute moral status to the fetus.

Abortion regulation became a tool in the political and economics-driven process of defining who should be allowed to practice medi-cine and a means of excluding groups such as midwives and abortion providers who were not medical doctors. Law et al. (1992) note,

> Physicians were the principal nineteenth-century proponents of laws to restrict abortion. A core purpose of the nineteenth-century laws, and the doctors in supporting them, was to control medical practice in the interest of public safety.... Anti-abortion laws would weaken the appeal of the competition and take the

pressure off the more mar-ginal members of the regulars' [regular physicians] own sect.

While physicians at the time argued that abortion regulation was for the purpose of protecting the safety and health of women, there is ample evidence of a general resistance to the increasing independence and self-determination of women. Similar arguments were waged at the idea of women receiving college educations, and women seeking education were warned that college would be both physically and so-cially damaging to them. Specifically, it would damage their ability to bear children and would certainly make them less attractive to po-tential husbands (Palmer, n.d.).

Law et al. (1992) argue that the enforcement of sharply differenti-ated concepts of the roles of men and women underlay efforts to reg-ulate abortion and contraception in the nineteenth century:

Physicians persuaded political leaders (who were, of course, uniformly male) that "abortion constituted a threat to social order" and to male authority. Since the 1840s, a growing movement for women's suffrage and equality had generated popular fears that women were departing from a purely maternal role—fears fueled by the decline in family size during the nineteenth century. A central rhetorical focus of the woman's movement was framed by a new perception of women as the rightful possessors of their own bodies.

Opposition to abortion and contraception were closely linked, and can only be understood as a reaction to the uncertainties generated by changes in family function and anxieties created by women's challenges to their historic roles of silence and subservience. These challenges were critical factors motivating the all-male state legislatures that adopted restraints on women, including restrictions on abortion. In opposition to the feminist demand for control of reproduction, the federal gov-ernment in 1873 took the lead in banning access to information about both contraception and abortion.

Law et al. (1992) argue that contraception and abortion regulation also reflected ethnocentric fears about relative birthrates of immigrant and white Protestants during a period of intense immigration at the end of the nineteenth century:

Beginning in the 1890s, and continuing through the first decades of the twentieth century, nativist fears coalesced into a drive against what was then called "race suicide." The "race suicide" alarmists worried that women of "good stock"—prosperous, white, and Protestant—were not having enough children to maintain the political and social supremacy of their group. Anxiety over the falling birth rates of Protestant whites in comparison with other groups helped shape policy governing both birth control and abortion.

Abortion became a focal point in the debate about women's lives. In-terestingly, during the post-Civil War period, when the women's suf-frage movement was gaining momentum and the first wave of feminism was attempting to redefine women's roles, there were feminists opposed to abortion. Mary Krane Derr, in a 1991 amicus curiae brief, notes:

Early feminist opposition to abortion was deep-seated, and addressed the causes of abortion, not just the practice. In this way, it was distin-guished from other anti-abortion efforts including those of the Amer-ican Medical Association. Feminists documented that abortion was caused by, among other things, culturally enforced ignorance about sexual and reproductive physiology, especially family planning and fetal development; cultural construction of pregnancy as a patholog-ical condition; a sexual double standard which permitted men to be sexually and parentally irresponsible; the social valuing of "legitimacy" over children's lives and women's well-being; and lack of social and economic support for mothers, especially single ones.

For women, the choices were never simple or free of stigma, but be-fore 1973, upper- and middle-class patients with the right health care resources could obtain "therapeutic abortions" (Adler et al., 1992) if they declared themselves suicidal and received the appropriate docu-mentation from one or two psychiatrists. In 1970, more than 98 per-cent of the legal therapeutic abortions were for mental health reasons (Adler et al., 1992).

LEGAL CASES

The Supreme Court has been the arena for promoting and challeng-ing abortion in the United States. While *Roe* v. *Wade* (1973) established a woman's legal right to obtain an abortion, subsequent cases have ad-dressed efforts to define and restrict that right.

Roe v. *Wade:* A Fundamental Privacy Right

In *Roev. Wade* (1973), the U.S. Supreme Court described a woman's right to have an abortion as part of a fundamental right of privacy, similar to that in *Griswold,* and government interference with that right would be subject to strict judicial scrutiny.

Justice William Brennan, writing for the majority, noted that bans on abortion were relatively recent:

It perhaps is not generally appreciated that the restrictive criminal abortion laws in effect in a majority of States today are of relatively re-cent vintage. Those laws, generally proscribing abortion or its attempt at any time during pregnancy except when necessary to preserve the pregnant woman's life, are not of ancient or even common-law origin. Instead, they derive from statutory changes effected, for the most part, in the latter half of the 19th century....

It is thus apparent that at common law, at the time of the adoption of our Constitution, and throughout the major portion of the 19th century, abortion was viewed with less disfavor than under most American statutes currently in effect. Phrasing it another way, a wom-an enjoyed a substantially broader right to terminate a pregnancy than she does today [p. 720].

He went on to describe the "person" for whom the Constitution was intended and then introduced the issue of "viability," or the point at which the state has a "compelling interest" in the unborn child:

The Constitution does not define "person" in so many words.... But in nearly all these instances, the use of the word is such that it has ap-plication only postnatally None indicates, with any assurance, that it has any possible prenatal application.... In short, the unborn have never been recognized in the law as persons in the whole sense.

... We repeat, however, that the State does have an important and legitimate interest in preserving and protecting the health of the preg-nant woman, whether she be a resident of the State or a non-resident who seeks medical consultation and treatment there, and that it has still another important and legitimate interest in protecting the po-tentiality of human life. *These interests are separate and distinct* [ital-ics added]. Each grows in substantiality as the woman approaches term and, at a point during pregnancy, each becomes "compelling."

... The end of the first trimester mortality in abortion may be less than mortality in normal childbirth. It follows that, from and after this point, a State may regulate the abortion procedure to the extent that the regulation reasonably related to the preservation and protection of maternal health.

With respect to the state's important and legitimate interest in po-tential life, the "compelling" point is viability [p. 163].

Doe v. *Bolton:* Health of the Mother

In *Doev. Bolton* (1973), the companion case to *Roev. Wade,* the Su-preme Court held that the decision of whether a woman requires an abortion for the health of the mother is a medical judgment to "be ex-ercised in the light of all factors—physical, emotional, psychological, familial, and the woman's age— relevant to the well-being of the pa-tient" (p. 212).

Hyde Amendment and *Maher v. Roe:* Medicaid Funding

Since *Roe* v. *Wade,* the Supreme Court has used abortion cases to refine its position and define the limits to a woman's access to abortion. As states have enacted increasingly restrictive abortion laws, the Supreme Court has had to determine the boundary between a state's legitimate interest and an unreasonable interference in access to abortion.

Federal regulations have also implemented limitations on access and funding of abortions. The Hyde Amendment, passed by Congress in 1976, excludes abortion from the health care coverage provided to low-income women through Medicaid, except when a woman's life is at risk (Lichtman, 2003). Congress later amended the Hyde Amend-ment to allow coverage for abortions in cases of rape or incest.

States enacted legislation with similar restrictions. In *Maher*'v. *Roe* (1977), the Court was presented with the question of whether the right of access to abortion described in *Roe* v. *Wade* included an en-titlement to Medicaid payments for abortions that are not medically necessary. At issue in *Maher* was a Connecticut welfare regulation un-der which Medicaid recipients received payments for medical services incidental to childbirth but not for medical services incidental to non-therapeutic abortions. The Court held that the constitutional freedom recognized in *Wade* and its progeny "protects the woman from unduly burdensome interference with her freedom to decide whether to ter-minate her pregnancy" (pp. 473-474) such as the severe criminal sanc-tions at issue in *Roe* v. *Wade,* or the absolute requirement of spousal consent for an abortion challenged in *Planned Parenthood of Central Missouri* v. *Danforth* (1976), but did not prevent Connecticut from being free to make "a value judgment favoring childbirth over abor-tion, and... implement that judgment by the allocation of public funds" (p. 474):

Although government may not place obstacles in the path of a wom-an's exercise of her freedom of choice, it need not remove those not of its own creation. Indigency falls in the latter category. The financial constraints that restrict an indigent woman's ability to enjoy the full range of constitutionally protected freedom of choice are the product not of governmental restrictions on access to abortions, but rather of her indigency [p. 478].

The Court stated that indigent women do not even have a right to funding for a medically necessary abortion:

Although Congress has opted to subsidize medically necessary services generally, but not certain medically necessary abortions, the fact re-mains that the Hyde Amendment leaves an indigent woman with at least the same range of choice in deciding whether to obtain a med-ically necessary abortion as she would have had if Congress had cho-sen to subsidize no health care costs at all. We are thus not persuaded that the Hyde Amendment impinges on the constitutionally protected freedom of choice recognized in Wade [p. 478].

The Hyde Amendment sets a floor, but permits states to use their own funds to underwrite abortions for low-income women. As of Feb-ruary 2004, only four states (New York, Maryland, Hawaii, and Wash-ington) have done this voluntarily. Thirteen other states have done so under court order (Lichtman, 2003). Thirty-two states and the Dis-trict of Columbia follow the federal standard and provide abortions in cases of life endangerment, rape, or incest. One state, South Dakota, pays for abortions only when necessary to protect the woman's life (Alan Guttmacher Institute, 2004).

Congress has passed restrictions similar to the Hyde Amendment affecting programs on which an estimated 20 million women rely for their health care or insurance. According to the American Civil Lib-erties Union (2002), those denied access to federally funded abortion include poor women on Medicaid, Native Americans, federal employ-ees and their dependents, Peace Corps volunteers, low-income resi-dents of Washington, D.C, federal prisoners, and military personnel and their dependents.

New health initiatives are also being burdened by the legacy of the Hyde Amendment. The Children's Health Insurance Program, a pro-gram providing expanded health insurance for children aged nineteen or younger, includes a ban on the use of federal funds for abortions unless the pregnancy endangers the teenager's life or results from rape or incest. The Omnibus Appropriations Act for fiscal year 1999 also extended the Hyde Amendment to Medicare for the first time, pro-hibiting abortion coverage for disabled women, except in cases of rape, incest, or life endangerment (American Civil Liberties Union, 2002).

Planned Parenthood of Central Missouri v. *Danforth:* Spousal Consent

The Court held in this 1976 case that legislative bodies or courts could not properly determine the specific point in the gestational period when viability occurred, holding instead that such a determination varies with each pregnancy and should be left to the individual judg-ment of the attending physician.

Webster v. *Reproductive Health Services:* Use of Public Facilities and Public Personnel

In *Websterv. Reproductive Health Services* (1989), five state-employed health professionals and two nonprofit corporations brought a class action suit challenging Missouri's 1986 act. The act declared in its pre-amble that life begins at conception. It prohibited the use of public funds to counsel women to have an abortion unless necessary to save her life, and it prohibited the use of public hospitals or state employ-ees for abortions unless necessary to save the woman's life. It also required physicians to perform viability tests on fetuses after twenty weeks' gestation. The Court articulated the position that a state may make a value judgment, as Missouri did in its preamble, which favored childbirth over abortion. The Supreme Court maintained that this act only restricted "a woman's ability to obtain an abortion to the extent she chooses a public facility" and did not examine the cost differences between a public and private facility, or the actual effect on access to abortion for poor women.

Planned Parenthood of Southeastern Pennsylvania v. *Casey:* Restrictive State Abortion Laws

In *Planned Parenthood of Southeastern Pennsylvania v. Casey* (1992), the Supreme Court reaffirmed the right to an abortion as part of a con-stitutionally protected right to privacy but simultaneously upheld a state's ability to pass restrictive abortion laws (Lichtman, 2003). It also lowered the standard of review for abortion legislation from "strict scrutiny" to "unduly burdensome," making it easier for such restric-tions on abortion to be found constitutional.

Under a "strict scrutiny" analysis, legislation infringing on the right to privacy was treated with the most rigorous level of review, reserved for certain fundamental constitutional rights such as free speech, reli-gious freedom, or freedom from racial discrimination. It is rare for leg-islation infringing on these rights to survive strict scrutiny. By lowering the standard of review to the more ambiguous "unduly burdensome," the Court opened the door to a number of restrictions that would make it more difficult for women to obtain abortions but did not go so far as to prohibit them.

At issue in this case were the provisions of the Pennsylvania Abor-tion Control Act of 1982, which

1. Required informed consent before an abortion and specified that certain information must be provided at least twenty-four hours before the abortion
2. Required consent of one of the parents of a minor seeking an abortion with the option of judicial bypass in certain circum-stances
3. Required spousal notification by married women seeking abortions
4. Defined a "medical emergency" as a condition that necessitates an abortion to avoid death or serious, irreversible harm to the mother and exempted women in that condition from the above requirements

5. Imposed various reporting requirements for facilities that per-form abortions

Justices Sandra Day O'Connor, Anthony Kennedy, and David Souter, writing for the majority, reaffirmed the essential holding of *Roe* v. *Wade*—a woman's right to an abortion before fetal viability— but rejected its trimester framework. The medical emergency defini-tion and exemption, informed-consent requirement, parental consent requirement (with judicial bypass), and record-keeping provisions were upheld using an "undue burden" standard. The spousal notifi-cation requirement was held unconstitutional, because it imposed an undue burden on women who fear abuse from their husbands, as were the reporting requirements pertaining to it.

Public Policy Consequences of Restrictive Abortion Laws

Beginning with *Roe* v. *Wade,* the legal discussion of abortion has been one of physiology. A pregnant woman and her fetus are presented as two beings that happen to be temporarily interconnected. Becker, Bow-man, and Torrey (1994*)* note "that the woman and her life are almost absent from the discussion of abortion in Roe v. Wade, which becomes instead the story of the fetus and the doctor... resulting from the fact that the Court typically reasons about reproductive regulation in phys-iological paradigms, seeing regulation as state action that concerns women's bodies rather than women's roles, despite the fact that the social role of women was clearly the central concern in the historical debate about abortion" (p. 378).

From the beginning of abortion case law, the Court introduced the idea that the interests of a pregnant woman and those of the "poten-tiality of human life" are "separate and distinct" *(Roe v. Wade).* This ar-guably artificial distinction between a pregnant woman and the child she carries encouraged a line of reasoning that would not be accept-able in other areas of the law. While discrimination based on pregnancy has been prohibited by legislation and case law, including discrimina-tion in health insurance, the Court allowed exactly this discrimination in the Hyde Amendment by excluding insurance coverage when the pregnant woman needs an abortion, even when her life or health are at risk, which is surely the definition of "medically necessary."

Current legislation continues to set mother and unborn child against one another, and the value of the mother's life is explicitly dis-regarded. Before the movement to regulate abortion, when "quicken-ing" was the criterion for a fetus's viability, it was the pregnant mother who determined whether she experienced evidence of life in the un-born child. Since *Roe* v. *Wade,* legislators have increasingly sought to regulate women as if they were simply vessels that happened to be physiologically connected to the unborn child.

Lichtman (2003) argues that states' restrictive abortion laws reduce access to abortions for low-income women and result in increases in unwanted births to low-income women and increases in the number of children needing and receiving public assistance. Underserved wom-en are the first to lose their right to choose, because limitations on fund-ing and access make abortion effectively unavailable to them. Lichtman compared three states: South Dakota, which has the most restrictive abortion laws and only one abortion provider in the entire state, and Vermont and Connecticut, which protect a woman's right to repro-ductive choice in their state constitutions. She found that by looking at indicators such as abortion rates, birthrates, child poverty levels, and public assistance caseloads, one can identify a link between abortion access and the number of unwanted births to underserved women. In contrast to Vermont and Connecticut, South Dakota has not been able to reduce its high number of children living in poverty. Lichtman states, "While motivations are both political as well as ethical, anti-abortion legislators and judges are imposing their own ethical beliefs on whom-ever they can control. In most instances, low-income women and mi-nors are those with the least bargaining power and are thus easiest to control. If these anti-abortion legislators impose their moral beliefs about abortion on low-income women, by removing their access to abortion, these women's reproductive right to privacy is terminated" (p. 361).

CURRENT LEGISLATION

A series of legislative acts have emerged that illustrate the ongoing challenge to *Roe v. Wade* and abortion rights. Rather than trying to overrule the decision in *Roe,* opponents of abortion have used the strat-egy of incremental legislation, restricting abortion further and further until access is effectively unavailable.

The Partial-Birth Abortion Ban Act of 2003

The Partial-Birth Abortion Ban Act of 2003 represents the most re-cent challenge to *Roe v. Wade* and is a response to the 2000 Supreme Court decision *Stenberg* v. *Carhart*, in which the Court struck down a similar state law in Nebraska.

In *Planned Parenthood v. Casey* (1992), the Court rejected the *Roe* trimester framework and held that the point of viability is the dividing line for determining when the state's interest in potential life outweighs a woman's interest in choosing whether to have an abortion. The *Casey* Court determined that the state's interest in potential life exists through-out pregnancy and thus a regulation on abortion is constitutional at any point during pregnancy so long as it does not place an "undue bur-den" on a woman's right to choose.

In *Stenberg*, the Court applied the *Casey* test to a Nebraska statute banning partial birth abortion. The statute in question banned partial birth abortion except when "necessary to save the life of the mother" (Holsinger, 2003). Though ostensibly aimed at prohibiting the abor-tion procedure known as "dilation and extraction" (D&X), the Nebraska law did not refer specifically to this procedure, and instead defined par-tial birth abortion as "an abortion procedure in which the person per-forming the abortion partially delivers vaginally a living unborn child before killing the unborn child and completing the delivery" (*Stenberg* v. *Carhart*, 2000, p. 922). The statute specifically prohibited the delib-erate and intentional delivery "into the vagina a living unborn child, or a substantial portion thereof, for the purpose of performing a pro-cedure that the person performing such procedure knows will kill the unborn child and does kill the unborn child" (*Stenbergv. Carhart*, 2000, p. 922).

The Court examined the Nebraska statute as it applied to pre- and postviability abortions and found that the statute's vague language ren-dered it unconstitutional with regard to previability abortions. In ex-amining the definition of partial birth abortion, the Court found that the language applied to both D&X and to a different procedure "dila-tion and evacuation" (D&E). D&E is the most common procedure used for previability second-trimester abortions. Because the statute had the effect of banning the previability use of D&E, it constituted an undue burden on a woman's right to choose (Holsinger, 2003). In her concurrence in *Stenberg,* Justice O'Connor noted that if the Nebraska statute were limited to D&X and included a health exception, "the ques-tion presented would be quite different from the one we face today" (*Stenbergv. Carhart,* 2000, p. 950).

The language of the Partial-Birth Abortion Ban Act of 2003 is sub-stantially the same as that of the Nebraska statute. The bill's drafters claim to have remedied one of the constitutional problems that plagued the Nebraska statute by defining partial birth abortion more precise-ly so as to exclude D&C procedures from the scope of the bill's pro-hibition (Holsinger, 2003). Holsinger argues that the bill easily could have been drafted to exclude D&E by specifically limiting the prohi-bition to either D&X or postviability procedures. Instead, like earlier versions, the bill employs nonmedical terminology to define the pro-cedures prohibited under the bill. This intentional ambiguity is ar-guably intended to allow the broadest possible interpretation of the prohibition and thus to restrict abortion procedure by procedure.

Carhartv. Ashcwft

The Center for Reproductive Rights legally challenged the federal abortion ban. This case, known as *Carhartv. Ashcwft,* went to trial in 2004 in a Nebraska federal court. Representing doctors from Ne-braska, New York, Virginia, and Iowa, the center argued that the ban on safe abortion procedures violates the U.S. Constitution and puts women's health and lives in serious jeopardy. To stop the federal ban from taking effect, a lawsuit was filed on October 31,2003, on behalf of Dr. LeRoy Carhart, the lead plaintiff in the earlier Supreme Court case. When President Bush signed the new federal law, U.S. District Court Judge Richard G. Kopf, for the District of Nebraska, issued a tem-porary restraining order blocking enforcement of the abortion ban, allowing Dr. Carhart and the other physicians challenging the law to continue to perform abortions without fear of prosecution. Pending further legal decisions, the law was blocked by federal courts in Ne-braska, New York, and California (Center for Reproductive Rights, 2004). In September 2004, Judge Kopf handed down a decision find-ing the Partial-Birth Abortion Ban Act of 2003 unconstitutional:

After giving Congress the respectful consideration it is always due, I find and conclude that the ban is unreasonable and not supported by substantial evidence. In truth, "partial-birth abortions," which are med-ically known as "intact D&E" or "D&X" procedures, are sometimes nec-essary to preserve the health of a woman seeking an abortion. While the procedure is infrequently used as a relative matter, when it is needed, the health of women frequently hangs in the balance.

Therefore, I declare the "Partial-Birth Abortion Ban Act of 2003" un-constitutional because it does not allow, and instead prohibits, the use of the procedure when necessary to preserve the health of a woman.

In addition, I decide that the ban fails as a result of other constitutional imperfections. As a result, I will also permanently enjoin enforcement of the ban. Importantly, however, because the evidence was sparse re-garding postviability, I do not decide whether the law is unconstitu-tional when the fetus is indisputably viable [pp. 2, 5].

FACE: Freedom of Access to Clinic Entrances Act

Increased family planning and abortion clinic violence compelled Con-gress to pass the Freedom of Access to Clinic Entrances Act (FACE) in 1994, which prohibits the use of force, threats of force, and physical obstruction of clinic entrances. FACE appeared to be effective in de-creasing the violent attacks on clinics. Although bomb threats, arson, death threats, and stalking still persist at 20 percent of clinics, the fig-ure is down from 52 percent of clinics in 1994 (Smith, 2002).

While there have been challenges to FACE based on the First Amendment freedoms of speech and assembly, the U.S. Supreme Court has refused to hear these challenges. Lower courts have determined that the legislation is content-neutral and is thus is not biased against the expression of a particular viewpoint or political position. Courts have also determined that the First Amendment does not protect the types of activities that FACE seeks to prohibit (Smith, 2002). In May 2002, an en banc panel of the Ninth Circuit ruled that "wanted-style" posters and an Internet "hit list" identifying abortion providers are also threats under FACE. The court upheld the injunctive relief in the case, but remanded the case for further review regarding the size of the punitive damage award (Feminist Majority Foundation, 2004).

RU486

The violence that FACE tried to address also frightened away poten-tial manufacturers of RU486, thereby denying American women a safe and more easily obtained early abortion procedure. According to Eric Schaff, M.D. (1999), the threat of physical violence is a major reason that potential manufacturers of RU486 are reluctant to step forward. Schaff notes that the escalating violence targeted at abortion providers and abortion facilities has decreased the number of physicians who are willing to risk their lives and careers to provide these services. Eighty-four percent of counties in the United States have no abortion provider. As a result, fewer services make it more difficult for women to access abortion, thus undermining their ability to control their fer-tility and health.

RU486, also known as mifepristone, represents a new class of med-ications that block the action of progesterone, a naturally occurring hormone produced by the ovaries. This causes a nonsurgical abortion in over 95 percent of early pregnancies. RU486 has also been shown to have many significant nonabortifacient-related benefits such as emergency contraception, once-a-month contraception, labor induc-tion, and cervical dilation. It has also been used in the treatment of endometriosis, fibroids, meningioma, Cushing's syndrome, and pro-gesterone-sensitive tumors such as some breast cancer, endometrial cancer, and prostate cancer (Schaff, 1999).

In November of 2003, the RU-486 Suspension and Review Act of 2003 was introduced by Sen. Sam Brownback (R-KS) and Rep. Mike DeMint (R-SC). This legislation was intended to prevent the use of mifepristone and called for a review of the process by which FDA ap-proved the drug. It was not passed.

This legislation was viewed by many as blatantly antichoice politics, rather than reflecting a concern for women's health. The RU-486 Sus-pension and Review Act challenged the integrity of the FDA to deter-mine the medical and scientific safety of the drugs it approves. In fact, the FDA has approved 557 new drugs since 1995, yet Congress has never attempted to impose such onerous and burdensome distribution re-quirements on any other drug. Legislating the approval or disapproval of any drug sets a dangerous precedent. The effort to restrict FDA ap-proval of mifepristone on the basis of an antichoice viewpoint under-mines the integrity of the drug approval process and prevents FDA's reliance on science as the sole determining factor in judging the safety of drugs. As is the case with all FDA-approved drugs, mifepristone was put through rigorous scientific research to determine its safety and ef-ficacy (American Association of University Women, 2004).

Ideologically driven legislation such as this disregards other possible benefits of nascent medications and limits access both to safer means of abortion and to potentially effective treatments for other disorders, further undermining a woman's right to choose.

FETAL RIGHTS

The question of whether a fetus has rights independent of its mother has been the subject of political debate and has presented challenges to well-established rights of privacy, opportunities for valuable stem cell research, and the basic concept that a woman should have control over her own body. Issues of gender, race, and poverty discrimination are all raised in reference to the populations immediately affected by these policies.

In what has been referred to as a frontal assault on abortion rights, legislators at the state and federal levels have sought to define life as starting at conception, thus making abortion illegal as a form of mur-der. Congressman Duncan Hunter (R-CA) introduced a bill titled the "Life at Conception Act of 2003." Hunter's bill asserts that life begins at conception, and the California congressman hopes that if it ever be-comes law, abortion supporters will have no legal leg on which to stand: "The only way that we're going to legislatively overturn Roe v. Wade is to establish personhood early on—and that is at conception," Hunter said (Tennessee Right to Life, 2003). Beyond abortion access, this type of legislation has implications for a woman to be held criminally ac-countable for the outcome of her pregnancy.

Ferguson v. *City of Charleston* (2001) accentuates the distinct prob-lems behind conceptually separating a woman from her fetus for the purpose of law. Heard by the Supreme Court, *Ferguson* v. *City of Charleston* addressed matters of self-incrimination, right to privacy, and discrimination.

In 1989, in response to concern over the apparent increase in the use of cocaine by pregnant patients and "crack babies," the

Medical University of South Carolina (MUSC) implemented a policy order-ing drug screening to be performed on urine samples of pregnant women suspected of using cocaine. MUSC developed and imple-mented this policy in conjunction with local law enforcement officials. Police could be involved in one of two ways: identification of drug use during pregnancy and the identification of drug use after delivery. In the first way, the patient faced arrest only if she tested positive a second time or refused to enter and complete a substance abuse pro-gram. In the second way, the police promptly arrested the patient. Ten women who received care at MUSC were arrested after testing posi-tive for cocaine. In *Ferguson* v. *City of Charleston*, they challenged the policy, stating that warrantless and nonconsensual drug tests con-ducted for criminal investigatory purposes were unconstitutional searches (Leslie, 2001).

The Supreme Court found that the state hospital's policy violated the constitutional rights of the women who were tested. It held that "a state hospital's performance of a diagnostic test to obtain evidence of a patient's criminal conduct for law enforcement purposes is an unreasonable search if the patient has not consented to the procedure" (Leslie, 2001, p. 95). The Court described the invasion of privacy in *Fer-guson* as far more substantial than similar cases in that the hospital did not provide these pregnant women with an understanding about the purpose of the test, the potential use of the test results, or protections against the unauthorized distribution of the results to third parties. The Court noted that it was apparent that "the focus of the policy was on the arrest and prosecution of the drug-abusing mothers." While the ultimate goal of the program may have been substance abuse treatment for the women in question, the immediate goal of the searches was to generate evidence for law enforcement purposes. The Court found that the primary purpose of the Charleston program was to use the threat of arrest and prosecution in order to force women into treatment. Be-cause of police involvement, the strictures of the Fourth Amendment should be strictly adhered. State hospital employees had a duty to in-form patients of the potential ramifications of the urinalysis if the spe-cific purpose for the test is to obtain evidence of potential drug abuse. The maternity patients should have been made aware that their urine drug tests were going to be reported to law enforcement if their urine tested positive for cocaine (Leslie, 2001). The South Carolina case focused on women ingesting drugs or al-cohol while pregnant, with the propensity for the women affected to be African American. Gagan (2000) reported that in a rehabilitation program generated for this "criminal" population, "forty-two women arrested under the program between 1989 and 1994 were black [all but one]. The single white woman allegedly had a black boyfriend, a fact which was noted on her chart" (p. 491).

Fried (1990) suggests that gender discrimination plays a role in these cases, in that a woman is being charged for criminal activities against the fetus while men who commit equal or greater degrees of violence are not prosecuted. Fried (1990) illustrates this in an example:

While the behavior of pregnant women has, in some cases, led to crim-inal prosecution, there have been no prosecutorial efforts to arrest men for the damage that secondhand cigarette smoke may cause to a fetus; men have not been required to avoid exposure to drugs or chemicals known to cause damage to the sperm; nor have the male partners of pregnant battered women been targeted by prosecutors for their in-fliction of injury to the fetus in the course of physically abusing the woman [p. 265].

Efforts to legally establish fetal rights, and particularly life at con-ception, also threaten the possibility of scientific gains from embryonic stem cell research. Stevens (2003) emphasizes, "Because the Catholic Church, pro-life activists, and other religious groups believe that life starts at conception, they oppose embryonic stem cell research. These groups argue that benefiting from the destruction of a human embryo is 'no less a crime than abortion'"(p. 631).

Questions raised about the ethics of acquiring the embryonic stem cells must be matched with questions of the ethics of withholding pos-sible medical treatments. Regardless of what stance is taken in this de-bate, medical advances that save lives are valuable.

PSYCHOLOGICAL AND CULTURAL PERSPECTIVES ON ABORTION

In 1969, the American Psychological Association (APA) Council of Representatives adopted a resolution that identified termination of un-wanted pregnancies as a mental health and child welfare issue. It re-solved that termination of pregnancy be considered a civil right of pregnant women, to be handled like other medical and surgical pro-cedures in consultation with her physician (Adler et al., 1992).

In 1980, in response to governmental attempts to suppress research on abortion, the APA Council of Representatives passed a resolution supporting the right to conduct scientific research on abortion and reproductive health, stating that the APA "affirms the right of quali-fied researchers to conduct appropriate research in all areas of fertil-ity regulation" (Adler et al., 1992, p. 1194).

In February 1989, the APA, wishing to improve the accuracy of the debate, convened a panel of experts to review the best scientific stud-ies of abortion outcome. In August 1989, the APA Council of Repre-sentatives, concerned about the distortions of the research findings in the press, passed its third abortion resolution. This resolution, which cited the work of the panel, initiated a public awareness effort to cor-rect the record on the scientific findings of abortion research (Adler et al. 1992).

Psychological Research on the Effects of Abortion

The psychological research on abortion has focused on postabortion emotional responses (Adler et al., 1992).

Stress and coping

From the stress and coping perspective, an un-wanted pregnancy is seen as an event that can be challenging or stress-ful. Stress has been defined as emerging from an interaction of the individual and the environment in a situation that the person appraises as "taxing or exceeding his or her resources and endangering his or her well-being" (Lazarus & Folkman, 1984, p. 19). Termination of an un-wanted pregnancy may reduce the stress engendered by the occurrence of the pregnancy and the associated events. At the same time, the abor-tion itself may be experienced as stressful (Adler et al., 1992).

Research on the psychological effects of abortion has found that most women do not show any long-term harm after having had an abortion. According to Cozzarelli, Sumer, and Major (1998), "Although most women do not appear to experience severe, negative, postabor-tion psychological responses, abortion is perceived as an acute stres-sor by a large number of women." In general, individuals who feel efficacious have been found to handle stressful life events, including abortion, more effectively. Furthermore, self-efficacy beliefs have been found to mediate the positive effects of more global personal resources such as self-esteem, optimism, and locus of control on adjustment.

Adler et al. (1992) note the methodological difficulties in the psy-chological research literature on abortion, including researcher bias, too narrow a focus on pathological or negative outcomes of abortion, and questionable validity and reliability of outcome measures such as in-terviews. The varied quality of these studies makes it difficult to draw conclusions from the entire body of existing research literature. Many reports are clinical observations of small numbers of women. Some pro-vide no data, or data are inappropriately or inadequately analyzed. Some studies report responses of women having illegal or therapeutic abor-tions rather than legal, elective procedures. Some studies, particularly those that are retrospective, may have a mix of women who had illegal, therapeutic, and elective abortions that are not analyzed separately.

In order to try to draw some conclusions from existing research, Adler et al. (1992) reviewed research that met the following minimum criteria: the study must be empirical (involving the collection of data subjected to statistical analysis) and use a definable sample. The stud-ies used only samples of women who had abortions under legal, non-restrictive conditions in the United States. The studies involved a range of medical settings, and the subjects covered a range of ethnicities and ages. The weight of the evidence was that legal abortion, as a resolu-tion to an unwanted pregnancy, particularly in the first trimester, does not create psychological hazards for most women undergoing the pro-cedure. In fact, psychological distress has generally been found to drop from before the procedure to immediately after and from preabortion or immediately postabortion to several weeks afterward.

Self-esteem

Russo and Zierk (1992) examined the relationship of abortion and childbearing to self-esteem in a national sample of 5,295 U.S. women interviewed annually from 1979 to 1987 in the National Longitudinal Study of Youth. Controlling for preexisting self-esteem, employment, income, and education, neither having one abortion nor having repeat abortions in the period from 1980 to 1987 was related to self-esteem. This study demonstrates that up to eight years follow-ing an abortion, no negative associations occur with self-esteem (Cen-ter for Human Resources Research, 1988).

Demographic and social factors

Younger and unmarried women without children were relatively more likely than those who were older and who had already given birth to experience negative responses. So too were women whose culture or religion prohibits abortions and those who attended church more frequently (Adler et al., 1992).

The decision process

A number of studies have examined the rela-tionship between aspects of the woman's decision process regarding abortion and her emotional response afterward. Most women do not have difficulty with the abortion decision. Osofsky, Osofsky, and Rajan (1973) found that 12 percent of 100 first-trimester patients stated the decision to have an abortion was difficult, and 7 percent reported ini-tial indecision regarding continuation or termination of the pregnancy. Among 200 second-trimester patients in the study, 51 percent reported difficulty in deciding, and 36 percent reported initial indecision. Other correlates of difficult decisions or ambivalent feelings are being mar-ried and being Catholic (Adler et al., 1992).

Studies examining satisfaction with the abortion decision and post-abortion emotional response consistently found that women who were satisfied with their choice or reported little difficulty in making the decision showed more positive postabortion responses. Greater diffi-culty in making the decision has been associated with higher negative postabortion reactions, including feelings of guilt, anxiety, and inter-nally based negative emotions, such as regret and depression (Adler et al., 1992).

Women who initially want to be pregnant may react more negatively to abortion. Shusterman (1979) found an association between a wom-an's immediate affective response to learning that she was pregnant and her response to abortion. Women who reported the pregnancy as "high-ly meaningful" to them reported more physical complaints immediately after and anticipated more negative consequences from the abortion than did women who reported their pregnancy to be less meaningful (Adler et al., 1992).

Abortion in the Context of Culture

Catherine MacKinnon (1987) describes the aspect of abortion that the legal decision makers have chosen to overlook: that abortion is "inex-tricable from sexuality" and that men's and women's lives are very dif-ferent for that reason:

> I first situate abortion and the abortion right in the experience of women. The argument is that abortion is inextricable from sex-uality....
>
> Most women who seek abortions became pregnant while having sexual intercourse with men. Most did not mean or wish to conceive. In contrast to this fact of women's experience, which converges sexu-ality with reproduction with gender, the abortion debate has centered on separating control over sexuality from control over reproduction, and on separating both from gender and the life options of the sexes.
>
> ... Sexual intercourse, still the most common cause of pregnancy, cannot simply be presumed coequally determined. Sex doesn't look a whole lot like freedom when it appears normatively less costly for women to risk an undesired, often painful, traumatic, dangerous, some-time illegal, and potentially life-threatening procedure than to protect themselves in advance.
>
> In the context of a sexual critique of gender inequality, abortion promises to women sex with men on the same reproductive terms as men have sex with women [pp. 93, 94–96, 99].

Kathleen M. Sullivan and Susan R. Estrich (1989) noted,

> Abortion restrictions, like the most classic gender-based restrictions on women seeking to participate in the worlds of work and ideas, have historically rested on archaic stereotypes of women as persons whose "paramount destiny and mission... [is] to fulfill the noble and be-nign office of wife and mother" (Bradwell v. Illinois, 1873).... Legis-lation prohibiting abortion, largely a product of the years between 1860 and 1880, reflected precisely the same ideas about the natural and proper role of women as did the legislation of the same period—long-since discredited—that

prohibited women from serving on juries or partic-ipating in the professions, including the practice of law.

Abortion as an International Health Concern

The World Health Organization defined reproductive health as "com-plete physical, mental and social well-being in all matters related to the reproductive system" (cited in Murphy, 2003, p. 205). It defined sexual health as "a part of reproductive health that includes healthy sexual de-velopment, equitable and responsible relationships and sexual fulfill-ment, and freedom from illness, disease, disability, violence and other harmful practices related to sexuality" (p. 205). Henry David (1994) noted that the most significant development in reproductive behavior over the past few decades has been the political commitment to the worldwide expansion of more effective contraceptive practice:

Historically, the human rights rationale emerged when women began to assert their rights as equal partners. A woman who lacks control over her fertility has considerable difficulty completing her education, maintaining gainful employment, and making independent marital decisions. The demographic rationale evolved in response to concerns about the negative effects of rapid population growth on socio-economic development and environmental degradation. The health rationale became the basis for advocating that pregnancy be delayed until the most appropriate time and for preventing high-risk unin-tended pregnancies [p. 344].

The human rights rationale is inextricably intertwined with a wom-an's role in decision making, cultural traditions, and access to educa-tion. In societies in which a woman's value is based on the number of children she has, her ability to regulate and control her fertility will be limited. Women in developing countries with seven or more years of education tend to marry, on average, four years later and have two or three fewer children than women with no schooling (David, 1994).

UNWANTED CHILDREN

One of the arguments in favor of access to abortion involves concern for the psychological and physical health of unwanted children, born because a woman did not have access to abortion. According to David (1994), unique circumstances combined to make available for detailed medical, psychological, and social assessment 110 boys and 110 girls born between 1961 and 1963 to Prague women twice denied an abor-tion for the same pregnancy: once on initial request to an abortion com-mission and again on appeal.

In order to study the impact of being the result of an unwanted pregnancy, these 220 children were pair-matched with 220 children born to women who had purposely discontinued con-traception or had accepted unplanned pregnancies. Matching criteria included age, sex, number of siblings, birth order, and school class. The mothers were matched for age, marital status, and socioeconomic sta-tus as determined by their male partner's occupation and presence in the home. All of the children were born into intact families, in which both the mother and father (or father substitute) were present.

The children were about nine years old at original assessment and have been followed over many years. Differences between the two groups of subjects widened over time, always to the detriment of those born from unwanted pregnancies. For example, at ages twenty-one to twenty-three, the subjects born to women twice denied abortion for the same pregnancy reported significantly more often than did the control subjects less job satisfaction, more conflict with coworkers and supervisors, less satisfying relations with friends, and more disap-pointments in love. A larger proportion had had sexual experience with more than ten partners, judged their marriages to be less happy, and more often expressed the desire not to be married to their cur-rent partner. There was considerable evidence that in the aggregate, being unwanted and subsequent compulsory childbearing had a detri-mental effect on psychosocial development (David, 1994).

Romania represents the most striking failure of a coercive public policy designed to influence reproductive behavior, according to David (1994). After years of liberal abortion legislation and ready access to abortion services, on October 1,1966, without prior warning, Roma-nia severely restricted access to legal abortion, except for women over forty-five years or who met narrowly defined medical criteria, pro-hibited the importation of contraceptives, and threatened clandestine abortion providers with fines and imprisonment. The birthrate rose from 14.3 per 1,000 population in 1966 to 27.4 births in 1967, but gradually declined again to 13.8 in 1983. Public policy clashed deeply with societal values (David, 1994).

In 1986, President Nicolae Ceausescu proclaimed, "The fetus is the socialist property of the whole society. Giving birth is a patriotic duty... those who refuse to have children are deserters, escaping the law of natural continuity" (cited in David, 1994). To qualify for a legal abor-tion, a woman had to have five living children, all under the age of eighteen. The state required employed women to undergo periodic gynecological examinations and imposed special taxes on unmarried individuals over the age of twenty-five and on marital partners who were childless after two years. Modern contraceptives were available only on the black market. The World Health Organization reported a sharp increase in maternal mortality. It nearly doubled, from 86 deaths per 100,000 live births in 1981 to 169 per 100,000 in 1989, the highest rate ever recorded in Europe. After the overthrow of Ceausescu in De-cember 1989, the new government, on its first day in office, revoked all prohibitions on abortion services and the availability of contraceptives. In 1990, the maternal mortality rate dropped by more than one-half from its previous peak and continues to decline (David, 1994; David, Dytrych, & Matejcek, 2003).

CONCLUSION

While the intensity of feelings associated with abortion makes con-versation difficult, one group of women in Boston had the courage to talk directly to one another about their views. In response to the De-cember 30, 1994, shootings of several Planned Parenthood clinics in Brookline, Massachusetts, by John Salvi, a group of six women began to meet privately. They were leaders in their community. Three iden-tified themselves as prochoice and three as prolife. The Public Con-versations Project, a Boston-based national group that designs and conducts dialogues about divisive public issues, consulted many com-munity leaders about the value of top-level talks about abortion, and these six women began conversations that they discussed publicly only six years later. In a January 28,2001, *Boston Globe* article (Fowler et al., 2001), they described their experience:

These conversations revealed a deep divide. We saw that our differ-ences on abortion reflect two world views that are irreconcilable.

If this is true, then why do we continue to meet?

First, because when we face our opponent, we see her dignity and goodness. Embracing this apparent contradiction stretches us spiritu-ally. We've experienced something radical and life-altering that we de-scribe in nonpolitical terms: "the mystery of love," "holy ground," or simply, "mysterious."

We continue because we are stretched intellectually, as well. This has been a rare opportunity to engage in sustained, candid conversations about serious moral disagreements. It has made our thinking sharper and our language more precise.

We hope, too, that we have become wiser and more effective lead-ers. We are more knowledgeable about our political opponents. We have learned to avoid being overreactive and disparaging to the other side and to focus instead on affirming our respective causes.

Since that first fear-filled meeting, we have experienced a paradox. While learning to treat each other with dignity and respect, we all have become firmer in our views about abortion.

We hope this account of our experience will encourage people everywhere to consider engaging in dialogues about abortion and other protracted disputes. In this world of polarizing conflicts, we have glimpsed a new possibility: a way in which people can disagree frankly and passionately, become clearer in heart and mind about their ac-tivism, and, at the same time, contribute to a more civil and compas-sionate society.

8

Insurance Coverage of Contraceptives

Access to safe and reliable contraception is an es-sential component of health care for women. Despite the fact that pre-scription contraceptives were first made available over forty years ago, many health insurance plans have a history of excluding coverage for prescription contraceptives even while covering other prescription drugs and devices and preventive care, as well as sterilization and abor-tion. This inequity did not get national attention until the mid-1990s, when a national survey of insurance coverage of reproductive health care revealed for the first time the extent to which women were being denied contraceptive coverage.

Shortly after the release of this study, Viagra, a drug used in treat-ing male impotence, was approved by the Food and Drug Administra-tion and was immediately covered by many insurance companies. The sharp contrast between insurance companies' willingness to cover Vi-agra and their reluctance to cover contraceptives, even in the face of studies demonstrating the need, captured the attention of the media and the public. Not surprisingly, the public broadly supported requir-ing contraceptive coverage. A 1998 Kaiser Family Foundation poll found that 75 percent of Americans believed contraception should be covered by insurers even if such coverage added to the cost of their in-surance. This support has been steady. A 2001 poll found that 77 per-cent of Americans support laws requiring health insurance plans to cover prescription contraception (NARAL, 2001).

Energized by the increased awareness and support that developed in the mid-1990s, women's advocates and legislators began pushing for change and have had a great deal of success in challenging the de-nial of contraceptive coverage in a variety of ways. Since this problem came to the forefront just ten years ago, legislation has been adopted in twenty states across the country, and is being considered in Congress, to specifically mandate contraceptive equity in health insurance cov-erage. In addition, legal rulings have established the principle that singling out contraceptive coverage for exclusion from an otherwise comprehensive employee health plan is unlawful sex discrimination in employment. Although the battle for equity in health care coverage continues, the past ten years have witnessed a dramatic transforma-tion in the legal landscape surrounding contraceptive coverage as this gender gap in health care coverage narrows.

WOMEN'S CONTRACEPTIVE NEEDS HAVE NOT BEEN MET

Despite public recognition of the importance of contraception to women's health and equality, health insurance has historically failed to provide adequate coverage of prescription contraceptive drugs and devices and related services. In 1994, the Alan Guttmacher Institute (AGI) released the first study establishing the extent to which women have been denied comprehensive insurance coverage. That survey showed that almost half of all fee-for-service large-group plans (those covering over one hundred employees) did not cover any form of con-traception at all, and only one-third covered oral contraceptives, the most commonly used reversible contraceptive in the United States. Al-though managed care plans have typically provided better coverage than traditional fee-for-service plans, the study revealed that only 39 percent of health maintenance organizations routinely covered all methods of reversible contraception. Only 49 percent of large-group plans and 39 percent of small-group plans covered outpatient annual exams, which are essential for women using prescription contracep-tive drugs or devices. In 2004, AGI released an updated study and found that coverage of contraceptives in employee health benefits plans is increasing. The percentage of plans routinely covering all methods of reversible contraceptives increased from 28 percent in 1994 to 86 percent (Alan Guttmacher Institute, 2004). But the fact that 99 per-cent of employee plans cover prescription drugs generally means that a contraceptive coverage gap remains (Kaiser Family Foundation/ Health Research Education Trust, 2003). These statistics indicate that although progress has been made in the fight to obtain full coverage of contraceptive drugs, devices, and services, many women are still not receiving the contraceptive coverage they require.

WHY CONTRACEPTIVE COVERAGE MATTERS

The gender gap in health care coverage that is created by the reluc-tance of health insurance companies to cover contraceptives affects women and their families adversely in several ways. Women who do not have health insurance coverage for contraception, but who nonetheless wish to avoid pregnancy, are often forced to use a less expensive, but also less effective, method of contraception (Darroch, 1998).A woman without insurance coverage also may not be able to afford to use the contraceptive method that is most appropriate for her medical and personal circumstances (Gold, 1998). For example, where oral contra-ceptives are contraindicated for medical reasons, an intrauterine device (IUD) or implant may be the most appropriate form of con-traception, but these devices have the highest initial cost and there-fore can be the hardest to pay for out-of-pocket.

Because pregnancy is a condition that is unique to women and be-cause the only forms of prescription contraception available today are exclusively for women (oral contraceptives, injections like Depo Pro-vera and Lunelle, implants like Norplant, IUDs, and barrier methods like the diaphragm and cervical cap), the exclusion of prescription contraceptives from health insurance coverage unfairly disadvantages women by singling out for unfavorable treatment a health insurance need that only women have. Failure to cover contraception forces wom-en to bear higher health care costs to avoid pregnancy and exposes women to the unique physical, economic, and emotional conse-quences that can result from unintended pregnancy.

Pregnancy prevention is central to good health care for women. Most women have the biological potential for pregnancy for over thirty years of their lives. For approximately three-quarters of her reproductive life, the average woman is trying to postpone or avoid preg-nancy (Alan Guttmacher Institute, 1998a). Nearly half of pregnancies in the United States are unintended, including 31 percent of preg-nancies among married women (Henshaw, 1998).

Access to contra-ception is critical to preventing unwanted pregnancies (and thus also to reducing the number of abortions). It also enables women to con-trol the timing and spacing of their pregnancies, which in turn reduces the incidence of maternal morbidity, low-birth-weight babies, and in-fant mortality (U.S. Office of Disease Prevention and Health Promo-tion, 2000; Alan Guttmacher Institute, 1998b).

Moreover, oral contraceptives are sometimes prescribed for health reasons other than birth control—for example, for medical conditions like dysmenorrhea and premenstrual syndrome or to help prevent ovar-ian cancer. Some insurance plans do not cover oral contraceptives even when they are prescribed for these purely medical reasons. Thus, in ad-dition to the dangers to women's health presented by the failure of in-surance to cover pregnancy prevention, the exclusion of contraception from insurance coverage causes other harmful consequences for wom-en's health. For all these reasons, as a federal court declared, "the exclu-sion of prescription contraceptives creates a gaping hole in the coverage offered to female employees, leaving a fundamental and immediate healthcare need uncovered" (*Erickson* v. *Bartell Drug Co.*, 2001).

The lack of insurance coverage for contraceptives is also a matter of gender equity. When effective contraception is not used, it is wom-en who bear the risk of unwanted pregnancy. When unintended preg-nancy results, it is women who incur the attendant physical burdens and medical risks of pregnancy, women who disproportionately bear the health care costs of pregnancy and childbirth, and women who of-ten face barriers to employment and educational opportunities as a result of pregnancy. These occur even today despite the fact that the law clearly prohibits this form of discrimination in the workplace and in educational institutions.

CLOSING THE GENDER GAP IN HEALTH CARE COVERAGE

Galvanized by the 1994 Alan Guttmacher Institute study revealing the common exclusion of contraceptives from health insurance plans, ad-vocates for women's health and equity began pursuing a multitrack ap-proach to ensure that women receive access to needed contraceptives. At the federal level, this effort includes enforcing Title VII of the Civil Rights Act of 1964 as well as seeking passage of the Equity in Prescrip-tion Insurance and Contraceptive Coverage Act (EPICC). At the state level, efforts include both legislative and administrative approaches to establishing explicit legal requirements for contraceptive coverage. These approaches are complementary, and all are necessary.

The ability of women to obtain the contraceptive insurance cover-age they need advanced significantly with two interpretations of the federal civil rights laws in 2000 and 2001. Both the Equal Employment Opportunity Commission (EEOC) and a federal court held that it is unlawful sex discrimination in the workplace under Title VII of the Civil Rights Act of 1964, and specifically the Pregnancy Discrimina-tion Act of 1978 (PDA) that is incorporated in Title VII, for an em-ployer covered by Title VII to exclude prescription contraceptive drugs and devices and related services from a health insurance plan provided to its employees, when the plan covers other prescription drugs and devices and preventive care generally.

Title VII prohibits all private employers with at least fifteen em-ployees, as well as public employers, from discriminating on the basis of sex in the terms and conditions of employment, including fringe benefits. And as amended by the PDA, Title VII's prohibition against discrimination "on the basis of sex" includes discrimination "on the basis of pregnancy, childbirth, or related medical conditions." This language was enacted by Congress to overrule the decision in *General Electric Co.* v. *Gilbert* (1976), which held that excluding disabilities arising from pregnancy from an employee's disability plan did not vi-olate Title VII. As the Supreme Court has held, the PDA now makes it clear that for purposes of Title VII, such singling out of pregnancy coverage is sex discrimination on its face (*Newport News Shipbuilding and Dry Dock v. EEOC,* 1982; *UAWv. Johnson Controls,* 1991).

The PDA, moreover, is not limited to discrimination based on preg-nancy itself; it expressly applies to discrimination based on "pregnancy, childbirth, or related medical conditions." As the Supreme Court stated, "The 1978 Act makes clear that it is discriminatory to treat pregnancy-related conditions less favorably than other medical conditions" (*New-port News Shipbuilding and Dry Dock v. EEOC,* 1982, p. 684), and the EEOC has long interpreted the PDA to mean that "any health insur-ance provided [to employees] must cover expenses for pregnancy-related conditions on the same basis as expenses for other medical con-ditions" (Questions and Answers on the Pregnancy Discrimination Act, 2002).

Contraception—the prevention of pregnancy—is plainly pregnancy related. Moreover, contraception addresses a woman's potential for pregnancy, and the Supreme Court held in 1991 that an employer's classification of employees on the basis of potential for pregnancy is covered by the PDA's language. In *UAW v. Johnson Controls* (1991), the Court noted that an employer's policy barring fertile women from cer-tain jobs was a classification on the basis of potential for pregnancy, and concluded that "under the PDA, such a classification must be re-garded, for Title VII purposes, in the same light as explicit sex dis-crimination" (p. 199). The Court cited PDA legislative history to show that "this statutory standard was chosen to protect female workers from being treated differently from other employees simply because of their capacity to bear children" (p. 205).

In 1999, based on this analysis, sixty women's, civil rights, and health groups submitted a petition to the EEOC arguing that Title VII, as amended by the PDA, prohibits employers from excluding pre-scription contraceptive coverage from an employee health plan that otherwise covers prescription drugs and devices generally, as well as other preventive health care. The EEOC agreed, and in a ruling re-sponding to two pending charges against employers, reasoned that Title VII's "prohibition on discrimination against women based on their ability to become pregnant... necessarily includes a prohibition on discrimination related to a woman's use of contraceptives" (U.S. Equal Employment Opportunity Commission, 2000). The commis-sion issued a ruling that in order to be in compliance with Title VII:

Respondents must cover the expenses of prescription contraceptives to the same extent and on the same terms, that they cover the expenses of [preventive] drugs, devices, and preventive care.... Respondents must also offer the same coverage for contraception-related outpatient services as are offered for other outpatient services. Where a woman visits her doctor to obtain a prescription for contraceptives, she must be afforded the same coverage that would apply if she, or any other employee, had consulted a doctor for other preventive or health main-tenance services. Where, on the other hand, Respondents limit cover-age of comparable drugs or services (e.g., by imposing maximum payable benefits), those limits may be applied to contraception as well. Respondents' coverage must extend to the full range of prescription contraceptive choices. Because the health needs of women may change—and because different women may need different prescrip-tion contraceptives at different times in their lives—Respondents must cover each of the available options for prescription contraception. Moreover, Respondents must include such coverage in each of the health plan choices that it offers to its employees [p. 5].

Although the EEOC's decision was disposing of two specific pend-ing charges, it constitutes a formal statement of commission policy and applies to all similarly situated employers. As the federal agency charged with administering and enforcing Title VII, the EEOC's in-terpretation of the law is authoritative.

The EEOC's ruling was followed by the court's decision in *Erickson* v. *Bartell Drug Co.* (2001). In *Erickson,* the U.S. District Court for the Western District of Washington cited the EEOC ruling favorably and found that the defendant's exclusion of prescription contraceptives from its otherwise comprehensive employee health benefits plan constituted a violation of Title VII. The court's decision, granting summary judg-ment to Jennifer Erickson and the plaintiff class she represented, was the first court decision ever to rule definitively on the merits of this issue. Other courts have subsequently ruled in favor of the plaintiffs in similar cases, denying the defendants' motions to dismiss and allowing the cases to proceed *(Cooleyv. Daimler Chrysler Corp.,* 2003; *Equal Em-ployment Opportunity Commission* v. *United Parcel Service,* 2001; *Wess-ling et al.* v. *AMN Healthcare and Medical Express,* 2001).

In the *Erickson* decision, the court carefully reviewed the legislative history of Title VII and the PDA, relevant precedents, the EEOC deci-sion, and each of the arguments presented by the defendant. The court concluded:

Bartell's exclusion of prescription contraception from its prescription plan is inconsistent with the requirements of federal law. The PDA is not a begrudging recognition of a limited grant of rights to a strictly defined group of women who happen to be pregnant. Read in the con-text of Title VII as a whole, it is a broad acknowledgment of the intent of Congress to outlaw any and all discrimination against any and all women in the terms and conditions of their employment, including the benefits an employer provides to its employees. Male and female employees have different, sex-based disability and healthcare needs, and the law is no longer blind to the fact that only women can get preg-nant, bear children, or use prescription contraception [p. 1271].

On this basis, the court ordered Bartell Drug Co., the defendant, to cover each of the available options for prescription contraception to the same extent, and on the same terms, that it covers other drugs, de-vices, and preventive care for its employees, as well as all contraception-related outpatient services.

As a result of the EEOC and court rulings, all employers covered by Title VII are now on notice of their legal obligation to include coverage of prescription contraceptives if they are providing health insurance that otherwise covers prescription drugs and devices and preventive care. Some employers have responded by promptly adding this cover-age to their employee health plans. Others have been more resistant to their obligations. In response, women have followed in Jennifer Erick-son's footsteps and filed charges with the EEOC and Title VII suits against their employers for the exclusion of prescription contraceptives from their health plans. For example, one suit is currently pending against Wal-Mart Stores (*Mauldin* v. *Wal-Mart Stores*, 2001,2002), and another suit has been filed against Union Pacific Railroad (Planned Par-enthood of the Columbia/Willamette, 2004).

Many other women are demanding the contraceptive coverage to which they are legally entitled and hoping to obtain that coverage with-out embarking on formal legal action. Some have been successful. For example, after several female faculty and staff members at the Uni-versity of Nebraska urged the university administration to add con-traceptive coverage, the university regents agreed ("University Health Plan to Cover Birth Control After Vote," 2001). Dow Jones and Com-pany also agreed to provide coverage for all FDA-approved prescrip-tion contraceptives and related medical services in all of its health plans for its employees, as part of a settlement of charges that had been filed with the EEOC by employees and their union (Planned Par-enthood Federation of America, 2002b). In November 2003, Lenox Hill Hospital in New York City, in response to a demand for coverage by one employee, announced that it was adding this coverage for all employees. In addition, a number of unions have begun to press this issue on behalf of their members, spurred on by the Contraceptive Equity Project of the Coalition of Labor Union Women. A local coun-cil of the American Federation of State, County and Municipal Em-ployees (AFSCME), for example, secured contraceptive coverage in the benefits package for employees of the city of Eugene, Oregon.

Students have begun to press for complete contraceptive coverage in their student health plans as well. They have argued that Title IX of the Education Amendments of 1972, which extends federal protection against sex discrimination to students at educational institutions that receive federal funds, must be interpreted, like Title VII, to prohibit the exclusion of prescription contraceptives from plans that include other prescription drugs and devices. This argument has proved successful. For example, in response to demands relying on this argument by sev-eral students, George Washington University added insurance cover-age for prescription contraceptives to its student health insurance plan.

Employers sometimes resist adding contraceptive coverage to an employee health benefit plan on the grounds that it would raise em-ployers' health care costs. As it turns out, however, as is true for other key forms of preventive health care, coverage of contraceptives actu-ally saves money. For every dollar spent to provide publicly funded contraceptive services, an average of three dollars is saved in Medic-aid costs alone for pregnancy-related health care and medical care for newborns (Forrest & Samara, 1996). In addition, studies by business groups and employer consultants have concluded that employers can save money by including contraceptive coverage in their employee health plans, thereby reducing unintended pregnancies and their as-sociated costs, as well as promoting maternal and child health (Bonoan & Gonen, 2000; William M. Mercer, 2000).

For example, the Wash-ington Business Group on Health, which represents 160 national and multinational employers, has estimated that failing to provide con-traceptive coverage could cost an employer at least 15 percent more than providing this coverage. This report concluded, "For health and finan-cial reasons, employers concerned with providing both comprehen-sive and cost-effective health benefits ought to consider ensuring that they are covering the full range of contraceptive options" (Bonoan & Gonen, 2000, p. 7).

Moreover, any direct premium costs to an employer who adds con-traceptive coverage to its benefits plan are at most extremely modest, and likely to be nonexistent. The experience of the Federal Employ-ees Health Benefits Program (FEHBP) is most instructive. It showed that adding contraceptive coverage to the FEHBP caused no increase in the federal government's premium costs. When the FEHBP contra-ceptive coverage requirement was implemented, the Office of Person-nel Management (OPM), which administers the program, arranged with the health carriers to adjust the 1999 premiums in 2000 to reflect any increased insurance costs due to the addition of contraceptive cov-erage. However, no such adjustment was necessary, and OPM reported that "there was no cost increase due to contraceptive coverage" (J. R. Lachance to M. D. Greenberger, Jan. 16, 2001). Another study found that on average, it costs a private employer only an additional $1.43 per month per employee to add coverage for the full range of FDA-approved reversible contraceptives (Darroch, 1998).

Of course, even if the cost of contraceptive coverage were substan-tial (which, as shown, it is not), such costs could not justify short-changing women or sacrificing their health. Cost is never recognized as a defense to discrimination, as has been noted by both the EEOC and the court in *Erickson.*

Erickson and the EEOC ruling are also influencing the interpreta-tion of state employment discrimination laws. Almost every state has a law against sex discrimination in employment that is similar to fed-eral law (Title VII). Given that Title VII has been interpreted as placing a contraceptive coverage requirement on employers who are covered by federal law, advocates have suggested that similar state laws should be interpreted the same way. In Wisconsin, the state attorney general is-sued an opinion that does just that (P. A. Lautenschlager to G. Moore, October 17,2003). The opinion cites *Erickson* and the EEOC decision and finds that Wisconsin's Fair Employment Act should be interpreted, like Title VII, to require employers to include contraceptive coverage. In addition, the attorney general's opinion states that Wisconsin's law prohibiting sex (or pregnancy) discrimination in education applies the same principle to coverage for students by Wisconsin colleges and universities.

Advocates for women's rights and women's health are also press-ing for the enactment of new legislation, at both the state and federal levels, to guarantee that all health insurance plans that provide cover-age of prescription drugs include the same level of coverage for FDA-approved prescription contraceptives, as well as coverage for outpatient contraceptive services.

Maryland, in 1998, became the first state to enact a comprehensive contraceptive equity law (Maryland Insurance Code Annotated, 2003). Since that time, nineteen other states have passed laws requiring health plans that cover prescription drugs to include prescription contra-ceptives. Similar legislation has been introduced in other states as well. In general, each of the state contraceptive equity laws provides that a health insurance policy that is issued in that state and provides cov-erage for prescription drugs generally must provide coverage for any prescription drug or device that has been approved by the FDA for use as a contraceptive. Most also direct that if an insurance policy pro-vides coverage for outpatient health care services, it must provide coverage for outpatient contraceptive services, such as consultations, examinations, procedures, and other medical services. Most of the laws further provide that any deductible, copayment, or coinsurance that is applied to contraceptives may not be greater than the deductible, copayment, or coinsurance applied to other prescription drugs. Sev-eral of the laws mandate that the contraceptive coverage requirement apply to both the insured and the insured's covered spouse and other dependents.

Fifteen of the states with contraceptive equity laws have enacted re-ligious refusal clauses, that is, exceptions to the contraceptive equity mandate for religious employers or insurers (or individuals enrolled in the plan) whose religious tenets prohibit the use of contraceptives. These clauses vary in scope. About half of the states with religious re-fusal clauses require employers to cover contraceptives when they are used for noncontraceptive medical reasons. Two of the narrower re-ligious refusal clauses are being challenged, so far unsuccessfully, by religiously affiliated employers in New York and California who are not covered by the exemption.

At the federal level, advocates are urging passage of the EPICC, which has been introduced in the U.S. Senate and House with bipar-tisan support. EPICC does not require special treatment of contra-ceptives, only equitable treatment within the context of an existing prescription drug benefit. EPICC will extend protection to plans not provided by an employer to its employees, such as nonemployment group and individual plans, and to employer plans not covered by Title VII, thereby guaranteeing contraceptive coverage for the millions of women who receive their insurance from a source not covered by Title VII. Enactment of EPICC would represent an additional and im-portant step forward for women's health.

CONCLUSION

It is long past time for health insurance plans to cover women's con-traceptive needs when they cover other prescription drugs and devices. The evidence is clear that denying such coverage is harmful to wom-en's physical and fiscal well-being. In the past few years, this persistent gender gap in health care coverage has begun to narrow, due to recog-nition of the need by the public and policymakers alike and new legal mandates. There is reason to hope that this momentum will continue and that women across the country will soon receive the contracep-tive insurance coverage to which they are entitled.

9

Women and Depression

Venice Beach window and see a familiar face. There is a Mexican American woman whose name I have asked but never was able to understand because of her thick accent and my poor Spanish. She for-ages through the neighborhood recycling bins daily, collecting re-deemable materials. Today, Super Bowl Sunday, she has brought her daughter. The girl cannot be more than ten years old, and the man-ner in which the young one bounces from bin to bin makes the task look more like a treasure hunt than labor that those of us watching million-dollar commercials would not tolerate. Does she not know her indigence, or has she just known nothing else? Or is it a matter of culture and familial foundation?

Mary Pipher (1994, p. 281) reminds us, "Properly faced, adversity makes us stronger." But what befalls the girls whom adversity over-whelms? What consequences of insufficient coping skills carry into womanhood and pass on to the next generation? Depression is one manifestation of these consequences, and cultural context plays an in-tegral role in how depression is perceived, experienced, and expressed. The goal of this review of the research literature is to clarify some of the key issues that women encounter when coping with depression in the framework of specific cultural influences.

Women have endeavored throughout history to employ a voice of fortitude, faculty, and accord. The effects of poverty, abuse, discrimina-tion, and restrictive gender roles extend beyond the social ramifications generated and into a woman's mental health. In an exposition written for the United Nations Division for Advancement of Women, Del Vec-chio Good (n.d.) relates that "depression, hopelessness, exhaustion, anger and fear grow out of hunger, overwork, domestic and civil vio-lence, entrapment and economic dependence. Understanding the sources of ill health for women means understanding how cultural and economic forces interact to undermine their social status" (para. 3).

A woman's willingness to seek aid for her symptoms puts her among the 12.4 million women reported by the National Institute of Mental Health (2002) to suffer from depression. The Depression and Bipolar Support Alliance (2004) reports that women experience depression at twice the rate of men, regardless of ethnicity. The majority of research conducted on women's depression has been on women of European descent, excluding other ethnic populations that need mental health care.

The development of gender-sensitive services is an attempt to offer treatment that can distinguish between gender role expectations and those characteristics that leave women more vulnerable to depressive symptoms. The Department of Health (2002) published a strategy for the development of women's mental health that emphasized service characteristics such as providing women with a choice of type of treat-ment, creating a safe environment, and recognizing specific gender, religious, and cultural needs.

This chapter explores the distinctive features associated with de-pression among women in the African American, Latina, Caucasian, and Asian populations. The explanation of each ethnicity's experience of depressive symptoms will raise issues of diagnostic bias, discrepancy in symptom reports by different groups, misdiagnosis, treatment plan-ning, and utilization of services. There are broad implications when la-beling groups that include different cultural and religious factions.

For the purpose of this chapter, the definitions provided by the National Women's Health Information Center (2002) are used. Latina women are of Cuban, Mexican, Puerto Rican, South or Central American, or other Spanish culture or race. African Americans have origins in any of the black racial groups of Africa, and Caucasians are descendants of Europeans, Middle Easterners, and North Africans. Finally, the Asian population entails those of the Far East, Southeast Asia, and the Indian subcontinent. Heeseung (2002) describes the "universal orientation" perspective of culture and mental health as one that considers both bi-ological and cultural, or environmental, factors in human behavior. This perspective allows the clinician to integrate a range of therapies in treatment, providing more options to the client.

THERAPIST BIAS

Therapist or diagnostic bias complicates the accuracy of assessments and the proper treatment of specific populations. When cultural in-consistency exists between therapist and client, the client's expression of symptoms and the clinician's interpretation of that expression may result in inaccuracy in the perceived tendency of a population toward a specific mental illness (National Association for Mental Health, 2003). The experience of culture also includes common health con-cerns, similar educational opportunities in combination with socioe-conomic level, family dynamics, religious inclinations, and worldviews. All of these factors influence a population's attitude toward mental health, which bears on how services are accessed and the effectiveness of treatments not culturally specified (VanderVoort & Skorikov, 2002).

An important component in considering a cultural view of depres-sion is locus of control. Rotter (1975) describes locus of control as the individual's perception of life as experienced with an internal or ex-ternal influence. The determination of the influence dictates an indi-vidual's type of coping mechanisms, worldview, and confidence in problem-solving skills (Sue & Sue, 2003). Religious affiliation can en-courage the inclination to view external forces as destiny or fate, and in turn create opportunities for reflection and growth, but may hinder acceptance of personal responsibility (Ellison, 1993). Identifying locus of control is essential to determining the client's motivations, values, sense of personal responsibility, and relationship to society in treat-ment (Sue & Sue, 2003). The merging of these experiential components creates a unique cultural dynamic that has implications for a woman's experience of depression.

In this chapter, the review of literature will be done from the uni-versal orientation perspective (Heeseung, 2002), beginning with broader gender and cultural issues and then exploring the specifics of each population. The function of gender roles, discrimination, and social status in the contribution to depression will be accentuated. In the review of these issues, the examination of racial, gender, and so-cioeconomic prejudice will be relevant in and outside the clinical set-ting in relation to depressive features. Next, research describing distinctions between cultural trends, perspectives, and the experience of depression is evaluated in terms of implications for treatment. Spe-cific cultural dynamics of each population will be reviewed in relation to specific abilities to impose or prevent depression.

DISCRIMINATION AT THE ROOT: THE FOUNDATION OF DEPRESSION

Gender and culture play a large role in the formation of an individ-ual's identity and life experiences, both in the way others respond to him or her, and in the way these encounters are interpreted, internally (as in depression) or externally (as in stereotyping and bias).

Gender Bias

Current research on gender and depression indicates that women suf-fer depressive symptoms at twice the rate of men (National Institute of Mental Health, 2002). There have been questions raised about the cri-teria on which the *Diagnostic and Statistical Manual of Mental Disorders* (DSM-IV-TR; American Psychiatric Association) diagnosis is based. McLaughlin (2002) notes that diagnostic bias has been defined as "an error in judgment that counselors make when they collect or interpret information... [and] as a differential prevalence of either false posi-tive diagnosis... and/or false negative diagnosis" (p. 256). Joiner and Blalock (1995) elucidate three theories that may explain the increased diagnosis of women's depression: the artifact hypothesis, the biologi-cal theory, and psychosocial aspects (Joiner & Blalock, 1995).

The artifact hypothesis states that women are more likely to report symptoms of stress and depression (Joiner & Blalock, 1995). In com-bination with diagnostic criteria inclined to support the description of female depression, a disproportionate number of women diagnosed is not surprising. Gender-stereotyped behavior leads to a common di-agnosis, whether or not based on valid observation (Cook & Warnke, 1993). Kopper and Epperson (1996) discuss the association of the ex-pression of anger and depression. The results of their study suggest that "depressed women reported engaging in more verbal hostility than depressed men," and when under stress, they "were more likely to express their anger and feelings" (Kopper & Epperson, 1996). Cook and Warnke (1993) remind clinicians that gender differences in diag-nostic criteria do not necessarily imply bias. This point emphasizes the role of the clinician's judgment as the ultimate determinant in bias. McLaughlin (2002) discusses three important concepts of clinical bias: data availability and vividness, self-confirmatory bias, and self-fulfilling prophecy. Data availability and vividness implies that a clin-ician will diagnose a patient based on information most familiar to him or her and the characteristics that are regarded as obvious rather than the patient's actual presenting complaints. Self-confirmatory bias refers to a situation in which the clinician makes a diagnosis (possi-bly based on a stereotype or prejudice) and then notices only evidence that is consistent with that diagnosis. McLaughlin defines *self-fulfilling prophecy* as when a clinician responds to an individual in a way that confirms the clinician's expectations, in spite of incongruous evidence. These unconscious cognitive processes tend to confirm those beliefs and stereotypes that the clinician brought into the therapeutic en-counter, regardless of the characteristics of the client. The merging of these factors creates the risk of gender and culture bias in therapy be-cause of the strength and pervasiveness of gender and racial stereo-types throughout society.

Culture Bias

The factors that play the largest role in ethnocentric views of depres-sion and cultural bias are issues of misdiagnosis, improper treatment, inequality and poverty discrimination, differences in exposure to phys-ical and mental illness, and unequal access to care. The principal fac-tor in these issues is the level of socioeconomic status. Furthermore, each of these factors is a contributor to the onset of depression. Myers et al. (2002) discuss the relationship between the rate of depressive symptoms in Latina, African American, and Caucasian women and socioeconomic status. Initially, more depressive symptoms were re-ported in the Latino population, but no significant difference was found when the affluent group was included (Myers et al., 2002). An-drew Solomon (2001), writing extensively on the cyclical epidemic of poverty and depression, points to the significance of parenting style: "Mechanisms by which one achieves positive change in life are in-credibly basic, and most of us learn them in infancy in maternal in-teractions that demonstrate a link between cause and effect" (p. 350).

Finkelstein, Donenberg, and Martinovich (2001) concluded that the stringent parenting style, intended to cultivate coping mechanisms, of African Americans decreases susceptibility to adolescent depression. The Latino population has shown a high number of high school drop-outs in addition to a lack of medical insurance. The 37 percent rate of Latino high school dropouts is two and four times more than in Cau-casian and African American populations, respectively (Moore, 2001). In addition, Latina women are likely to be employed at low-paying jobs that supply a low social status (National Women's Health Infor-mation Center, 2002). Del Vecchio Good supports this statement by adding, "In the world of work, we find employment may bring self-esteem and independence; however, low paid or unpaid labor may con-tribute to oppression rather than independence" (n.d., para. 6). These low-paying positions are less inclined to offer job-related health ben-efits, resulting in the 30 percent of the Latino population that remains uninsured (National Women's Health Information Center, 2002). Fur-thermore, policy that surrounds allocating funds to indigent popu-lations is scrutinized for the lack of intended accuracy in who benefits. After speaking to members of Congress, Solomon remarked, "The ques-tion of whether [the community health programs] are serving the in-terest of the well is often examined; whether they are helping their target community seldom comes up" (2001, p. 377).

CULTURAL FEATURES AND DYNAMICS OF DEPRESSION

The diagnostic features of depression have historically been based on the symptoms displayed by Caucasians. As a consequence, treatment models have been assumed effective when applied across cultures (Sue & Sue, 2003). As mental health providers begin to accept the need for gender-specific treatment, the call for culturally sensitive services has emerged. Sociologist David Karp poses the important point that the question of culture "is a global question about what we owe to our-selves, what do we owe to others, and what do we think society owes us?" (2001, p. 235). Within each culture, the answer to this question is variable in terms of gender, but it is more prominently swayed by socioeconomic status. Asian, Latina, African American, and Caucasian women are highlighted as significant populations to be evaluated. The availability of research on each group differs, suggesting that a well-founded assessment of diagnostic basis, perception of culture by client and clinician, and realistic treatment options are necessary to develop effective interventions.

Asian Women and Depression

Contrary to the perception that Asian culture generates a healthy and "model" way of living, there is a disparity between reality and this per-ception that leads to what Sue and Sue (2003) describe as a myth of success. The depression rates reported by the National Asian Women's Health Organization (2003) illustrates this fact. Asian American girls exhibited the highest depression and suicide mortality rates across all ethnic groups considered. In addition, senior Asian women held the highest female suicide success rates amid all taken into account.

The Asian cultural attitude toward and experience of depression stems from facets of psychosocial, spirituality, and physical health ele-ments (Cochrane & Hussain, 2002). In contrast to Western ideas of men-tal health, Eastern cultures take a holistic approach to illness (Cochrane & Hussain, 2002; Sue & Sue, 2003). This results in the incorporation of physical symptoms reported with mental health complaints. Asian Americans may experience culture-bound syndromes such as *hwa-byung* (American Psychiatric Association, 2000).

Hwa-byung, or "sup-pressed anger syndrome," is characterized by symptoms such as constriction in the chest, palpitations, flushing, headache, dysphoria, anorexia, anxiety, and poor concentration. Studies by the Center for Asian-Pacific Exchange showed service utilization by 17 percent of the population (U.S. Department of Health and Human Services, 2001). While Asian Americans tend to postpone mental health treatment until a crisis because of shame and social stigma, once they are involved in treatment, typically the rate of success is very high. Hicks (2002) iden-tified concerns about safety in reporting symptoms as one explanation of the low usage of public health care and specifically concerns that pub-lic health care utilization can threaten immigration status.

Spirituality may play a considerable part in treatment success in addition to physical healing. Techniques such as acupuncture and *qigong*, a Chinese breathing method combined with exercise, are looked to as viable alternatives to Western medicine (Solomon, 2001).

The re-ligious foundation of Asian culture teaches that answers are found within the individual experience. This is illustrated in a quotation from Buddha: "Be lamps unto yourselves" (Martin, 1999). However, because Asian society is collectivist, the locus of control tends to be one of externality (Sue & Sue, 2003). An effective psychotherapy must consider the complexity of social structures and religious factors that reinforce an external locus of control and a duty to family that is at odds with Western values of independence and autonomy.

Gender roles for Asian women are a significant factor in the onset of depression. Scattolon and Stoppard (1999) found that a woman's at-tempt to be consistent with the idea of a "good" woman was incorpo-rated in the onset and alleviation of depression. Marital troubles or the inability to fulfill the role of the proper mother, daughter, sister, or wife creates family conflict (Cochrane & Hussain, 2002). Gordon (2003) points out the negative implications if a woman remains unmarried or resists the traditional marriage ideal. In turn, it is the prospect of fulfilling that role that will often aid in treatment motivation. Family cohesion, stability, and status are functions of an Asian woman's de-pression and recovery from which the malady originates. Regaining her "proper" role in the family increases status and social support, in ad-dition to supplying a sense of worth that was otherwise absent (Coch-rane & Hussain, 2002).

The issue of acculturation inconsistency between generational val-ues is present when a woman's role is considered. Once a family has immigrated to the United States, the second generation of women is likely to pursue identification with a European American culture that clashes with traditional Asian values. Huang (1994) proposes identity development through biculturalism, which is the individual's amal-gamation of dominant societal standards and traditional Asian val-ues. Pipher's interview (1994) with an eighteen-year-old Vietnamese woman who had recently immigrated is an example of the complexity involved in biculturalism:

She was dressed casually in a Garfield sweatshirt and jeans, but she was carefully groomed with long ice-blue nails and an elaborate hairstyle. Only her crooked teeth betrayed the poverty she must have experi-enced in Vietnam.... When we discussed American teenagers, Leah hesitated, clearly concerned not to appear rude. Then she said, "I don't like how American children leave home when they're eighteen. They abandon their parents and get into a lot of trouble. I don't think that's right" [pp. 87, 88].

When direct and indirect racial discrimination are incorporated, issues such as abuse, social isolation, and increased vulnerability to poverty emerge (Cochrane & Hussain, 2002). Cochrane and Hussain note that the locus of control that most Asian women experience is explained as a coalescence of the acceptance of depression and the function of kismet, or fate. Treatment implications involve the consid-eration of client participation in design and a deeper understanding of religious influences on behavior. Goal setting should be family inclu-sive, with consideration of acculturation in order to create a familiar support network and to process generational value conflicts (Sue & Sue, 2003). Ito and Maramba (2002) report a preference for the me-dicinal model of treatment by Asian American therapists, while re-maining aware of the possible medication cure-all assumption by the client. An awareness of preexisting cultural ideas will prevent mis-communication and misdiagnosis and cultivate an encouraging and productive relationship between client and therapist.

Latina Women and Depression

There is a striking lack of information regarding Latina women's ex-perience of depression across subcultures. If our scientific community functions at this limited level of awareness, then what expectations shall be held for the layperson? If the mental health community is to highlight culturally specific, gender-sensitive treatments and services, it is critical to have accurate and comprehensive information about the culture.

In comparison to the 75.1 percent of the Caucasian population, the Hispanic or Latino population accounts for 12.5 percent of the U.S. population (U.S. Census Bureau, 2000). This does not include the un-authorized Latino residents, estimated to number an additional 7.8 million (Bean, Van Hook, & Woodward-Lafield, 2001). The 1999 Sur-geon General's Report estimated that fewer than one in eleven Lati-nos access mental health services, and fewer than one in five make contact with a primary care provider. Diversity among Latino popu-lations is an important consideration, as each subpopulation varies in terms of use of health care facilities. Puerto Rican American women have higher rates of poverty than the larger Mexican American sub-group, but they access health facilities at rates similar to Caucasian women (NAWHO, 2003).

When faced with stressful life situations such as acculturation, pov-erty, and marital problems, the Latina woman is inclined to confer with family-approved religious resources such as an *Espiritistas* or *curandero* (Heeseung, 2002; Stoeber, 2003; Sue & Sue, 2003). Stoeber (2003) attributes the preference of alternative treatments to a lack of concurrence in ethos between Latino culture and the traditional men-tal health provider. Religious or spiritually warranted services func-tion with the dual purpose of healing and maintaining psychological health (Ramirez de Leon, 2002). Latino culture operates as a collec-tive society, emphasizing commitment to family roles and relation-ships. Koss-Chioino (1999) observed the reaction of family shame to any display of aggressive behavior by Puerto Rican women. In place of the unapproved aggressive or assertive behavior, there are vindic-tive or malicious rumors circulated, a kind of indirect expression of aggression (Malgady, Rogler, & Cortés, 1996; Koss-Chioino, 1999). This is not to say that assertive behavior is discouraged in all circum-stances within the Latino family structure. Pipher's interview (1994) with a sixteen-year-old Hispanic young woman, whose family had a long tradition of social activism, demonstrates the support available within the *familio,* or family unit:

I wanted to fit in. I desperately tried to raise my coolness quotient. I even bought some Guess jeans, but they didn't help. The problem was my color.... Mom encouraged me to fight the pressure to be a certain way. She hates racism and elitism. [My brother] was a nonconformist and he teased me about those jeans. Later I did fight.... I was lonely and mixed up for awhile. I took everything personally, and I thought there must be something wrong with me. But [my brother] and my mom kept saying it wasn't me. They talked me into joining Amnesty International.... The people were great. Their friendship saved me [pp. 278,279].

Similar to Asian culture, the theme of suppressed anger is identi-fied in Latino culture as *obsesion simple,* the culture-bound syndrome that compares to depressive characteristics (Koss-Chioino, 1999). An-other culture-bound syndrome, termed *nervios* by the DSM-IV-TR (American Psychiatric Association, 2000), shares the symptomatic characteristics of depression, as well as features of somatoform, ad-justment, anxiety, dissociative, and psychotic disorders. The prom-inent identifiers of this culture-bound syndrome are the somatic indicia such as headaches, irritability, difficulty sleeping, and a ten-dency to weep. These somatic descriptors are an indicator of the man-ner in which most Latina women express and experience depression.

A noteworthy perception of variance between the mental illness of Mexican Americans and Puerto Ricans is accurately described by Lopez and Guarnaccia (2000), specifically the culture-bound syn-drome *nervios:*

Nervios among Mexican Americans and ataque de nervios among Puerto Ricans are similar in that the concept of nervios (nerves) re-flects both a mental and physical state. The two concepts differ as well; for example, ataque de nervios is usually thought to have a sudden onset whereas nervios is more of a condition that befalls individuals who are thought to be weak or vulnerable [para. 7].

A collective society promotes an external control worldview that deepens the significance of relationships as coping mechanisms, but also promotes a pessimistic and fatalistic outlook of life events. Dent and Teasdale (1988) confirmed that the extent of negative self-perception displays a predictive correlation to the proportions of de-pressive features, but also aggravates the tendency to perceive a gener-alized negativity of the self and the environment. A negative perception of the self in combination with the collectivist external locus of con-trol places emphasis on the feelings of helplessness that foster depres-sion in women. Latina women place significant importance on their respective gender roles and the resulting functions. Specific emphasis is placed on the role of mother and wife, therefore intensifying the stressors of marital problems or family discord. Aranda, Castaneda, Lee, and Sobel (2001) drew from their study that the self-efficacy of a Mexican American woman is jeopardized by the family and marital stressors that may hinder her proficiency as a mother or wife. Self-sacrifice for the family unit is commended within the culture if the difficulties encountered are viewed as successfully surmounted by the woman (Koss-Chioino, 1999).

Jean Baker Miller (1976) describes the idea of self-sacrifice and ser-vice as an integral aspect of feminine identity. She explains further that vulnerability to "involutional depression" increases and often takes the form of somatic symptoms. According to Koss-Chioino's assessment of Puerto Rican women's dominant depressive symptoms (nervousness or intranquility, sleep disturbance or hallucinations, prolonged crying, and headaches or other bodily aches), the role of self-sacrifice draws on sig-nificant aspects of Latina identity. In contrast, when collectivist versus individualist groups were analyzed for salience in social connectedness and depressive features, VanderVoort and Skorikov (2002) controlled for level of income and found no significant difference in display of so-matic symptoms. This indicates that it is possible that socioeconomic status accounts for the disparity in symptom expression. This assertion suggests multiple treatment implications that deemphasize cultural lim-itations and converge on economic and social facets. The restructuring of governmental policies that infringe on minority mental health will aid in the increased success of depression treatment.

African American Depression

African American women join the rest of the American women in reporting depression at twice the rate of their male counterparts. The unique characteristic of the African American woman is her perspective on emotional stamina and the role personal perspective plays in depres-sion. In Solomon's *Noonday Demon* (2001), Meri Danquah describes her experience of depression:

Clinical depression simply did not exist within the realm of my pos-sibilities, or that matter, in the realm of possibilities for any of the black women in my world. The illusion of strength has been and continues to be a major significance to me as a black woman. The one myth that I have had to endure my entire life is that of my supposed birthright to strength. Black women are *supposed* to be strong—caretakers, nurturers, healers of other people [p. 195].

The racism and discrimination endured by this population has cre-ated a sense of mistrust between African American culture and health care professionals. Sue and Sue (2003) regard historical hostility as a client's response to identification with present-day or past suffering due to discrimination. Solomon (2001) points out that "since the high rates of women's depression do not reflect a genetic predisposition that we can currently locate, we can say with some assurance that the rates of depression among women could be significantly reduced in a more equitable society" (p. 178).

Poverty, discrimination, and depression are potent reinforcers of one another. Individually, these social ills are arduous; when compounded, the burden created can overwhelm even a healthy individual, let alone one who is already lacking resources and coping skills. The accessibility to and relationship with a familiar, trusted primary care provider is an important component in the diagnosis of depression, accuracy of treat-ment, and view of depression in the African American community. O'Malley, Forrest, and Miranda (2003) found that although fewer African American women than Caucasian women are diagnosed with depression, physicians who provided thorough medical services were more likely to inquire about and treat for depression. Myers et al. (2002) report that African American women have a lower level of trust than do Caucasian women, which also contributes to the amount of treatment offered to female African Americans. The nature of the physician and patient relationship is considered a contributing factor in how fre-quently a primary care provider is used and consequently how often a treatment is implemented. A respectful relationship between provider and patient sets an environment for open communication with a greater possibility for quality health care, illness prevention, and proper treat-ment of depression (O'Malley et al., 2003). The perception of the pro-vider is also an issue of respect and trust that is present between the therapist and client. Sue and Sue (2003) explicate the importance of re-solving any unease between client and therapist that would provoke the client to investigate the sincerity and integrity of the relationship be-yond practical limits. Until this trepidation has ceased, the question of effective treatment taking place is at an impasse.

Similar to the collectivist natures of Latina and Asian cultures, the African American's cultural investment in religion can result in a view of predestination. The connection of spirituality and treatment is pow-erful in this community. "He [the Lord] brought me into the depres-sion and out of there too. I done prayed to the Lord for help and he sent me Dr. Marian" (Solomon, 2001, p. 351). Finding support within church and community can be a coping mechanism, though when the community is ill, effective support is difficult to maintain. Bell and Doucet (2003) describe the limitations of a support system among women enduring similar circumstances, in which focusing on the shared stressors may be demoralizing and exacerbate feelings of pow-erlessness. Dependency among peers that may not be reliable sources of help can result in a continued sense of instability and isolation (Bell & Doucet, 2003). Solomon (2001) queries a young woman about her encounter with depression: "Since I think positive... I made it. Ain't nothing that bad you can't get through.... I say that loud with these people, they just dogs eating dog. And anyone can be saved. I had one woman, she drank, smoke, had been with my husband... but when she come round, I gonna help her, 'cause in order for her to get better she gotta have someone to help her" (p. 352).

In addition to helping individual women develop more effective coping skills, an emphasis on educating religious leaders in mental health skills may support the African American community from with-in the culture's unique dynamic. Taylor, Ellison, and Chatters (2000) explored the considerable influence of clergy on mental health care decisions, qualities, and access for their community. Clergy who es-tablish trust within the community on a spiritual level and display per-sonal investment by engaging in the community through advantages such as home visits create accessibility to mental health care unequaled by alternate sources (Taylor et al., 2000).

When exploring depression in specific populations, it is imperative to keep in mind that race is not equivalent to culture (Phinney, 1996). Cultural influence on a client's worldview dictates the extent to which problem solving is effective and the manner in which treatment is approached. An external locus of responsibility, or the propensity to identify with imposed discrimination and prejudice, is common among African Americans, which encompasses the impact of the his-tory of slavery (Sue & Sue, 2003). The differentiating factor in the Af-rican American identity is the locus of control. Individuals who embody an internal locus of control tend to engender racial pride, while those who assume an external locus of control are more sensitive to outside influences (Sue & Sue, 2003). Martin and Hall (1992) ascertain an in-tegral consideration of an African American woman's role prioritiza-tion in reference to the fortification of African Americans. Specifically important to account for in regard to treatment planning is the unique aspect of the inclination to forfeit power in the belief that it will strengthen racial solidarity.

Caucasian Women and Depression

The depression that a Caucasian woman experiences often stems from a lack of cohesiveness and the conflict formed when facing feminine socialization and ideals of American autonomy. Gender roles, the amount of value that is placed on them, and the woman's ability to ful-fill those roles are significant factors across cultures. The non-Hispanic white woman seems to struggle with the lack of clarity and consis-tency within American gender roles. Karp (2001), in *The Burden of Sympathy*, discusses the extent to which Americans have learned and prioritized self-interest and profit. He applies this to the concept of caring for the mentally ill and postulates that because there are no dis-tinct cultural definitions and motivations, as a society we rely on out-dated gender roles to create structure in caring. He relates this to women in the statement, "In a culture otherwise dedicated to expressive in-dividualism, women—mothers in particular—often measure their morality through an ethic of care and willingness to subordinate self-interest to the greater good of the family" (p. 246).

Sullivan and Neale's meta-analysis of the genetic epidemiology of major depression (2000) provided evidence that genetics accounts for 40 percent of the risk in major depression. Depression within the fam-ily can complicate caretaking if none of those affected are being prop-erly treated. Martha Manning (1994) speaks of her own undertaking with her grandmother:

My grandmother sits at the kitchen table.... The lazy Susan spins in the center, with the host of prescription bottles, holy cards of dead people, Avon products, and napkins.... I watch the objects move as I circle my grandmother's depression.... Other people deal with it bet-ter than I. They have more distance. Her sorrow is not separate from me. It is in me too. I know it. I've known it all along. I have lived all my life with parallel visions of her: my magical creative wonderful grandmother who calls me golden and loves me like crazy, and the sad angry woman who gave up on life so long ago [pp. 26-28].

Women construct their identity on the equality of intimacy and re-lationships in their lives. Aspects that create a healthy identity, such as respect, meaningful work, safety, and loving relationships, may be mis-directed or undeveloped, bringing vulnerability to depression (Pipher, 1994). A woman's adult identity dictates the quality of interpersonal relationships concerning family, spouse, and outside interactions. Uebelacker, Courtnage, and Whisman (2003) discovered that marital dissatisfaction was correlated with depressive symptoms in both men and women due to self-silencing. The significant factor in the women's depression was explained by the inability to express dissatisfaction with the marriage for fear of unsettling or compromising the relation-ship (Uebelacker et al., 2003).

The need to harmonize with outside relationships in addition to maintaining a cosmetically placid life creates stressors that are unique to women. Additional pressures of the worldview held by Caucasian women often accompany the consequence of self-silencing within and outside the home. American society generates an emphasis on pro-duction, ambition, and individuality (Sue & Sue, 2003). Self-blame is common when accountability is high in unrealistic goal setting, which is maintained by an internal locus of control and internal locus of re-sponsibility (Sue & Sue, 2003). In addition to the pressures that wom-en endure, there is an extension of the tendency to accept an ambitious, self-defining role without internalizing the relationship-dependent role and the autonomous role. Jean Baker Miller (1986) illustrates this as "paradoxical depression": "Such depressions may reflect the fact that the individual is forced to admit increased self-determination and to admit that [she], [herself], is responsible for what happens. [She] is not doing it for someone else or under the direction of someone else" (p. 92).

Miller postulates that the conflict of self-determination extends past accountability and into the basic issues of safety and love:

> If I can bring myself to admit that I can take on the determination and direction of my own life rather than give it over to others, can I exist with safety? With satisfaction? And who

will ever love me, or even tol-erate me, if I do that? Only after these questions are confronted, at least to some degree, can one begin to ask the even more basic question: what do I really want? And this question too, will not always be an-swered easily [p. 93].

Abuse and poverty are significant factors that impress on a woman's ability to cope with stressors. Physical, sexual, or emotional abuse that begins at an early age sets an interpersonal dynamic that is difficult to escape. Abuse from a dating partner is reported by 20 percent of wom-en, which illustrates the commonalty in violence against women (Sue & Sue, 2003). Lack of educational resources and vulnerability to pov-erty leave women without the proper aids to divert depressive symp-toms: the establishment of safe and equal relationships in treatment planning accompanied by access to basic resources. The relation be-tween assessment of self-concept and the woman's ability to empower and problem-solve is essential to track progress: the creation of a "per-sonal vision," as Miller (1986) describes it, and the search for the ideal authenticity that defines and determines "what we want."

CONCLUSION

Roosa, Dumka, Gonzales, and Knight (2002) state, "For interventions to be culturally competent, they must be designed and implemented in ways that not only fit the culture of the targeted group *but also* help the targeted group be successful in their context." Therefore, the em-phasis in clinicians' service is conditioned on the character and capa-bility of our empathy for the client. In order to do this, it is necessary that the key traits of a culture be kept at the forefront of considera-tions. Locus of control, the value of gender roles within that culture, and the client's extent of involvement in her culture are specific as-pects that require attention. Without these considerations, the incon-sistencies will continue to occur and the populations served will not benefit from the efforts put forth.

INTIMACY AND INJURY

The response of the law to the problem of violence in intimate relationships has not been swift. For centuries, legal actors neglected to notice or address the issue, an omission linked in large part to the broader problem of gender inequality deeply entrenched in the culture. Indeed, the common law of the Anglo-American world permitted the "master of the household" to "chastise" his wife using corporal punishment, as long as he did not inflict permanent physi-cal injuries (Siegel, 1996).

Although American judges had explicitly rejected the doctrine of chastisement by the late nineteenth century, they began substituting for it a common law doctrine of family privacy that justified legal non-intervention in the marital relationship, despite evidence that a hus-band was subjecting his wife to physical abuse. Since this shift in the justification for nonintervention coincided with the era of Recon-struction, it is not surprising that the understanding by which fami-lies were to be accorded privacy was racialized. When the customs of racial hierarchy were threatened by the abolition of slavery, intimate violence came to be understood as a problem of African American and poor immigrant men, such as those of German and Irish descent. Legal sanctions, particularly the punishment of flogging, were im-posed in some of these cases, but not in instances of intimate vio-lence committed by men of privileged classes.

For most of the next century, intimate violence was treated as an oc-casion for social services to be brought to bear on women, with family courts sending marital violence cases to social workers, who used coun-seling and urged reconciliation (Siegel, 1996). The problem was un-derstood as one in which women provoked violence. When framed in this manner, the appropriate intervention became one of teaching women better habits to prevent their provocations. Within this cul-tural framework, male violence receded from view. This notion of in-timate violence as a private family dispute that women could be taught better skills to address extended late into the twentieth century.

Due to this history of dramatic underenforcement of crimes of in-timate violence against women, feminist activists and an influential victim's rights movement combined their energies to remove the cloak of privacy from the problem of intimate violence and put the issue on the public political agenda of the 1960s and 1970s. Their efforts were tremendously successful at local, state, and national levels. In relatively short order, they were able to alter the cultural understanding of the problem of intimate violence.

Over the past three decades, battered women's advocates have es-tablished hundreds of battered women's hotlines, shelters, and vic-tim's advocacy programs. They have produced documentaries about battered women's experiences, generated a cross-disciplinary profes-sional literature on the subject, and in some instances, pioneered treatment programs for batterers (Adams, 1988). Medical schools have added course work about domestic violence to standard medical train-ing, and a number of law schools now offer both classroom courses examining issues of domestic violence and clinical programs in which student-attorneys provide legal representation for battered women. These extraordinary efforts have both reflected and promoted a grow-ing cultural awareness of the nature, scope, and severity of the prob-lem of violence between intimate partners.

These changing cultural attitudes have wrought many changes in law, particularly on the front lines of law enforcement. Many of these changes have involved toughening the criminal laws regarding vio-lence between intimates and educating both law enforcement and ju-dicial officials about the nature of the problem and the use of criminal laws to respond to it. Although the criminal justice system has been the primary locus of legal change on this issue, it has not been the ex-clusive one.

CONTEMPORARY LEGAL INTERVENTIONS

A variety of legal reforms have been undertaken to improve the re-sponsiveness of law enforcement systems to victims of intimate abuse. Legal commentators have characterized domestic violence not just as a crime, but as a violation of human rights (Copelon, 1994; Culliton, 1993; Holt, 1994; Thomas & Easley, 1995), hate crime statutes (Cope-land & Wolfe, 1991), and the prohibition on involuntary servitude found in the Thirteenth Amendment to the U.S. Constitution (Mc-Connell, 1992). Consequently, courts have been deluged in recent years with a variety of cases brought on behalf of domestic violence victims.

Civil Protection Orders

The major way in which courts now seek to address the danger posed by intimate violence is through the provision of a process by which those who have suffered violence may obtain civil orders of protec-tion, also known as restraining orders, against their batterers. Every American jurisdiction now has legislation by which courts can issue such orders to enjoin a batterer's abuse and threats (Finn & Colson, 1990). Different states have different procedural requirements by which victims may invoke the civil protection order process (Klein & Orloff, 1993; Kinports & Fischer, 1993).

Obviously, the effectiveness of the civil protection order process depends on how readily a victim of violence can access it and how will-ing local criminal justice officials will be to enforce it (Harris & Smith, 1996; Klein, 1996). Both of these are questions of resources. Jurisdic-tions vary as to how much outreach is provided to victims of intimate violence to assist them in using this process and in how many law en-forcement resources are directed toward responding to it (Fischer & Rose, 1995). These are significant issues: in some instances, the holder of a restraining order faces retaliatory actions and an escalation of in-timate violence.

Most states have enacted statutes criminalizing the violation of a restraining order, and others use criminal contempt laws to bolster the protection that a restraining order—a mere piece of paper—can pro-vide (Zlotnick, 1995). In these jurisdictions, the restraining order process provides formal notice to the abuser that continued coercive contact with the person who obtained the order can be prosecuted as a crime. Although the crime is defined and punished in various ways depending on the jurisdiction, it has often been made a felony carry-ing the risk of years of imprisonment and significant collateral con-sequences (Epstein, 1999).

Arrest and Prosecution

Beyond the prosecution of violations of civil restraining orders, legal reforms have resulted in dramatic increases in the arrest and prose-cution of batterers for the assaults and the batteries that they have committed. Some states prosecute intimate violence under their gen-eral laws against assaultive behavior, while others have enacted sepa-rate statutes with separate penalties for crimes of intimate violence (Hart, 1992). States have also enacted statutes that define new crimes related to the circumstances of intimate violence. For example, every jurisdiction adopted an antistalking law in the 1990s (Jordan, Quinn, Jordan, & Daileader, 2000). While the first such statutes faced consti-tutional challenges due to the breadth and vagueness of the conduct they covered, newer antistalking legislation benefited from the more precisely worded model statute drafted in 1993 by the U.S. Depart-ment of Justice and other federal agencies.

In most jurisdictions, the general rule is that police officers are forbidden to make arrests for misdemeanor offenses unless they first obtain an arrest warrant (James, 1994). Battered women's advocates worked to change this general policy, such that now most jurisdictions have statutes that permit arrests for the misdemeanor of assault and battery in domestic violence cases to be made without warrants (Zorza, 1992). Some locales also have mandatory domestic violence training for law enforcement officers (Gagné, 1998; Guinn & O'Dell, 1993).

In responding to reports of intimate violence, police in some ju-risdictions are permitted to exercise their discretion in making arrests, while other jurisdictions have removed that discretion. The 1984 pub-lication of an experiment with mandatory arrest in Minneapolis spurred a number of states to adopt mandatory arrest statutes or poli-cies. These require police officers to arrest domestic violence sus-pects whenever the officers have probable cause to believe that a crime such as assault or battery has been committed. Other states have pre-ferred discretionary arrest laws in these situations.

Some jurisdictions have mandatory prosecution policies as well, such that prosecutors have no discretion to dismiss domestic violence charges once they are filed (Hanna, 1996). Even if the victim of the crime re-quests that the charges be dismissed and refuses to cooperate in press-ing the charges, the prosecutor will be required to pursue the case nonetheless. In addition, most states have mandatory reporting laws that require medical professionals, and occasionally other social services workers, to file reports with police whenever they suspect that a patient's symptoms or injuries are caused by intimate violence (Mills, 1990).

Mandatory reporting, arrest, and prosecution are legal reforms in-tended to counter the long and notorious history of law enforcement's failure to respond to victims of intimate violence. Supporters of man-datory legal interventions believe that they provide powerful deter-rents to batterers, demonstrating strong cultural condemnation of battering behavior and reducing the likelihood of discriminatory law enforcement. Therefore, they consider these policies the most effec-tive available tool for reducing intimate violence (Hanna, 1996; For-um, 1997; Stark, 1996; Guinn & O'Dell, 1993; Zorza, 1994).

By contrast, opponents of mandatory interventions are deeply con-cerned when decisions to arrest and prosecute intimate violence are made without regard to the victim's wishes (Mills, 1990). They are con-cerned that especially when victims remain in relationship with abusers, as many do, mandatory criminal justice interventions can be harmful to the victim in a number of ways. These harms are compounded for women who come from communities with historically troubled rela-tionships with law enforcement, immigrant women whose batterers may be deported, and women living on the edge of poverty (Fedders, 1997; Ruttenberg, 1994; Klein & Orloff, 1993; Crenshaw, 1993). More-over, researchers are in dispute as to the long-term effectiveness of man-datory policies in reducing intimate violence (Zorza, 1994; Symposium on Domestic Violence, 1992).

A criminal conviction for a crime of domestic violence may in some instances result not in immediate incarceration, but in a sentence of probation with required conditions (Hanna, 1998). These conditions, enforced through the threat of future imprisonment for failure to comply, often require that the batterer enter individual counseling, an anger-management program, or other available social services (Adams, 1988; Harrell, 1991). In some jurisdictions, such as Boston, Seattle, and San Diego, there are therapeutic programs to which convicted bat-terers can be sentenced that are designed exclusively to treat men who perpetrate intimate violence (Rosenfeld, 1992).

Some commentators argue that encouraging and facilitating the use of therapeutic services in domestic violence cases would be more effective than mandating their use through the criminal justice sys-tem. They worry that the coercive qualities of criminal penalties im-pede the effectiveness of these services (Mills, 1990). Others suggest that in some cases, providing intimate violence victims with the ma-terial resources that many of them lack, such as independent housing and income, may be preferable to policies of punishing abusers through criminal justice sanctions (Coker, 2000).

While these controversies about the appropriateness of various kinds of legal interventions continue, there is no doubt that prosecu-tions of domestic violence cases have become features of the landscape in criminal courtrooms around the country. Some criminal courthouses hold specialized domestic violence sessions, and a handful of juris-dictions have established a court devoted exclusively to domestic vio-lence (Keilitz, Efkeman, & Casey, 1997). The underlying rationale for the latter arrangement is that specialized domestic violence courts, overseeing all related civil and criminal matters, will more effectively address the complex issues—potentially involving divorce, property, child custody, and other issues—that may be implicated when efforts are underway to end an abusive relationship.

Civil Lawsuits

While far less common than criminal prosecutions, some victims of in-timate violence have filed civil lawsuits, known as tort actions, against their abusers. Through these lawsuits, plaintiffs seek monetary com-pensation for the harms that they have suffered due to the defendants' abusive behavior (Scherer, 1992). The harms compensated need not be physical injuries alone, but might include the traumatic consequences of living under the coercive control of one's intimate partner. Many jurisdictions recognize a tort action for intentional infliction of emotional distress, and some commentators have suggested that claims based on this legal theory might be used as a source of redress for victims of in-timate abuse in conjunction with tort actions for physical harms such as assault and battery (Scherer, 1992; Dalton, 1997).

Tort actions as a source of redress in these situations have some ob-vious constraints. First, victims will need the assistance of lawyers to pursue such actions, and there is a profound shortage of lawyers for those who are unable to pay for their services. Second, a batterer with-out sufficient financial means may be unable to pay a monetary judg-ment if it is imposed. Therefore, even in situations where plaintiffs are able to hire lawyers to file such suits and their claims are upheld by courts, the victories will be merely symbolic unless the defendants have significant resources. Hence, the deterrence picture provided by this legal remedy is a limited one, although there may be some individual cases where it is a viable avenue of redress.

Another kind of civil lawsuit that does not depend for its success on the resources of an individual defendant is a lawsuit against police departments and municipalities, alleging civil rights violations in the failure of police officers to respond to complaints of intimate violence. Evidence that the police had policies or practices of nonintervention in domestic violence cases led to a number of prominent lawsuits and multimillion-dollar judgments in the 1980s. The prospect of liabil-ity at this level of financial magnitude encouraged police departments to increase their responsiveness to victims of intimate violence. In-deed, the fear of liability may well have led some communities to favor mandatory arrest programs (Dalton & Schneider, 2001).

The 1989 Supreme Court decision in *DeShaneyv. Winnebago County Department of Social Services* seems to prohibit lawsuits against police departments and municipalities for failure to protect victims from pri-vate violence that the police could not control. Nonetheless, a plain-tiff may still be able to prevail in such litigation on a claim that police enabled private violence (Borgmann, 1990) or engaged in discrimi-natory enforcement (Choundas, 1995). Although lawsuits of this sort may be advisable in particular situations, they are not a feasible ap-proach in most cases of intimate violence.

Alternative Forms of Dispute Resolution

In cases involving family law, many courts prefer mediation as an alternative to litigation. This preference for mediation is sparked by a desire to reduce both case congestion and levels of antagonism in matters related to the family. Indeed, a number of states require media-tion in cases involving child custody and visitation.

The preference for mediation is controversial in cases involving intimate violence. Those who oppose mediation in cases of intimate vi-olence argue that the posture of mediator neutrality prevents the me-diator from giving the abused partner the support that she may need and inhibits any signaling of disapproval of the batterer's behavior. Con-sequently, mediation opponents fear that the ethos of mediation is such that it enables the batterer—and, even worse, the system—to overlook the extent of the harm that the batterer has inflicted and to avoid tak-ing it into account in reaching agreements (Fischer, Vidmar, & Ellis, 1993; Cobb, 1997).

Supporters of mediation in at least some of the cases involving in-timate violence believe that many of the opponents' concerns can be addressed through the manner in which the mediation setting is struc-tured. The mediator can meet separately with the parties and can en-courage the batterer to take responsibility for his behavior. This less adversarial mediation process is characterized as more potentially em-powering to the battered woman than the formality of the courtroom setting (Joyce, 1997).

The controversies concerning the appropriateness of mediation in cases that entail intimate violence have influenced the legal regulation of access to mediation. Some of the jurisdictions that mandate medi-ation relinquish that requirement in cases where intimate violence has occurred. Some jurisdictions go so far as to ban mediation in these cases, whereas others permit the judge to make a discretionary judgment concerning the appropriateness of mediation in a particular case (Bart-lett, Harris, & Rhode, 2002).

Mediation is not the only potential alternative setting for resolving disputes in cases that involve intimate violence. Coker (1999) has de-scribed the Navajo practice of peacemaking as a kind of forum that may provide assistance to battered women in some circumstances. Peacemaking processes may be initiated by the battered woman or by referral from the Navajo legal system. The peacemaker facilitates a con-versation between the parties, those with a stake in the parties' lives, such as family and friends, and those with special expertise related to the pertinent issues. The group then works to try to create a plan for addressing the problem. This kind of model has been adopted by pro-ponents of restorative justice programs, some of whom believe that these represent promising alternative interventions for at least a por-tion of the cases involving intimate violence.

SELF-DEFENSE

Against the backdrop of the centuries-old reluctance to address the problem of intimate violence, all of these developments in the law were hard won and recently so. Nevertheless, attitudes often change more slowly than the law. As battered women's advocates have observed, legal decision makers' perceptions of battered women are often still plagued by stereotypes and misperceptions. These problems manifest them-selves acutely when the legal interventions detailed in the preceding section have not succeeded in preventing intimate violence and bat-tered women find themselves on trial for killing their abusers.

In an intimate relationship that becomes violent, the violence may become lethal. When it does, the violence in the relationship has gen-erally escalated to the extent that the abuser in the relationship kills the abused. Studies show that approximately one-third of female mur-der victims, compared to one-twenty-fifth of male murder victims, are killed by their intimate partners (Rennison, 2003).

Occasionally, lethality runs in the opposite direction from the pat-tern of abuse, such that a person who has suffered repeated and severe violence at the hands of her intimate partner responds by killing her batterer. Often these killings are charged as crimes, ranging from man-slaughter to first-degree murder. A third of the women incarcerated for homicide have been convicted for killing an intimate partner. Re-search shows that a considerable percentage of these partners had his-tories of abusing the women who killed them (Browne, 1987).

In such cases, the likely defense is self-defense. To meet the criteria of self-defense and thereby avoid conviction for acts of violence against a batterer, a defendant must convince a jury that she acted from a rea-sonable belief that she was in imminent danger of serious bodily harm or death (Gillespie, 1989). In other words, self-defense in this context entails a claim that the intimate violence had reached a point at which either the abuser or the abused would be maimed or killed. Stated more plainly, when the abused, now a criminal defendant, took the abuser's life, she did so to save her own.

Battered Woman Syndrome

Over the past three decades, psychologists have sought to understand more clearly the dynamics of abusive relationships, the experiences of battered women, and the psychological consequences of living for an extended period in an intimate relationship with a batterer. In the 1970s, psychologist Lenore Walker (1979) coined the term "battered woman syndrome," a subspecies of posttraumatic stress disorder, to explain the perceptions and behavior of women in such situations. Following the publication of Walker's research, lawyers representing women charged with violence against their batterers saw that prose-cutors, judges, and jurors might learn more about how the world looks to women trapped in violent relationships and might view them more sympathetically if these decision makers were able to become better educated about battered women's lives.

Consequently, activists and lawyers for battered women developed a trial strategy of seeking to admit experts who could offer testimony to educate jurors about battering relationships and their consequences. Since "battered woman syndrome" had a scientific flavor, similar to other sorts of psychological and scientific testimony that experts were permitted to offer at trial, the educational process that occurred in the course of battered women's litigation took the form of admitting the expert testimony of psychologists. When permitted to testify, these ex-perts would describe for the jury the nature of battered woman syn-drome and explain how it might illuminate what occurred in the case at bar.

Battered women's lawyers believed that through the admission of expert testimony about battered woman syndrome, which focused on the experiences, perceptions, and mental states of women caught in abusive relationships, jurors could come to appreciate how the de-fendant reasonably believed that she had to use violence to repel the imminent life-threatening violence of her batterer. In the absence of ex-pert testimony, battered women's advocates feared that the law of self-defense would be applied in a gender-biased fashion, since judges and jurors might fail to apprehend the contextual conditions of battered women's lives (Schneider, 2000).

Initially, litigants' efforts to admit expert testimony of battered woman syndrome met with little success. Judges often refused the ad-mission of such testimony, disputing its relevance, its scientific basis, or the notion that it would assist a jury. Battered women's advocates re-sponded with campaigns to liberalize the evidentiary rulings to more readily allow for the admission of expert testimony in these cases. These campaigns yielded statutes adopted by some state legislatures that au-thorized the admission of such testimony and case law from the high-est court of many states that reached the same conclusion. By the end of the 1980s, the admission of expert testimony on battered woman syn-drome had become a far more commonly accepted practice in trials of battered women charged with violence against batterers.

When expert testimony of battered woman syndrome was admitted, it did not always work as battered women's advocates had hoped. Al-though some women whose self-defense trials featured testimony about battered woman syndrome did receive acquittals or convictions of lesser charges, many others were convicted of the crimes with which they had been charged. Some argue that this pattern of results relates to inher-ent limitations in the concept of battered woman syndrome itself.

While testimony about battered woman syndrome can be a vehicle for educating jurors about battered women's relationships, perceptions, and experiences, it can also reinforce a view of battered women as mentally impaired. Commentators observe that battered woman syn-drome focuses attention on the psychology of the battered woman rather than on the batterer's pattern of coercive behavior. As a result, new stereotypes about battered women have been created, such that those who fail to meet the stereotypes are perceived to be less credible when they claim self-defense. As several commentators have noted, the battered woman stereotype has worked to the particular disadvan-tage of black women, lesbians, women perceived to have assertive per-sonalities, women with substance abuse histories, and others who for a variety of cultural reasons may not be as readily perceived to embody the passive virtues that fit constrained understandings of the battered woman profile.

Success in court has been particularly elusive for battered women defendants who raise self-defense in cases in which the self-protective violence that they inflicted on their batterers did not occur in the mid-dle of a threatening confrontation. Rather, the violence they inflicted may have been during a lull in the abuse, when the batterer was sleep-ing or otherwise off guard. While battered women's advocates have never contended that women should kill batterers in these noncon-frontational situations, they also suggest that it is not unreasonable in certain of these situations to view these women as acting in self-defense, similar in fashion to hostages overtaking their captors (Marcus, 1994; Cohen, 1996).

In cases in which the battered woman defendant had previously sought aid from police, courts, and social services, only to find them nonresponsive or ineffective in their efforts to protect her, a predicate may well be laid for an argument that she honestly and reasonably believed that she was able to protect her life from the batterer's impend-ing lethal violence only by the assaultive actions for which she is now on trial. Indeed, decision makers would have no context within which to understand her actions and perceptions unless they heard exten-sive evidence of the violent dynamics in the relationship, the history of abuse, and prior efforts to escape or halt the violence. Nevertheless, women have not fared well in cases of nonconfrontational assaults, likely due to fears that if the imminent harm requirement of self-de-fense doctrine is stretched beyond confrontational episodes, battered women may be encouraged to take violent retaliatory actions and then claim self-defense.

Problems in Representation of Battered Women as Defendants

Problems inherent in the interpretation and application of the con-cept of battered woman syndrome are not the only problems that bat-tered women face as defendants in courtrooms. The failure of women who have defended their lives against their batterers to successfully defend themselves against criminal convictions has multiple causes. Sometimes it is related to inadequate representation, a problem that pervades the criminal justice system for those without access to con-siderable financial resources.

Unfortunately, it is not an aberration to find practicing in crimi-nal courtrooms around the country attorneys who are unschooled in the phenomenon of domestic violence, hold misconceptions or biases about battered women, or simply lack knowledge about the complex-ities of representing battered women and lack the desire to remedy this deficit. Due at least in part to their misapprehension of the na-ture and the legal implications of the incidents underlying the charges, such attorneys may fail to effectively investigate the battered woman's claim of self-defense. They may fail to identify or interview potential defense witnesses such as family members or friends, find other sources of information such as medical records or employment records that corroborate the defense, or seek expert assistance to bolster an avail-able defense.

Attorneys who are not fully aware of the story of abuse that under-lies the current charges may permit a biased jury to decide the case. This can happen when an attorney fails to properly question prospective ju-rors, through a procedure known as voir dire, about the misperceptions that they may hold of battered women. It can also happen when the attorney fails to challenge the selection of jurors who reveal such biases. These attorneys may also fail to request that judges instruct jurors on how credible evidence of battering relates to a claim of self-defense. In addition, attorneys may fail to develop relationships of trust with their clients, which when combined with the confusion and memory lapses that frequently plague battered women who have used lethal vi-olence, may lead them to give poor advice to their clients regarding de-cisions to accept a plea bargain or to testify at trial.

Despite the fact that the Sixth Amendment to the U.S. Constitution guarantees the effective assistance of counsel at a criminal trial, the Supreme Court has made it exceedingly difficult to overturn a con-viction on the grounds of ineffective assistance. This is so even when there is substantial evidence of significant inadequacies in represen-tation. In a number of appellate cases, courts have refused to find that the ineffective assistance of trial counsel rose to the level of a consti-tutional violation, although counsel failed to develop a full eviden-tiary record of the history of battering in the defendant's relationship with a violent partner.

Problems of Judge and Juror Bias

In addition to receiving inadequate representation, women raising self-defense claims have sometimes met judicial hostility. Judges un-sympathetic to defendants generally, or to women raising self-defense claims in particular, have sometimes refused to admit evidence, ex-pert or otherwise, proffered in support of self-defense on the grounds that it is not relevant or would not be helpful to the jury. In some in-stances, judges have refused to permit questioning of prospective ju-rors during the voir dire process to uncover specific attitudes that may bias them against a claim of self-defense in these circumstances. Judges may also refuse to instruct juries to consider self-defense in these cases (*State v. Norman*, 1989).

Recent case law and legislation in a number of jurisdictions requires the admission of evidence bearing on self-defense when a factual pred-icate can be established that the defendant on trial suffered a history of abuse at the hands of the person she is charged with assaulting or killing. Nevertheless, judicial hostility remains an obstacle to fair tri-als in some instances, as judges still retain considerable discretionary authority over the presentation of evidence. After a careful study of appellate cases concerning battered women's claims of self-defense, Holly Maguigan (1991) concluded that the major obstacle to fair tri-als in these cases is error by the trial court judge in the application of self-defense doctrine to the evidence that the defense presents.

If the trial judges in these cases do not instruct jurors properly on self-defense, the jurors will be unable to determine the appropriate legal relevance of any evidence that the defense has been able to pre-sent. Yet even in the absence of judicial error or hostility, when jurors receive the evidence and are fairly instructed about how to consider it as bearing on self-defense, some juries, for a variety of reasons, reject it. Especially in situations of inadequate defense representation, these reasons may include the jurors' misconceptions of the nature of the abuse and its consequences, which may lead them to misinterpret as aggression or retaliation the self-defensive violence for which the bat-tered woman is now on trial.

After conviction, women in these circumstances may face severe penalties, ranging from a term of years, to life in prison with or with-out parole, to the death sentence. Sometimes the jurisdiction's statu-tory structure is set up such that the judge has no discretion about the sentence imposed after conviction on particular charges. In other cir-cumstances, judges who have sentencing discretion and harbor mis-conceptions of battered women's situations have exercised it harshly An unduly stiff sentence imposed by a judge may result from inade-quate defense representation, bias, or other factors that block the judge's apprehension of the mitigating features of the underlying events that were the subject of the trial. The penalties flowing from conviction in-volve not just the potential loss of life or liberty, but other serious col-lateral consequences, such as the loss of custody of children, future employment opportunities, and the right to vote (Mauer & Chesney-Lind, 2002).

THE EMERGENCE OF CLEMENCY PROJECTS

The nationwide difficulties that battered women encountered in re-ceiving fair hearings on self-defense claims spawned another legal re-form effort to address this injustice. In the 1990s, regional women's groups organized clemency projects around the country to seek a reduction in the penalties that battered women suffered after they were convicted of crimes against their batterers. While the clemency movement has not concerned itself exclusively with battered women convicted of homicide, these are the cases to which the movement de-voted its primary attention. Aided by the clemency projects, women imprisoned for killing their batterers sought executive clemency.

The Nature of Executive Clemency

Executive clemency refers to the discretionary power of the president of the United States or the governor of a state to reduce the severity of a criminal sentence. Clemency implies mercy, the application of a kind of forbearance or forgiveness of an unduly harsh sanction (Dorne & Gewerth, 1999). While a form of executive clemency has existed since ancient times and can be found in virtually every country's legal system (Moore, 1989), the prerogative to provide sentence relief on the part of the executive branches of state or federal governments is rooted in their respective constitutions.

The clemency process as a means of ameliorating unduly harsh penalties varies from state to state. In many states, an advisory board, most frequently the state's parole board, considers petitions for clemency, gathers information to investigate the petitions, holds hear-ings in some instances, and makes recommendations to the governor about whether a pardon—signifying full absolution for the crime— or a commutation—signifying a reduction in sentence—should be granted. Although they typically have independent decision-making authority, governors tend to heed the advice of their advisory boards. In a few states, a governor's decision to grant clemency may need to be approved by another administrative body as well. In Massachusetts, this body is the Governor's Council, established as a check on guber-natorial power.

Battered women who have petitioned for relief through the clemency process have rarely sought full pardons. Although the assertion in a clemency petition that a claim of self-defense was erroneously denied at trial establishes a legitimate ground for a pardon, battered women incarcerated for homicide, after making pragmatic assessments of the relative probabilities of success, have generally sought to have their sen-tences commuted or reduced in duration. In these instances, the peti-tioners were seeking recognition that the self-defensive aspects of their cases established the mitigating grounds for sentence relief. From the petitioner's perspective, receiving a full pardon is a prefer-able remedy, in that it results in the petitioner's immediate release from prison as well as the erasure of the conviction and its attendant collat-eral disabilities. Nevertheless, a commutation provides substantial relief, as it can reduce a sentence to time served. In other words, receiving a commutation can also result in the petitioner's immediate release from prison—often the primary concern of the petitioner—even though in such an instance the conviction remains standing. Perceiving commu-tations to be more politically feasible and realizing that they too can result in grants of freedom from further incarceration, the battered women's clemency movement has focused primarily on sentence com-mutations.

A request for a sentence commutation was especially compelling in a case where self-defense had not been asserted as well as it might have been at trial or where it had encountered some apparent bias on the part of the judge or jury. Another compelling feature of clemency claims was that many of the incarcerated women faced trial before cul-tural understandings about the lives of battered women had evolved, before significant services had been made available to them, and be-fore legal reforms responsive to their situations had been incorporated. This was easily demonstrated in jurisdictions in which the incarcer-ated women were convicted prior to the enactment of laws that per-mitted the admission of expert testimony regarding battered woman syndrome and other types of evidence corroborating the extent and duration of the abuse the defendants had suffered at the hands of their batterers. Since these legal reforms were prospective in nature, apply-ing only to cases not yet finalized, those already serving sentences had not received the more enlightened legal treatment that they would have received had their cases arisen later. Hence, sentence commuta-tions came to be perceived as a form of equitable relief that substi-tuted for the inability to retroactively apply legal reforms.

The Ohio Experience: Leadership in Action

In the 1980s, issues of domestic violence were something of a *cause célèbre* for Governor Richard F. Celeste of Ohio, whose wife, Dagmar, had worked on these issues in the feminist community in Cleveland. In 1976, several women's groups in the Cleveland area had obtained a foundation grant to establish Ohio's first emergency shelter for bat-tered women. At that time, when Richard Celeste was lieutenant gov-ernor, he and his wife provided their own home to serve as that shelter.

Celeste became governor of Ohio in 1982, and he was elected to a second term in 1986. During these years, Dagmar Celeste was pro-vided an office and a staff in the statehouse and became an adviser to her husband's administration. Soon after his election, Dagmar Celeste began visiting the women's prison in Marysville, Ohio, learned that many of the incarcerated women had been victims of intimate vio-lence, and generated support for recovery programs and other services to be made available to them. These experiences led her to propose to her husband that he undertake a wide-ranging review of the cases of incarcerated battered women to determine who among them might be deserving of gubernatorial clemency (Gagné, 1998).

The political prospects for clemency improved when the Ohio Su-preme Court changed state law regarding the admission of expert tes-timony in trials of women charged with assaulting or killing their batterers. In 1981, just before Richard Celeste had become governor, the Ohio Supreme Court had decided *State* v. *Thomas*, upholding the murder conviction of a battered woman despite the trial judge's ex-clusion of expert testimony on battered woman syndrome. In March 1990, the court reversed itself. In the landmark case of *State v. Koss* (1990), the court overturned a battered woman's conviction for vol-untary manslaughter against her batterer due to the exclusion of ex-pert testimony concerning battered woman syndrome. Later in 1990, the state legislature adopted a statute permitting the admission of ex-pert testimony about battered woman syndrome in the trial of a de-fendant who raised self-defense to charges that she committed violence against her batterer (Ohio Rev. Code. Ann. § 2901.06,1990).

Governor Celeste was responsive to concerns that women tried be-fore the passage of the legislation and the decision in the landmark case might have been unjustly convicted and sentenced. He understood ar-guments that they had been denied a fair opportunity to explain how battering and its consequences influenced their situations and supported their defenses. The first lady and her staff were undoubtedly helpful in formulating these arguments and urging them as a basis for political ac-tion. Consequently, the governor initiated a clemency process.

In November 1989, while the legislation was under discussion and the landmark case was pending, Governor Celeste instructed his staff to review the cases of battered women convicted of crimes against their batterers. He wanted to identify women whose crimes grew out of their victimization by a violent partner. After instructing the state cor-rectional authority to cooperate in obtaining this research, the gover-nor received a report recognizing over two hundred such women.

Many of them were serving sentences on the order of twenty-five years to life, and a few were under death sentence. The candidates for clem-ency were selected from among this group.

Over the course of a year, the governor's staff educated themselves and the Ohio Parole Board concerning battering, self-defense, and the trial process of those who had been convicted of violence against their batterers. The education process included meetings with the incarcer-ated women themselves. Since most of these women had been involved in support groups that the first lady's previous advocacy had helped to create, they were better able to articulate their experiences with both battering and the court system, and they were better able to advocate for clemency on their own behalf. After exhaustively reviewing the incarcerated women's case files, the governor's staff distributed ap-plications for clemency to more than a hundred women. The women's groups in the prison and their supporters played a central role in dis-seminating information about the clemency process and in obtaining assistance for individual women in preparing their petitions.

The governor and his staff reviewed over one hundred cases, seek-ing to document and verify the history of abuse described in the clemency petitions. After eliminating cases of women who had con-victions for prior violence or records of disruptive prison behavior, the staff sought to identify the cases in which the women had been un-able to defend themselves adequately at trial. They isolated a group of cases in which they were persuaded that had jurors been able to hear expert testimony about battered woman syndrome and evidence about a well-documented history of abuse, they may have decided differ-ently. The Ohio Parole Board recommended clemency in eighteen of these cases (Gagné, 1998).

The national clemency movement was ignited when, in the winter of 1990, a few weeks before he left office, Governor Celeste exceeded the board's recommendations and commuted the sentences of twenty-seven women who had served or were serving sentences for violence, typically lethal violence, against their batterers. The governor pardoned a twenty-eighth woman who had already been released on parole. As a condition of their release from prison or from parole supervision, the women were required to perform two hundred hours of community service in a domestic violence context (Ammons, 1994).

An outcry immediately erupted in the media from those, most of them law enforcement officials, who opposed the governor's commu-tations. Others praised his courage, personal integrity, and sense of fair-ness. Some petitioners who had shared support groups with the twenty-eight women who received clemency from Governor Celeste were devastated when they did not receive clemency as well, and some of their supporters believed that the governor would have been justi-fied in granting an even greater number of petitions (Gagné, 1998).

Despite the controversies about whether Governor Celeste had done too much or too little, none of the cases in which he granted relief came back to haunt him in the future. Although a few of the battered woman he released were convicted of minor crimes later, recidivism proved a negligible problem. Of the few women who returned to the criminal courts, none returned for a crime of violence. Rather, in support of the view that Governor Celeste exercised his discretionary power cautiously, most of the women who were released after receiving clemency are living and working in their communities to this day (Am-mons, 2003).

Events in Ohio caught the attention of feminist activists and bat-tered women's advocates nationwide. Governor Celeste's precedent-setting grants of clemency to a group of battered women convicted of violent crimes against their batterers reverberated widely. Drawing on the strategies and experiences of those involved in the Ohio clemency project, a legal reform movement was born.

The Maryland Experience: The Power of Narrative

In the 1980s, while litigation and legislation efforts on behalf of bat-tered women were underway in Ohio and other states, battered wom-en's advocates in Maryland were unsuccessful in obtaining legal rulings through the courts that authorized the admission of expert testimony on battered woman syndrome when battered women faced trial for violence against their batterers (*Kriscumas* v. *State*, 1987; *Friend v. State*, 1988). Responding to this failure, Maryland's battered women's advocates organized a powerful educational initiative. This initiative formed the backdrop to a larger project of law reform.

The public education initiative in Maryland drew from the consciousness-raising methods that had emerged in the feminist movement and from the related storytelling strategies that groups of women and other disempowered groups had been using to convey their all-too-often-ignored experiences. Exposure to these experiences was conceived as a vehicle for promoting insights that might generate social change. In furtherance of its educational strategy to promote this exposure, the coalition of advocates arranged a number of set-tings in which women convicted of violence against their abusers could tell the stories of their relationships, the abuse they had suffered, and the circumstances leading to their acts of violence against their intimate partners.

In order to disseminate these gripping, poignant, and horrifying sto-ries to a broader audience, the Maryland advocates produced a short film, *A Plea for Justice*, which was released early in 1990. In the film, four women serving sentences on the order of fifteen years to life for killing their batterers tell the stories of their experiences with their violent part-ners. The advocates' intentions were to create conditions under which viewers might experience vicariously the women's life-threatening predicaments and their suffering, fear, and isolation. Their hope was that the film would render battered women as sympathetic and their claims of self-defense—that they killed their batterers because they saw no other way to save themselves—credible and understandable.

Unlike Governor Celeste of Ohio, Governor William Donald Schae-fer of Maryland had shown no prior interest in issues of domestic violence. Yet after he viewed the film with members of his staff, he re-quested a meeting at the Maryland women's prison with the women interviewed on video. The meeting was arranged, giving Governor Schaefer the opportunity to communicate in person with the women in the film and to hear from other similarly situated women as well. Later the governor told reporters that the meeting had altered his un-derstanding of the problems that battered women face. Subsequently, he expressed interest in receiving petitions for clemency, promoted the adoption of state legislation to improve domestic violence training for judges, and supported legislation that required in appropriate cases the admission at trial of testimony about battering and its effects.

Many other state officials in the executive, legislative, and judicial branches of government viewed *A Plea for Justice.* The media covered the release of the film and the issues depicted in it as well. When bat-tered women's advocates eventually prevailed in obtaining legislation that authorized the admission of evidence of battered woman syn-drome in battered women's self-defense cases, this success was in no small measure due to the far-reaching persuasive power of the widely viewed thirty-minute video.

Following their dramatically effective educational and legislative campaign, the coalition of battered women's advocates embarked on a clemency project. After identifying women who had suffered abuse and were incarcerated for crimes related to that abuse and notifying them about the possibility of filing petitions for clemency, thirty women requested interviews for clemency purposes. On January 23,1991, after a process of interviewing and verification, the advocates filed a volumi-nous confidential report seeking clemency for twelve women serving extended sentences for violence against their batterers.

Relying on the increased awareness of the plight of battered wom-en, the petitions detailed the individual experiences of each petitioner, her background, the abuse she suffered, and the events leading to the crime of which she was convicted. The request for clemency was rooted in the fact that much of this information had not been offered or con-sidered prior to the verdict or the sentence in each of the cases. In se-lecting twelve women to recommend for clemency, the advocates decided to pursue relief in those cases most likely to win the gover-nor's approval (Gagné, 1998).

On February 19,1991, Governor Schaefer commuted the sentences of eight of the incarcerated battered women (Schneider, 1991). When he received further advocacy on behalf of the remaining four, he de-cided to grant early parole to two of them. The women's advocates helped those who had received clemency with the considerable tran-sition difficulties—including housing, job placement, psychological adjustment, and media attention—that they would face upon reen-tering society. Through this assistance, the advocates hoped to facilitate the released women's social reentry and thereby reduce the potential political repercussions for Governor Schaefer (Gagné, 1998). By so do-ing, they would enhance the chances that other battered women might receive clemency in the future.

Fueled by its rapid success and national acclaim, the notion of clem-ency as a kind of partial justice for battered women incarcerated for killing their batterers had caught fire. With Governor Schaefer's clem-encies in Maryland following so closely on the heels of Governor Ce-leste's path-breaking actions in Ohio, the national clemency movement took hold. Feminist activists and battered women's advocates orga-nized clemency movements in many states and began requesting state governors to provide sentence relief to battered women incarcerated for crimes of violence against their batterers.

The Massachusetts Experience: The Framingham Eight

In the late 1980s and the early 1990s, eight women who were incarcer-ated in the women's prison in Framingham, Massachusetts, for having killed their batterers were meeting in a support and consciousness-raising group facilitated by a human rights activist. Due to similarities in their experiences, the incarcerated women took on a collective iden-tity (Goldfarb, 1996). They called themselves the Framingham Eight, a name that implied solidarity among them and that, in part as a re-sult of this implication, caught the media's attention. The battered wom-en's advocates in Massachusetts consciously developed a media strategy to try to cultivate public understanding of battered women forced to defend their lives (Gagné, 1998).

By 1991, sympathetic stories prominently featured in the Boston press exposed the lethality of violence against women and linked cases of women killed by intimate partners to the cases of the Framingham Eight (Grossfeld, 1991; Kabat, 1991). In that year, the legislature ad-dressed questions of legal protection for victims of intimate violence (Gagné, 1998). Subsequently, Governor William Weld, a socially mod-erate Republican who had also adopted a tough-on-crime persona, amended the guidelines for commutation of sentences to include "a his-tory of abuse [that] significantly contributed to... the offense" (Wong, 1994). This amendment was the first official action in the country that formally increased battered women's access to clemency relief.

In response to this perceived invitation, a coalition of women's advocacy groups recruited attorneys to represent each of the Fram-ingham Eight in a quest for a commutation of her sentence. On February 14,1992, each of the eight respective defense teams filed a petition for commutation, detailing the petitioner's history of abuse and arguing that because each was tried before recent improvements in legal protections, she was therefore deserving of equitable relief (Locy, 1992a). Public hearings before the Advisory Board of Pardons and Parole were held in seven of the cases. Although some of the pe-titioners received other forms of relief, Governor Weld officially com-muted just two of the sentences (Locy, 1993).

Before the clemency process in Massachusetts had concluded, the legislature had enacted a law that guaranteed the admission in appro-priate cases of a history of abuse and expert testimony about bat-tering and its effects (Mass. Gen. Laws, chap. 233, sec. 1, §23E). An independent film, *Defending Our Lives*, which featured interviews with four of the Framingham Eight, won an Academy Award as the year's best short documentary film (Biddle, 1994). The Framingham Eight had not only obtained some sentence relief, but their stories had re-ceived national attention as part of a public educational movement.

California: Many Requests, Little Relief

As in Massachusetts, the California clemency movement began with the formation of support groups for incarcerated battered women. In March 1991, members of the group that met in Frontera, the major women's prison in southern California, wrote to Governor Pete Wil-son asking him to consider sentence commutations for all of the California women who were serving time for killing their batterers. Wilson responded by indicating that he would not conduct a statewide review of all of the cases of women incarcerated for killing their bat-terers, but that in the absence of any other requisite clemency proto-cols, he would consider the letter an application for clemency by the thirty-four women who had signed it. He proceeded to conduct a re-view of the signatories' cases (Gagné, 1998).

Inspired by the governor's apparent openness to considering such clemency requests, activists in California's battered women's move-ment decided to organize a large group of attorneys to prepare clem-ency petitions for all of the women incarcerated for killing their batterers. While they were engaged in the petition-drafting process, the California legislature considered a bill creating a right to introduce expert testimony on battered woman syndrome in appropriate cases (Gross, 1992). A number of legislators traveled to Frontera to hear the testimony of several incarcerated battered women who spoke about their abuse, their efforts to secure help, and their need to protect them-selves (Morrison, 1991). When the battered woman syndrome bill was subsequently enacted, the petitioners had an additional argument for clemency, as all of them were convicted before the right to expert tes-timony was guaranteed.

In 1992, attorneys filed clemency petitions for thirty-four battered women, a group that contained only some of the signatories to the ini-tial letter to Governor Wilson ("Thirty-Four California Killers Seek Clemency," 1992). In May 1993, Governor Wilson announced that he had reviewed six of these petitioners' cases and ten of those who had signed the letter. He reduced the sentence of two petitioners, one a seventy-eight-year-old inmate in failing health, and another, Brenda Aris, who after killing her abusive husband while he slept and failing to obtain relief through the courts, became eligible for parole a number of years earlier than her original sentence provided (Lucas & Moore, 1993).

Over the next several years, Governor Wilson denied either relief or review in virtually all other battered women's clemency cases. Al-though in 1992 he signed legislation that required parole commissioners to receive training concerning battered woman syndrome and domestic violence (Gagné, 1998), in 1993 he vetoed broadly supported bipartisan legislation that would have afforded battered women con-victed before the guarantee of expert testimony an opportunity for re-view of their original trials (Baker, 1994). Despite a benefit showing of *Defending Our Lives* in California in 1994, combined with a concerted media campaign by incarcerated battered women and their support-ers, Governor Wilson could not be moved to provide significant relief (Gagné, 1998). With the base of his political support lying squarely among social conservatives, he apparently determined that his polit-ical future as a law-and-order politician was best protected by dis-tancing himself from the movement to assist incarcerated battered women.

Governor Wilson's successor to office, Governor Gray Davis, bor-rowed the same political calculus. Seeking to bolster support among conservative voters, Davis vowed during the gubernatorial campaign to let no murderer go free during his term of office (Mydans, 1992). Under a new state law, however, the parole board was required to con-sider information regarding battered woman syndrome in any cases tried before such evidence had been rendered admissible. Although the parole board reviewed a few dozen cases, found battered woman syndrome to exist in a number of them, and recommended parole in eight of those cases, Governor Davis endorsed release on parole in only two of these cases (Warren, 2002).

Florida: Selective Advocacy

Florida has restrictive rules for seeking gubernatorial clemency. No one convicted in Florida may apply for a pardon until at least ten years after the completion of any sentence or parole conditions. No one may apply for a commutation without the consent of the governor, two cabinet members, and a recommendation of the Florida Parole Commission. The first stage of battered women's clemency activism in Florida took the form of modifying these restrictions to enlarge the prospects for clemency ("Can Panels Blaze Legal Trail for Battered Women?" 1992). Aided by a media campaign, these efforts prevailed (Schweers, 1993). Effective January 1992, Governor Lawton Chiles revised Florida's clem-ency procedures to enable a woman who was incarcerated for killing her batterer and who could demonstrate a history of abuse to ask the Parole Commission to waive the usual application consent policies and refer her case to a panel of experts on issues of intimate violence. If the panel determined that the petitioner suffered from battered woman syn-drome at the time of the offense, then the Parole Commission would recommend that the governor and the cabinet review the case for a pos-sible commutation of sentence (Gagné, 1998).

In *Rogers v. State* (1993), the Florida Court of Appeals authorized the admission of expert testimony on battered woman syndrome in appropriate cases. Despite the new case and the new rules for clem-ency, Florida's battered women's activists chose to proceed cautiously, avoiding mass applications for clemency and recommending that each petitioner file an individual request for commutation. By the end of

1993, sixteen battered women had filed an individual application for clemency under Florida's revised procedures (O'Neal, 1993). After sep-arate hearings, two women were granted clemency and released from prison in 1993 (Orlando & Willon, 1993). Seven others ultimately were granted commutations and released, but only after completing a pris-on work-release program (Gagné, 1998).

Given the potential for politicization of the clemency issue, bat-tered women's advocates chose not to file additional clemency peti-tions during the Lawton Chiles-Jeb Bush gubernatorial campaign of 1994.

After Chiles was reelected, efforts to obtain more commutations

increased. Attorneys prepared and filed ten battered women's clemency petitions in 1996, focusing on the cases that had the greatest chance of success, and then submitted more petitions in 1998 (Gagné, 1998). After granting a couple of additional clemencies, Governor Chiles died late in 1998 ("Six Women Who Killed Abusive Men Are Granted Clemency," 1998).

When interim Governor Buddy MacKay took office, he granted the clemency petitions of six more women incarcerated for killing their batterers ("Six Women Who Killed Abusive Men Are Granted Clem-ency," 1998). The clemency prospects for incarcerated battered women in Florida were significantly diminished when Jeb Bush was elected governor in the next election. Battered women's advocates accuse Governor Bush of ignoring the legitimate claims to relief filed by bat-tered women incarcerated in Florida's burgeoning prison system (Talan, 2000).

Illinois: Electoral Strategizing

After two Chicago defense attorneys obtained individual commuta-tions for four incarcerated women, they decided to organize a broader clemency project, staffed by attorneys, activists, law professors, and law students. Founded in 1993, the Illinois Clemency Project con-ducted inmate outreach leading to the submission of twelve clemency petitions in 1994. After hearings before the Illinois Prisoner Review Board, which forwards its recommendation to the governor confi-dentially, Governor Jim Edgar granted four commutations in May 1994 (Gagné, 1998).

Governor Edgar's commutation decisions were likely influenced by his reelection strategy. His 1994 gubernatorial opponent was a liberal woman. As long as he could justify his decision to grant clemency to four battered women, he could capitalize on an opportunity to appeal to some of his opponent's potential supporters without risking the transfer of any of his conservative support to her (Gagné, 1998). Al-though the clemency petitioners had consciously avoided using the concept of battered woman syndrome in their requests for relief, based on concerns about the message that such psychological language con-veys, Governor Edgar framed his justification for granting relief in those terms (Gagné, 1998).

In July 1995, the Illinois Clemency Project filed eighteen additional petitions for commutation. In this wave of applications, the petition-ers included the language of battered woman syndrome, because the governor had previously favored granting relief on that basis. This time Governor Edgar decided to release one woman after she had served fif-teen years of a twenty-nine-year sentence and to deny the seventeen other requests for commutation (Gagné, 1998).

Although additional commutation petitions were filed on behalf of incarcerated battered women during Governor Edgar's term of of-fice, the governor granted relief in just a few more cases (Grunman & Kiernan, 1998). Without an election strategy to be advanced by his clemency decisions, Governor Edgar approved battered women's pe-titions for clemency on an extremely meager basis. His successor in office, Governor George Ryan, celebrated for his blanket commuta-tions in death penalty cases, denied three requests for clemency by bat-tered women but commuted the sentence of one (Brotman, 2003).

Kentucky: A Sympathetic Governor

In *Commonwealth* v. *Craig* (1990), the Kentucky Supreme Court em-braced an expansive understanding of battered woman syndrome. Re-versing prior law, the court indicated that battered woman syndrome was not a psychological condition about which only a mental health professional could attest, but one about which information on the dynamics of battering and its consequences was broadly relevant. After this case was decided, battered women's advocates filed a number of petitions for clemency. In December 1991, just before he left office, Gov-ernor Wallace Wilkinson pardoned one petitioner who had already served her prison term and denied relief to two other incarcerated bat-tered women who had petitioned for clemency (Gagné, 1998).

In 1992, the Kentucky legislature enacted a law concerning battered women's self-defense that also established various reforms without re-lying on the concept of battered woman syndrome. Instead, the legisla-tion reconceived the notion of imminent harm for purposes of battered women's self-defense. In self-defense cases involving domestic violence, the 1992 law permitted a defendant's asserted belief that danger was im-minent to be supported by evidence that the victim had a history of se-rious and repeated abuse of the defendant (Kentucky Revised Statutes 503.010).

The 1992 act also amended certain requirements that violent felony offenders serve prison terms of a prescribed minimum duration, pro-viding an exemption from these requirements for those convicted of killing their batterers. Finally, for offenders who had not previously had the opportunity to present evidence of their history of abuse, the act afforded a right to file motions to present such evidence in their original trial courts. This provision proved less consequential than it might have been, because few trial court judges complied. Their non-compliance apparently stemmed from their failure to appreciate the rationale for providing this admittedly unusual rehearing of a set of facts concerning a case in which the offender was already serving a pris-on sentence (Gagné, 1998).

These legislative changes became effective soon after Governor Brereton Jones took office. In 1993, he appointed Helen Howard-Hughes, who had expressed interest in domestic violence issues, to chair the Kentucky Parole Board. Howard-Hughes was responsive to the suggestions of battered women's activists that she review for clem-ency consideration the cases of women incarcerated for assaulting or killing their batterers (Gagné, 1998). In 1995, she arranged for all members of the Parole Board to receive training in domestic violence issues. Thereafter, the Parole

Board reviewed a number of battered women's cases that had been identified by Howard-Hughes and de-veloped for clemency by attorneys in the public defender's office ("Jus-tice for Abused Women," 1995).

The Parole Board determined that fourteen incarcerated battered women should be considered for release on early parole. Five of these cases were scheduled for an early parole hearing, but under law, nine others were prohibited from early parole review until they had served a longer minimum prison sentence. Since these nine women had pe-titioned for clemency, the Parole Board recommended that the gov-ernor commute their sentences to a level at which they could receive hearings for early parole as well (Gagné, 1998).

Due to positive relations with the media that had been developed by battered women's advocates, the press became an ally in the quest for clemency. The media had shown particular interest in the life sto-ries of the incarcerated women, especially in a quilt that they had made in their prison support group to depict their experiences with violence. Indeed, the governor had reportedly been moved on viewing the quilt in 1995 when it was displayed at the Kentucky State Fair. The governor had also received many letters describing and documenting these experiences from the women themselves, and some members of the Parole Board had viewed a video in which the incarcerated women de-scribed their experiences with violence (Ellers, 1996).

On December 11,1995, Governor Jones granted the requested clem-encies, resulting in the release of nine women in January 1996 on early parole. The governor also pardoned a woman who had already served her prison sentence (Ellers, 1995). The governor denied four subse-quent clemency requests, but the Parole Board released other battered women who did not need clemency in order to be considered for pa-role (Gagné, 1998). In the course of a few years and with the help of a sympathetic governor, battered women's activists in Kentucky had achieved considerable success.

Clemency Nationwide

Before the 1990s had ended, hundreds of battered women had peti-tioned dozens of governors for clemency. In some cases, the clemency movement yielded significant victories, in others, searing disappoint-ments. Across the country more than one hundred of the battered wom-en who petitioned for clemency were successful in obtaining it.

In addition to the clemencies in the states examined here, a limited number of battered women received sentence relief from several other governors. Governor Roy Romer of Colorado granted sentence com-mutations to four battered women at the same time that he denied clemency to four other petitioners (Mitchell, 1999). Governors George Pataki of New York, Steve Merrill of New Hampshire, Terry Brandstad of Iowa, and Barbara Roberts of Oregon each granted clemency to one battered woman who had petitioned for relief (Ammons, 2003). Even a law enforcer as harsh as U.S. Attorney General John Ashcroft reduced the sentences of two battered women when he was governor of Mis-souri (Young, 1992). Other governors who have granted clemency to battered women on at least one occasion are Fife Symington of Ari-zona, Charles Roemer of Louisiana, James Martin of North Carolina, and Gary Locke of Washington (Ammons, 2003).

Many of the governors defended their clemency decisions on the grounds that they believed the petitioners had been suffering from bat-tered woman syndrome at the time of the crime, had been trapped in abusive relationships, and had been unable to offer a complete account of their abuse to a jury. Most used a rhetoric of justice and propor-tionality to support their decisions. Occasionally notions of mercy and compassion were invoked as well (Ammons, 2003).

CONTINUING CHALLENGES

Victims of Intimate Violence

As illuminated by the battered women's clemency movement and recent efforts to address the problems of intimate violence, the past generation's cultural support for battered women has both wrought tremendous changes and revealed profound challenges. Perhaps the most significant change is that groundbreaking legal and political de-velopments have reconceived intimate violence as no longer a personal matter in a private relationship, but one of major social dimensions. Nevertheless, the problem of violence in intimate relationships remains frighteningly frequent and severe, and battered women's mortality rates remain tragically high.

Battered women confront continuing problems, beyond the phys-ical and psychological harm that they suffer and the disruption that their efforts to obtain help can entail. For a variety of reasons, some women may wish to remain in a relationship with their batterers and have difficulty finding interventions that are supportive of that choice and effective in reducing the violence that they suffer. Some of these women resist the mandatory nature of criminal court involvement and resent the new reality that obtaining assistance during violent episodes is conditioned on an arrest and a prosecution that they may not support (Mills, 1990).

Many of those who wish to sever relationships with their batterers still find that the threat of violence actually increases with an attempt to end the relationship. Moreover, even in these high-risk situations, legal and social services for battered women—just as for other needy populations who cannot pay for services—remain significantly under-funded and are especially vulnerable to further funding cuts in a de-clining economy. This lack of material resources for programs and individuals makes independent living exceedingly difficult for many who try to leave their abusive partners (Coker, 2000). Those with chil-dren have an additional need for material resources and for negotiat-ing continuing relationships with batterers in many circumstances, due to the requirements of child custody and visitation.

The law of child custody and visitation has formally acknowledged the problem of domestic violence. Nevertheless, decision making in child custody cases is often insufficiently sensitive to the problems gen-erated by intrafamily violence. Moreover, a perceived failure to ad-equately protect children from witnessing or experiencing a partner's violence can jeopardize an abused parent's own liberty or custodial rights.

Battered Women as Defendants

The extraordinary difficulties that battered women face even in an improved social and legal climate become more pronounced if she uses self-defense. In some respects, the perception that help is now available to her deepens her plight when she defends herself phys-ically. Despite, or perhaps because of, public education concerning do-mestic violence, the reality that many battered women have greater recourse than in the past can turn the "Why didn't she leave?" ques-tion in any particular case into an even more haunting refrain. When battered women are prosecuted for assault or homicide against their batterers, their accounts of underlying events continue to be re-garded with skepticism. Criminal defendants in general tend to con-front disbelief of their claims. The charges against them render their mitigating or exonerating accounts of events inherently suspect. Even when these accounts are truthful, they may be disbelieved because they are self-serving.

Once charges have been filed, the adversary nature of the criminal justice system exacerbates skepticism, such that those who are allied with law enforcement feel professionally impelled toward disbelief of a battered woman's accounts. This disbelief carries a particular bite, as it often takes the form of an expression of support for battered women as a class, followed by an assertion that this defendant is not a member of that class. The problem of intimate violence seems to have more credibility and visibility in the abstract than it does when particular human beings—imperfect as they are—in a particular context— factually complex as it will be—are said to embody the problem.

Oversimplification

The adversarial legal system tends to reject com-plexity and insist that all human conduct be distilled into simple explanations. Explaining that battering relationships are typically characterized not just by physical violence but by other manifestations of coercive control requires a more sophisticated analysis of the long-term dynamics of the relationship rather than descriptions of violent episodes. Suggesting that a battering relationship may also include genuine forms of connection may be threatening to the listener—whether a judge, a jury member, or anyone else—because it invites comparison to one's own intimate relationships rather than facilitat-ing the psychological distancing that makes sitting in judgment more comfortable.

Women who take self-defensive measures during a lull in the abuse rather than during a confrontation with their abuser are especially vul-nerable to the simple assertion that they acted in angry retaliation rather than in fear for their lives. Explaining how it can be reasonable to believe that they risk serious, imminent harm during a lull in the abuse requires considerable psychological and contextual knowledge (Willoughby, 1989). It is far easier to ignore or dismiss these com-plexities, and the adversarial legal system, built around the human de-sire for simplicity, facilitates this reaction.

GENDER STEREOTYPING

Despite significant social progress in coming to understand the problem of intimate violence, traditional notions of gender remain a powerful force in the assessment of any battered woman's self-defense claims. Actual women—diverse, flawed, and complex—often fall short of the cultural ideal and are found less cred-ible. If understanding her situation requires understanding the long and psychologically complex dynamic of a relationship, the adversar-ial system is a poor forum for conveying that truth. The consequence is that many battered women are disbelieved. In these circumstances, disbelief can have dire consequences, including incarceration, injury, and even death.

The more the accused diverges from the internalized cultural un-derstanding of the good battered woman, the greater her credibility problems are. Perhaps not surprising, experience has shown that the features of the good battered woman stereotype are drawn from the traditional female stereotype to the extent that the less demure, docile, and deferential the battered woman is seen to be, the more credibility problems she has encountered. Battered women's survival strategies, such as self-medication with drugs or alcohol, and previous instances of fighting back, may lead to a counterstory that she provoked inti-mate violence. Women who are perceived to fall outside narrow and traditional gender role expectations of mainstream culture, whether by dint of personality (for example, independent, assertive) or iden-tity (for example, lesbians, African American women), face particular difficulties in having their claims to have acted out of fear for their lives seen and heard.

Impeaching credibility

Battered women's credibility problems are exacerbated by the fact that the techniques routinely used by the legal system to assess credibility do not comport with psychological under-standings of reactions to trauma. For example, a standard technique in the adversary system is to impeach a witness's credibility by showing that the witness made prior inconsistent statements about pertinent events, making it more likely that her current statements are manufac-tured. Psychologists indicate that among the consequences of trauma are confusion, disorientation, and memory repression, such that soon after a violent event, a woman may provide the police an account that during a recovery process she comes to know as false or incomplete. A court's evidentiary system is organized around an understand-ing that contemporaneous accounts are more accurate than subsequent accounts. Therefore, battered women may confront a paradox. The memory complications that can flow from the violence that some bat-tered women suffer are regarded as undermining the reliability of cur-rent accounts of that violence. Yet with respect to the psychological reality of the situation, initial memory problems may actually support a finding that she suffered significant trauma, and subsequent ac-counts may be the most accurate versions of events.

EXPERT TESTIMONY

If a psychological expert's testimony on battered woman syndrome is admitted during such a case, the expert can ad-dress the impact of trauma on memory and try to mitigate the harm done by standard evidentiary practices. But the admissibility of ex-pert testimony remains a double-edged sword in these cases. With its admission typically linked to the concept of battered woman syn-drome, expert testimony can illuminate a battered woman's situation only to the extent that the features of the situation are understood as aspects of the syndrome.

As many commentators have observed, viewing a victim of abuse as suffering from a syndrome deflects attention from the abuser and undermines an understanding that she conducted herself reasonably, albeit in desperate circumstances (Coughlin, 1994; Mahoney, 1991). This syndrome evidence, conjuring up images that the abuse victim suffers from pathology, can have an adverse impact on perceptions of her reliability. These adverse inferences can influence outcomes of legal proceedings and haunt other important efforts to achieve stability in her life as well.

Inadequate defense services

Another challenge for battered wom-en charged with crimes against batterers is that few locales have made significant progress in recent decades in improving the quality of in-digent defense systems. In many jurisdictions, battered women charged with assault or homicide against their batterers still receive woefully deficient representation, particularly when they are represented by ap-pointed counsel.

Given the poor quality of representation for many who cannot af-ford to hire competent counsel, the progress of the domestic violence movement in enabling fairer trials for battered women remains hy-pothetical for a defendant whose counsel does not appreciate the nature and circumstances of the underlying events, the context of the defendant's relationship, the need for psychological expertise, or the prospects for raising self-defense issues during the course of the case. In these circumstances, the factual record that might support self-defense can remain underdeveloped and fair outcomes impeded. Until indigent defense systems provide reasonably competent counsel on a reliable basis, battered women who have assaulted or killed their bat-terers, a subset of indigent defendants, will not be guaranteed the ben-efit of the progress that has been made in obtaining fairer treatment in the legal system for battered women.

Postconviction relief

Once a battered woman has been convicted of assault or homicide against her batterer, her chances for vindication through appeal, collateral attack, or executive clemency are low. Those who participated in obtaining the conviction often are institutionally invested in maintaining the original outcome and seek to preserve it. Decision makers with the power to overturn convictions or reduce sen-tences will naturally use this power quite sparingly. For battered women, these phenomena have become even stronger, since our cul-ture considers itself to have vastly improved its understanding and treatment of domestic violence. While this belief is partially true, it also generates limited interest in addressing the problems that remain.

Even for women who were convicted of crimes against their batterers before recent legal innovations, the clemency movement has achieved mixed success at best. Despite the approximately one hun-dred battered women across the nation who have received gubernato-rial clemency, hundreds more have been denied. Many of these women have strong arguments for clemency, yet their petitions did not find a receptive audience at the statehouse. As a result, they serve the re-mainder of their sentences as originally imposed.

CONCLUSION

Intimate violence is linked to inequalities in perceptions and alloca-tions of power within relationships. While any relationship can fea-ture power disparities, women remain especially vulnerable to male violence in heterosexual relationships in a world of continuing gen-der inequality. As long as gender inequality persists, the problem of intimate violence will remain intractable, although public attention to the problem can partially alleviate the extraordinary harm that in-timate violence creates.

The battered women's movement has changed the world, creating many more options than previously existed for women who suffer in-timate violence. Indeed, the considerable successes of the recent past create an especially challenging context for sustaining the energy of the movement today. Divisions within the movement about appro-priate future directions can also drain its energies, and a difficult eco-nomic outlook makes competition for shrinking social services funds especially contentious.

The hope is that the many eyes that have been turned to the prob-lem and the many voices addressing it will prove up to the task of mobilizing to face the challenges ahead and that the multiplicity of perspectives that high interest in the subject has generated will bring strength rather than fragmentation. The promise of a future contain-ing far less intimate violence is well worth the struggle.

10

Rape Resistance

Rape is widespread and persistent. It is one of the most prevalent and least recognized human rights issues in the world today (Heise, Ellsberg, & Gottemoeller, 1999; Rozee, 2000). Among in-dustrialized nations. rape prevalence is estimated at 21 to 25 percent (Koss, Heise, & Russo, 1994). Among nonindustrial nations, it is esti-mated to occur in from 43 to 90 percent of cultures worldwide (Rozee, 1993).

The United States has the highest rate of rape of any industri-alized nation—four times that of Germany, twelve times that of En-gland, and twenty times that of Japan. Research has shown little change in U.S. rape prevalence rates over time. A recent survey of rape preva-lence studies found that the U.S. rape rate has remained at approxi-mately 15 percent for the past quarter-century (Rozee & Koss, 2001).

This prevalence rate has not gone unaddressed by feminist schol-ars, activists, and individual women. There is a long and relatively suc-cessful history of women's resistance to sexual assault. The women's rights movement of the 1960s and 1970s spawned a powerful rape cri-sis movement that at its heart was a resistance movement. Like most other resistance movements, it sought changes at large-scale systems and institutional levels as well as at the individual level.

Resistance broadly defined includes challenging institutional, po-litical, religious, judicial, legal, law enforcement, and medical estab-lishments and their handling or interpretation of what is "real rape." This chapter addresses both the successes and continuing challenges of these efforts at each of the pertinent levels of intervention.

SYSTEMS-LEVEL INTERVENTIONS

Rape resistance at the systems level has occurred primarily in the way that legal systems define and prosecute rape.

Contested Definitions of Rape

One of the areas of contention in rape research concerns the defini-tion of rape (Koss, 1992). Feminist scholars wrestle with the contra-diction between the lived experience of rape survivors and the legal limits of prosecution. The legal definition of rape in the United States is so narrow as to severely limit the reporting, apprehension, prosecu-tion, and conviction of perpetrators. In many states, forced penile pen-etration of the vagina of an unwilling victim is required to constitute rape.

Yet many of the most violent rapes may not include penile pen-etration. Instead, penetration may be by fingers or other objects. Anal and oral penetrations are also common, as are penetration of a drugged or unconscious victim requiring no force. Feminist activists generally favor an expanded definition of rape that includes these other forms of violation, but many state laws use a more limited definition.

One of the most powerful effects of the resistance efforts of the rape crisis movement was on the definitions, legal and otherwise, of rape.

Feminist scholarship and activism have transformed the analysis of rape and led to a paradigmatic shift away from rape as a crime against the father, husband, or other male relative of the victim to a crime against the woman herself. In addition, pressure from women's orga-nizations resulted in the elimination in the 1970s of the "false accuser" jury instructions harking back to the seventeenth-century declaration by Sir Matthew Hale that rape accusations are easy to make but hard to prove and even harder to disprove (Sanday, 1996).

The 1990s saw the overturn of the so-called spousal rape exemption that enforced Hale's view that a woman cannot retract her matrimonial consent to sexual union with her husband. Thus, a woman could not accuse her husband of rape since it was part of the matrimonial agreement. The effort to change this legal exemption for marital rapists was lengthy and was waged by feminists on a state-by-state basis over twenty years.

Rape Myths and the Consent Defense

Feminist rape critics have pointed to larger social stereotypes about rape that are existent in every rape courtroom in the country. Legal scholars were able to effect a change in courtroom procedure, called the *rape shield* law, which prohibited introduction of the sexual back-ground of the victim into evidence under most circumstances. For-merly the strategy of exposing victim sexual history was used to show that she had had sex with other men, so her conduct with the defen-dant was likely consensual too. Despite the illogic in such a proposi-tion, there has been an increasing reliance on a consent defense for rape perpetrators. This leads to the proverbial "he said, she said" sce-nario that rarely favors victims' rights.

The consent defense strategy is effective because of the prevalence of a myriad of rape myths that are believed and acted on by juries of both men and women. Foremost among these is the widespread belief that many rape victims "ask for it" by their appearance, behavior, the situation in which they have placed themselves, or a combination of all three factors. This powerful myth persists despite the lack of research evidence to support it. An allied myth is that women secretly want to be forced or that many women like rough sex, despite women's protestations to the contrary. An additional rape myth is that men are basically unable to control their sexual impulses, especially if confronted with a particularly provocative female. This belies the fact that rape victims are on record from ages six weeks to up to ninety-five years old. In addition, most perpetrators have a legal source of sexual release with a wife or girl-friend and are not generally seeking a sexual outlet.

Juries are reluctant to convict if the victim is seen as somehow cul-pable in the assault. Ironically, the areas of culpability are basic to ex-pected heterosexual dating behavior, such as voluntarily leaving a place of relative safety (such as a bar or restaurant) with the assailant, con-senting to enter the home of her date, or consuming alcohol. What may be seen as typical dating behaviors becomes culpable behavior on the part of the victim when looked at through the lens of a rape trial. Victim blaming in rape cases is more extreme than in any other violent crime. Yet the predatory, manipulative, or coercive aspects of the assailant's behavior are of less concern in judicial procedures.

The consent defense often relies on evidence of victim resistance. Although feminist scholars were successful in removing the require-ment of resistance to prove nonconsent, physical resistance is fre-quently relied on by juries in assessing consent (Krulewitz & Nash, 1979; Ryckman, Kaczor, & Thornton, 1992; Warner & Hewitt, 1993). This expectation flies in the face of common advice given to women that resistance is both futile and dangerous (Rozee, 2003). Only a small mi-nority of consent defense rape cases result in convictions (Frazier & Haney, 1996).

RAPE: A GENDERED CRIME

There are two new areas of feminist legal scholarship that hold promise for future rape convictions. Both rely on the powerful finding of the gendered nature of rape. The examination of victim characteristics by numerous researchers has found that the only consistent predictor of being a rape victim is gender. In other words, women of all ages, ap-pearance, and behavioral category and in all situations are raped. Rape is predominantly a crime against women that is perpetrated by men (Koss et al., 1994). The research finding of gender as a predictor of rape is the strongest contraindicator of the victim precipitation argument that is so prevalent in a consent defense. It requires us to examine the power relations between the sexes that both enable and condone rape and pass this information on to succeeding generations.

"No Duty" Rules

This reform method would erect additional barriers to admission of testimony regarding victim behavior. Ellen Bublick (1999) described the "no duty" rule, which insists that women should have the consti-tutionally guaranteed rights to freedom of movement, association, and expression in where they go, with whom, and how they dress and be-have that men do. In other words, women have no duty to conduct themselves in fear of intentional rape, as if their every behavior will be judged as an indicator of a willingness to be raped.

"Reasonable Woman" Standard

The reasonable woman standard is consistently used in the prosecu-tion of sexual harassment cases due to the vastly different experiences and perceptions of women and men. This standard is intended to recognize the structural inequalities that are inherent in gender relations, particularly involving the contested territory of women's bodies (Ca-hill, 2001). As noted by Joan McGregor (1994), gender stratification and gender inequalities render the perceptions of a reasonable woman as different from those of a reasonable man. This difference requires a change in rape law that would include "requiring affirmative consent and relying upon the standard of the *reasonable woman* as evidence in rape cases" (McGregor, 1994, p. 232). Similarly, Caroline Forell, a University of Oregon law professor, and Donna Matthews, a Eugene attorney, in their book, *A Law of Her Own: The Reasonable Woman as a Measure of Man* (2000), argue that a woman-centered standard should be applied to the behavior of perpetrators in circumstances where women and men differ on their experiences of sexual violence and women are overwhelmingly the victims of male violence. They contend that because men have traditionally defined what is lawful, if we hold men to a "reasonable woman" standard it may challenge un-examined biases in the law that fortify the systematic subordination of women (Forell & Matthews, 2000).

RAISING THE SOCIAL COSTS OF RAPE

Feminist legal scholars contend that raising the social costs to rape perpetrators is essential to the prevention of future rapes. Rapists must know that rape is not condoned by our society, that rape is not sex, and that all legal sanctions will be brought to bear to punish perpe-trators. Committing rape must be seen as a costly endeavor for the rapist. Identifying and reporting rape is essential to raising the costs of rape to rapists.

However, narrow legal definitions of rape conflict with survivor de-clarations of rape. Because most researchers, activists, and even women themselves define "real rape" as a forceful attack by a stranger on an un-willing victim, many victims are reluctant to report rape (Estrich, 1987). This results in one of the lowest reporting rates for any violent crime, according to the Rape in America study (Kilpatrick, Edmunds, & Sey-mour, 1992). Only one in three rapes is reported, the lowest reporting rate since 1989 (Greenfield, 1997). The closer the relationship of the vic-tim to the offender, the less likely she is to report the rape to authori-ties. Although date and acquaintance rapes are no longer the hidden rapes that they have been throughout history, they are still functionally condoned by social myth. This is evidenced by the relatively low con-viction rate even though the perpetrator is typically easily identified.

Once reported, very few reported rapes ever reach the level of a trial (Gunn & Minch, 1992), and the few rapists who are tried rarely serve prison time.

Systems-level interventions are slow and difficult to achieve, but they can have a powerful impact on the successful outcomes of rape complaints for victims. The problem is multifaceted and will require resistance at multiple points.

INSTITUTIONAL-LEVEL INTERVENTIONS

Rape resistance efforts at the institutional level have taken place within those institutions having the most contact with rape survivors: med-ical providers, law enforcement, and educational institutions such as colleges and universities. The rape crisis movement resulted in the cre-ation of dozens of rape crisis centers that have worked with local hos-pital and law enforcement professionals to enact changes in the initial handling of rape cases. A notably successful program in Long Beach, California, involved the creation of cooperative Sexual Assault Re-sponse Teams (SART). When police receive a rape call, they notify the SART, representing hospital, police, rape crisis victim advocates, and prosecutors. All members of the SART meet at a special wing of the community hospital that is dedicated to rape investigations. The rape unit is located away from the emergency room in a private area staffed with forensic nurses. There, the rape kit is prepared, and microscopic evidence is collected using specialized equipment. The victim/survivor tells her story only one time since all interested parties are present at the rape unit. Such programs illustrate the potency of institutional re-sponses when territorial priorities take second place to serving victims. Colleges and universities responding to requirements of the Vio-lence Against Women Act of 1994 have conducted a wide range of rape education programs. These programs have occasionally been aimed at male fraternities or sports teams, but most rape prevention programs within both universities and communities have focused on avoidance strategies for women (Bachar & Koss, 2001). Although these programs have been effective in teaching women about personal safety, they lack information about precipitating perpetrator behavior and usually stop short of advocating physical self-defense as a prevention strategy for women (Rozee & Koss, 2001; Sochting, Fairbrother, & Koch, 2004). Bachar and Koss (2001), in a review of rape prevention programs, found that mixed-sex rape prevention groups are not as successful as single-sex groups due to the occurrence of gender polarization.

Only men can truly prevent rape; women can only avoid it. The prevalence of news reports regarding rape among organized male groups such as the military, sports teams, and fraternities communi-cates the desperate need to confront the distorted hypermasculinity among such groups and their negative effects on women. The few pro-grams that have been evaluated focused mainly on developing victim empathy or reducing rape-supportive behaviors, with mixed results. It has been suggested that future male-focused programs be developed based on research on male cognitive, emotional, and behavioral indi-cators for risk of rape behavior, such as power motivation, power-sex associations, high dominance, calloused and adversarial sexual beliefs, hostility toward women, and a preference for emulating pornography (Rozee & Koss, 2001).

INDIVIDUAL-LEVEL INTERVENTIONS

Individual-level interventions have been the special focus of the rape crisis movement. Rape crisis centers, universities, and various com-munity organizations have developed rape prevention and education programs offered in multiple settings in the community. Virtually all such programs are mixed-sex programs that deal with rape attitudes and myths. These programs often focus on information that is useful in avoiding rape by strangers. This strategy may be of questionable ef-fectiveness given that estimates hold that 80 to 90 percent of rapes are committed by acquaintances. In addition, most women already have a long and quite sophisticated list of precautions that they practice daily (Rozee & Koss, 2001). As Cahill (2001) pointed out, most women con-tinue to take these precautions because they believe that the risk of rape can be significantly reduced or even eliminated by correct behavior on the part of women.

Evaluations of rape prevention programs show a small but favorable attitude change that tends to decay or regress to pretest levels relatively quickly and no preventive effects on the occurrence of subsequent crimes (Bachar & Koss, 2001). Lonsway (1996) conducted a comprehensive re-view of all published rape education programs targeting women and men. Nearly all of them focused on attitude change, but only half actu-ally decreased rape-supportive attitudes. Even among these, the change did not hold up in long-term follow-up.

Recent studies of programs that assessed rape reduction as an out-come measure found disappointing results. For example, Breiten-becher and Scarce (1999) found no reduction in the incidence of sexual assault despite an increase in knowledge about sexual assault. An in-depth review of empirical studies by Sochting et al. (2004) confirms these findings across studies. Most researchers in this area have con-cluded that there is no evidence for the effectiveness of current rape prevention programs in preventing rape.

Interestingly, self-defense training is not generally taught as part of standard rape prevention programs. However, when all the avoidance strategies fail, there has to be a fail-safe. The best answer to this is self-defense. The evidence is clear that women who fight back are less likely to be raped, and most women who do not resist are raped. Despite the fact that the research literature has supported this finding for nearly two decades, there is almost no mention of the facts of rape resistance in rape prevention programs. This is due in part to the prevalence of strong cultural myths that prevent women from resisting.

Myths About Rape Resistance

Most women have been taught that to fight back against a rapist is both futile and foolish (Rozee, 2003). One common myth is that it is un-likely that a woman who is accosted by a rapist will be able to escape or fight him off because of his greater size and strength. In truth, wom-en are four times more likely to escape an attempted rapist than they are to be raped by him (Riger & Gordon, 1989). In addition, two liter-ature reviews of research on rape resistance have found that women who fight back, and do so immediately, are less likely to be raped than wom-en who do not (Furby & Fischhoff, 1986; Ullman, 1997). Self-defense is more a matter of technique and leverage than size and strength. In addition, women have a strong element of surprise since most rapists are not expecting resistance. Furby and Fischhoff (1986) found that these results held in both stranger and acquaintance rape situations and even in the presence of a weapon. There are fewer data on resistance in acquaintance rape situations, and this conclusion may require more research with more systematic definitions of resistance.

A second myth is that those who try to fight off an attacker are more likely to be injured. Injuries stemming from resistance tend to be mi-nor, consisting mainly of cuts and bruises, with less than 3 percent suf-fering more serious injury such as a broken bone (Ruback & Ivie, 1988). Despite evidence that risks for serious injury are not high, women are led to believe that such injuries are common in rape cases when the woman resists.

Recent evidence clearly shows that women who fight back are no more likely to be injured than women who do not fight back (Ullman, 1997). Ullman's research demonstrated that reports of women being hurt when they fight back have the sequence backward: women fought back when they were being hurt, not the reverse. Physical self-defense often occurred in response to physical attack. Thus, it does a real dis-service to women to dissuade them from resisting given that resistance is likely to prevent rape and result in no more injury than no resistance.

There are other advantages that can accrue to women who resist an attacker:

- Women who fight back experience fewer postassault symptoms (both physical and psychological) when their efforts prevent the completion of the rape (Koss, Koss, & Woodruff, 1991). It is im-portant not to underestimate the injury of the rape itself.
- Women who fight back have faster psychological recoveries whether or not they are raped (Bart & O'Brien, 1985). This may be due to the sense of control that fighting back imparts, despite the outcome.
- Fighting back strengthens the physical evidence should the sur-vivor decide to prosecute for rape or attempted rape.

Given the preponderance of evidence for the efficacy of physical re-sistance, it is perplexing that such information is so rarely presented to women as part of rape prevention and education programs.

Resistance to Resistance

Rape resistance in the form of physical self-defense is a controversial topic among feminist activists. There is often a split between activists who emphasize the need for physical resistance and those who think resistance is dangerous. It is notable that many rape activists have ig-nored the large body of empirical evidence on the effectiveness of phys-ical resistance that has been in existence for nearly twenty years (Rozee & Koss, 2001). Martha McCaughey (1998) suggests that some are ap-athetic or uncomfortable, especially with physical resistance, because they identify violence as the symbol of patriarchy. It may be thought of as using "the master's tools" and there may be ambivalence about the "failure to honor nonviolence" (p. 278). The goal of self-defense courses is to deconstruct femininity, writes McCaughey: "Femininity, as it is so-cially defined, is precisely what women must overcome when learning to fight" (p. 281). If femininity is deconstructed and women are learn-ing to fight, are they then becoming "like men"?

Other feminist authors have suggested that rape resistance train-ing for women appears to make the assumption that stopping rape is primarily the responsibility of women (Lonsway, 1996; Bublick, 1999). Yet the same conclusion could be made about any kind of rape pre-vention strategies aimed at women instead of men. Indeed, it is easy to see where the focus on women's behavior by the legal system has tak-en us. Almost any conduct by a woman can put her at blame for rape. As Bublick (1999) puts it, "According to the defendants, she is forever doing the wrong thing when a man is trying to rape her. She does not run soon enough, or far enough or fast enough" (p. 1433).

Many feminists have been silent on the issue of resistance due to fears of putting even further burdens on women and limits on their individual liberty. Constant worries about self-protection exact a toll on women's ability to participate in the world freely. In making her case for the legal notion of "no duty" (women's legal entitlement to act on the assumption that others will not rape them), Bublick (1999) points out that women may have an interest in not taking constant precautions against rape since it requires them to give up more of their liberties than men do in order to gain the same legal protections. Care must be taken not to define rape prevention as the sole responsibility of women. However, until we are able to change men's behavior, the need for women's resistance remains.

We do women a disservice by not focusing more efforts in standard rape prevention education on rape resistance. The unfortunate truth is that after they are raped, many women enroll in self-defense classes (Huddleston, 1991). Feminist efforts to get this information to women sooner would be well rewarded.

Cognitive Resistance

It is important for researchers to be aware that the legal definition of rape is not the whole story. The legal confinements of rape often deny the experiences of rape victims and survivors. A phenomenological approach to defining rape resistance requires one to set aside legal de-finitions of rape that are nearly always at odds with women's experi-ence. It also requires a focus only on the woman's experience of the unwanted sexual experience, expanding the parameters of what we label rape and what we label resistance.

Rape by its very definition implies resistance—psychological, if not physical. Women know when sex was not consensual and indeed may even declare it to be rape even if they did not resist or in any other way show a lack of willingness (Rozee, 1993). Ramos, Koss, and Russo (1999) illustrate this with the finding from their research with Mexican American women. Women in their focus groups reported that they consider it rape when husbands demand sex when she is not willing, even if she does not overtly indicate her unwillingness. Similarly, in my own research, many of the women described cognitive forms of resistance sometimes not evident to the rapist but nevertheless defining it as a rape for the victim. An examination of cognitive resistance re-quires us to think more creatively about what is and is not rape.

Several forms of cognitive resistance were described in the rape nar-ratives of 253 rape survivors (Rozee, 2001). Cognitive resistance is the bedrock of women's self-definition of rape. It is the first line of defense against the bodily assaults of rape. During the rape, many women re-ported praying as a strategy of cognitive resistance. Others reported that they concentrated on planning an escape, analyzing the risks, or memorizing details of the rapist for later description to the police. Many spent the time simply searching for explanations or reasons for the assault.

One of the most poignant forms of cognitive resistance involved various forms of *detachment:* a method of getting out of body and cognitively escaping the assault. One woman described this as follows: "I submitted myself, I neither wanted it nor did I fight it off. I men-tally was very separate from myself physically. It was almost like I was looking at myself from above" (Rozee, 2001). Common descriptions involved out-of-body experiences involving leaving the body and look-ing down at oneself as if at a stranger. Women also described feeling detached from what was happening, like an empty shell. As one wom-an describes it, "I was lying there like a dead person and I felt totally removed from the situation like I was somewhere else and that was just my body" (Rozee, 2001).

Many women fear rape at such an extreme level that they may offer no resistance whatsoever. This can best be described as *resignation.* Many women in my research reported that they simply submitted. They were resigned to "get it over with" and leave. Resignation can be a result of overwhelming force on the part of the perpetrator or overwhelming fear on the part of the victim. Resigned submission can also result from coercion. Strong coercion can result in unwanted sexual contact yet may appear as successful persuasion to the perpetrator. After repeatedly being raped by a family friend, one survivor recalled, "You put it out of your mind, when these things are happening, and you're not the person there that it's happening to" (Rozee, 2001).

These examples illustrate the vast separation between women's de-finition of rape and resistance and the legal definitions. They are pre-sented here as a way of opening the discussion of women's perceptions of rape and resistance, outside the constrictive legal definitions of rape. The issue is much bigger phenomenologically than just the constricted world of legally defined rape.

CONCLUSION

The study of rape resistance is an area that requires considerably more thought among feminist scholars. Men and women live in different worlds when it comes to male violence against women. Laws that at-tempt to make rape gender neutral do a disservice to rape victims. Such laws assume that the experience of female victims and male victims is essentially the same. Although the trauma outcome may be similar, men do not experience the cultural context of fear in which women live. In fact, men are generally shocked when they learn about the cog-nitive worlds of the women with whom they are acquainted. I have seen male students sit in total disbelief when women students write on the chalkboard all the daily strategies they use to be safe from rape. One young woman reported to me that her boyfriend, who was also in the class, said to her, "Yeah, but you don't do all those things, do you?" She said, "Yes, of course I do." It is important for us to share our worldview and our internal experience with the men in our lives who care about us. This is an important strategy to change the ignorance that men have about the restricted freedoms of women in this society.

It is time to break the culture of silence that surrounds rape. Part of how a rape culture renews itself is by making sure that women stay silent about abuse. Many survivors blame themselves for the rape; shame and fear keep them silent. This is bad for the survivor's recov-ery and bad for society. African American women have termed the breaking of silence as "giving testimony" or "bearing witness," and these are important cultural ways of reaffirming our truths (West, 2002). This is a way to heal oneself and gather together with other sup-portive women to acknowledge violence against women and work together to make change. Speaking up and speaking out breaks the trauma. It is cathartic.

Change starts with each individual and ultimately affects the struc-tural and institutional conditions that dictate the conditions of our lives.

11

Women's Human Rights Abuses in the Name of Religion

A woman remains in an abusive marriage because her husband refuses to consent to divorce. A young girl is forced to marry an older man with two other wives. A teenaged girl who is raped believes she is to blame because she kissed her date good-night. These three individuals live in different societies shaped by unique religious and cultural traditions, and yet all three suffer abuses justified in the name of religion. Although the global human rights and feminist movements have established gender equality as a fundamental human right, women continue to suffer gross human rights abuses that are frequently sanctioned by national governments as the free exercise of religion. Religion in its many forms has enriched cultures and commu-nities throughout the world, but certain religious movements, often referred to as fundamentalist, have used religion to advance political agendas extremely detrimental to the rights of women.

A WOMAN'S PLACE: THE FUNDAMENTALIST AGENDA

While fundamentalist religious movements are products of their own time and place, they share identifiable characteristics, especially regarding their attitudes toward women, gender, and sexuality. These movements share a deep commitment to a separate-spheres ideology— a belief that although men and women may be spiritual equals, they have different roles and responsibilities in the physical world. This be-lief system endorses a public-private division: men serve in the public sphere of work and politics, while women preside over the private, or domestic, sphere of family and home.

This artificial dichotomy is often reinforced by a belief in a divine hi-erarchy: men must obey God, and women must obey men in return for their protection and financial support. According to some fundamen-talist ideologies, women require men's protection in large part because a woman's sexual virtue is a measure of the family's honor. Restrictions on women's dress and their movement, as well as their reproductive choices, are attempts to control women's sexuality, which is frequently portrayed as dangerous—as the evil responsible for the sin and imper-fections of all human beings. As many human rights activists and schol-ars have noted, this separate-spheres ideology shields violations of women's human rights from outside intervention, hiding the contin-ued subordination of women within their homes behind protectionist language.

THE POLITICS OF RELIGION AND WOMEN'S RIGHTS

Fundamentalist religious movements are political movements. That is, they seek to gain political power and frequently seek to change or preserve laws to reflect their particular religious ideology. Not surpris-ingly, they often focus on laws affecting women's status within the family and society generally. For example, conservative Christian or-ganizations in the United States have invested substantial resources and time in securing the nomination and appointment of federal judges likely to limit or completely deny a woman's right to choose, as well as other fundamental rights. In addition, these same groups have suc-cessfully lobbied Congress for laws and funds that support their agenda. In 1996, Congress passed welfare legislation that allocated $50 million annually to abstinence-only sex education programs in public schools (Rose, 1999). These programs frequently provide adolescent students with misinformation or omit critical information concerning contra-ception and disease prevention in order to scare and shame students into abstaining from sex.

Moreover, at the heart of the abstinence-only curricula is the Chris-tian fundamentalist message that girls and women are responsible for controlling the sexual behavior of men. In one publication, a chart designates the "prolonged kiss" as the "beginning of danger" and the point after which male sexual desire is aroused. Female sexual desire, however, is not so easily aroused, sending the message that girls are in a better position to control sexual desire and male behavior (Rose, 1999). Having heard this message, if a girl allows her date to kiss her and he then sexually assaults her, she will likely blame herself instead of recognizing sexual violence as a violation of her basic human rights. Furthermore, evidence does not support proponents' claims that these programs reduce teen pregnancy and sexually transmitted diseases. In fact, in countries with lower rates of teen pregnancy, social attitudes toward sexuality and sex education are typically more liberal, as is ac-cess to contraception and health care.

Conservative Christian groups in the United States have not fo-cused solely on domestic policy; they have successfully influenced the flow of U.S. foreign aid, to the detriment of women all over the world. Shortly after President Bush was elected in 2000, he reinstated the Mexico City policy, popularly known as the global gag rule, which bars any foreign organization receiving money from the U.S. Agency for International Development (2001) from providing or promoting abor-tion as a method of family planning. For example, when members of an organization in Zambia counseled young people that unprotected sex and unwanted pregnancies can lead to unsafe and even fatal abor-tions, the organization lost approximately $30,000 in essential U.S. aid. The chair of the organization emphasized the dire consequences of the loss: "I think they are killing these women, just as if they are pointing a gun and shooting. There is no difference" (Loder, 2003). Oth-ers would agree with her characterization. In the summer of 2003, the United States cut $50 million in funds to the United Nations Popula-tion Fund (UNFPA) in response to the Christian right's accusations that UNFPA resources were involved in coercive abortion practices in China. Because of the loss in funds, the UNFPA estimates that ap-proximately "4,700 mothers, 77,000 infants and children, and 800,000 pregnancies will be lost" (People for the American Way, 2003). How the United States spends its dollars is truly a matter of life and death for women and girls.

Reproductive rights and access to safe abortions mean little if a wom-an is unable even to leave her home. In some societies, religious fundamentalism has resulted in severe violations of women's freedom of movement. The best-known example is the situation of girls and wom-en under Taliban rule in Afghanistan:

women could not leave their homes without a male chaperone and without being completely cov-ered by a dark heavy garment called the burqa. They could not be prop-erly examined by health care professionals, and they were denied the right to work. The Taliban promulgated decrees imposing draconian punishments on all those who violated these restrictions and justified them in the name of religion (Physicians for Human Rights, 1998). Although the Taliban's assault on women's rights is probably the best-known modern example, religion has been used in many other coun-tries to restrict women's freedom of movement. For example, in some countries, the law requires that a woman secure permission from her father or husband before she can obtain a passport to travel.

Even if a woman can leave her home, she may still feel she is a pris-oner if laws and social practices prevent her from escaping an unhappy or abusive marriage. In several countries, certain interpretations of Is-lamic law are codified into discriminatory family laws that allow men to divorce their wives arbitrarily and unilaterally with no judicial su-pervision (Alami & Hinchcliffe, 1996; Mayer, 1999). Frequently, a man can effect a divorce simply by saying, "I divorce you," three times, leav-ing the woman with no financial support and often without custody of her children. This practice clearly discriminates on the basis of sex because women are not given the same access to divorce as their hus-bands. Although most Islamic family laws contain grounds for a wife to divorce her husband, they are often limited, and they always require judicial consent. In other words, if she is unable to prove one of the limited grounds, such as her husband's desertion or failure to support her, she may be unable to secure a divorce. And because the codes fre-quently codify—either explicitly or implicitly—the principle that a wife owes her husband her obedience in return for his financial sup-port (Alami & Hinchcliffe, 1996; Heindel, 1999), domestic violence may be considered an acceptable means of correcting an "errant" wife rather than an acceptable ground for divorce, leaving her with no choice but to remain trapped in the marriage and suffering silently.

Religious family laws in many countries violate women's rights in other ways as well. For example, Islamic family laws often allow a man to marry as many as four women (Mayer, 1999). Although the first wife is sometimes granted the right to petition for divorce when her husband marries another woman (Esposito with DeLong-Bas, 2001), divorce may be an unattractive option if it leaves her with no finan-cial support and without custody of the children (Heindel, 1999). Sim-ilarly, although the law may require a woman's consent to be married, in reality she may have little choice: in societies that restrict women's rights to work and own property, marriage may be the only realistic option for survival.

Furthermore, even when governments enact legal reforms that ad-vance women's rights and gender equality in the public sphere (through affirmative action measures or antidiscrimination legislation), they frequently refuse to amend or repeal discriminatory family laws that are ostensibly based on religious law. For example, in Israel, a woman's access to divorce and other matters of personal status are governed by either Jewish, Muslim, or Christian law depending on the religion of her birth (Raday, 1999). Under Jewish law, a woman must obtain her husband's permission in order to obtain a divorce; if he refuses to give her a *get* (a divorce writ), she is not free to remarry, and if she has a re-lationship with another man, she may be labeled a "rebellious wife," jeopardizing her claims to alimony and child custody. Although the rabbinical courts have the power to order a husband to give his wife a *get*, if he chooses to disregard the order, his wife will remain married to him. This startling inequality exists alongside progressive secular laws advancing women's equality, such as laws on equal employment opportunity and equal pay for comparable work, comprehensive laws on sexual harassment, laws requiring affirmative action in the public sector, and laws recognizing women's right to participate in the armed services.

Discriminatory family laws, such as those in Israel, have historical origins in religious practice. Under Jewish law in Israel, women do not have the same right to preclude their husbands' access to divorce; if a woman does not grant her husband's request for a divorce, the hus-band may nevertheless seek a rabbinical license to remarry (Raday, 1999). This inequality is rooted historically in the practice of polyg-amy. Because Jewish law once allowed men to marry more than one wife, the law continues to support a man who has multiple partners over time, while it condemns a woman who has more than one part-ner during her lifetime (Raday, 1999). In fundamentalist strains of Ju-daism, a separate-spheres ideology prevails; a woman has a religious duty to care for home and family, while a man must devote himself to religious study and ritual (Yuval-Davis, 1999). Despite claims that gen-der roles are different but equal, women are clearly considered inferior beings: they may not lead prayers, hold public religious positions, or testify in a religious court. Most telling, in his daily morning prayer, a man thanks God for not making him a woman, while a woman be-gins her day by thanking God for making her according to his will (Yuval-Davis, 1999).

WOMEN'S RIGHTS AND RELIGIOUS FREEDOM UNDER INTERNATIONAL HUMAN RIGHTS LAW

These discriminatory laws and practices clearly violate numerous hu-man rights norms enshrined in national constitutions, international and regional treaties, and other international instruments. Widely rat-ified treaties, such as the International Covenant on Civil and Polit-ical Rights (ICCPR) and the Convention on the Elimination of All Forms of Discrimination Against Women (CEDAW), contain provi-sions prohibiting discrimination on the basis of sex and requiring that states reform laws and policies in order to prevent and eradicate gen-der discrimination.

Regional treaties, such as the African (Banjul) Char-ter on Human and People's Rights and the American Convention on Human Rights, contain similar provisions. Moreover, comments and recommendations by treaty-monitoring bodies, such as the Human Rights Committee (CEDAW, 1981), which monitors compliance with the ICCPR, plainly establish that religion may not be used to justify otherwise discriminatory laws.

Moreover, the right to equality within the family enjoys special recognition in international human rights law. In addition to nondis-crimination and equal protection provisions, both CEDAW and the ICCPR contain articles (respectively, Articles 16 and 23) specifically requiring states "to take appropriate steps to ensure equality of rights and responsibilities of spouses as to marriage, during marriage and at its dissolution."

Not surprisingly, several countries with religious fam-ily laws have entered reservations to Article 16(e) of CEDAW, which requires states "to eliminate discrimination against women in all mat-ters relating to marriage and family relations." The subarticles elabo-rate on this general prescription, detailing important rights, such as the right "to decide freely and responsibly the number and spacing of children and to have access to the information, education and means" necessary to exercise these rights.

Although the treaty does not specif-ically require states to provide access to abortion, this provision does suggest that girls and women have—at the very least—a right to com-prehensive sex education, suggesting the Christian right's abstinence-only education is not enough. Unfortunately, in part because of strong opposition by Christian fundamentalist groups, the United States has yet to ratify CEDAW.

Given the clarity of international human rights law (much of which is incorporated in national constitutions throughout the world), we may wonder why oppressive laws and practices continue to exist. From a legal perspective, fundamentalists often advance the argument that they have a right to these discriminatory laws and practices as a mat-ter of religious freedom.

But while human rights law certainly protects the freedom to practice one's religion of choice (ICCPR, Article 18), it does not do so at the expense of other rights and individual free-doms. Nondiscrimination clauses in various treaties place religion and sex on the same plane. One may not be used to justify discrimina-tion on the basis of the other. In fact, gender equality arguably occupies a privileged position. The ICCPR contains a separate article (Article 3) in addition to the general nondiscrimination clause requiring states "to ensure the equal right of men and women" to all rights in the treaty. Similarly, the UN Charter specifically notes the importance of gender equality in its preamble.

Furthermore, fundamentalists' claims to freedom of religion are dubious for another reason. Whose religion do they have the right to practice? No religion is monolithic or homogeneous; within every major religion, we find an abundance of interpretations, ideologies, and doctrines, each constantly contested and reinvented. When do-mestic laws codify religion, governments privilege one group's inter-pretation over another's, thereby endorsing one "right" religious view and marginalizing other religious views, which inevitably infringes on some people's freedom of religion. Moreover, even if a state allows each group to follow its own religious law, it cannot guarantee that all mem-bers of any given community participated in the creation of that law. In other words, if a state justifies its religious laws by claiming to defer to the wishes of each discrete religious community, we might ask how the state determines a "community."

In fact, in response to the Indian government's "policy of non-interference in the personal affairs of any community," a women's rights organization asked this very question. Before a community's religion becomes its law, women—who form at least half of the community—must have a voice in defining that reli-gion and its practice. To exclude them is to violate their freedom of re-ligion, in addition to their right to gender equality.

ADDRESSING THE PROBLEM: POTENTIAL CAUSES AND SOLUTIONS

But although international human rights law undoubtedly prohibits gender discrimination in the name of religion, eradicating such dis-crimination is a more complicated matter. Patriarchal attitudes and power structures do not change overnight. Before solutions are adopted, we must identify the causes and contributing factors to these move-ments and their misogynist doctrines. That is, we must first under-stand what fuels these movements in today's societies.

Scholars and commentators have offered numerous explanations. Some believe re-cent fundamentalist movements are a response to modernity. In the wake of globalization, overwhelming poverty and exploitation give rise to a "genuine sense of despair and disorientation," leaving people searching for the comfort and sense of identity religion can provide (Yuval-Davis, 1999, p. 34).

In addition, as communities of people his-torically fought for their right to self-determination, often in the con-text of colonial rule, "women were central to the definition of the cultural identity of a nation, and represented the spiritual sphere of the nation, away from colonial life and the public sphere" (Coomar-aswamy, 1999). Colonial powers contributed to this public-private di-vision, replacing local laws of business and commerce with their own laws but leaving family laws and other private matters to the indige-nous population. In addition, colonial governments often attempted to codify local practices into law, imposing a rigid legal framework on what would otherwise be a dynamic social order more susceptible to change. Consequently, colonial codes shielded laws and customs harm-ful to women from the vicissitudes of social change and time (Benha-bib, 2002).

The recent rise in fundamentalism might also be fueled by changes in the social order as a result of the women's rights movement. Men in many areas of society must now compete for power, wealth, and prestige in ways they did not previously: "When 'secondary-level' male elites are struggling to maintain male dominance in the middling areas of society where jobs are increasingly contested by women, they find that they can reassert themselves in the family, school, and church, which are the social institutions most accessible to them" (Rose, 1999, p. 19).

This might in part explain the popularity of the recent evan-gelical men's movement called the Promise Keepers, which has filled U.S. football stadiums full of men in search of their Christian mas-culinity. In *Seven Promises of a Promise Keeper* (quoted in Rose, 1999), Pastor Tony Evans characterizes the decline of the "traditional" family as a national crisis and identifies the "feminization of men" as the main cause for this crisis. In order to solve the problem, he exhorts men to fulfill their proper role as head of the family: "Unfortunately, however, there can be no compromise here Treat the lady gently and lovingly.

But *lead*!" In this case, the fundamentalist belief in a separate-spheres ideology, in what is often termed "traditional family values," seeks to preserve male dominance in areas where it is losing ground.

Even a brief inquiry into potential causes and contributing factors demonstrates that although fundamentalist movements and ideologies share similar views regarding women and gender equality, they are sit-uated in different political, historical, and cultural contexts. They there-fore require individualized strategies for change. In addition, women's actual lived experiences in the context of different fundamentalist movements are different both across cultures and within cultures. The solution is to create spaces in which women can speak and are em-powered to define their own religions and cultures, thereby changing laws and policies from within their societies. By recognizing that wom-en's lives are shaped by various factors and forces, advocates will be able to fashion strategies that respond to the specific contexts and to do so in partnership with the women and men directly affected.

But this does not mean international activists and organizations have no role to play. The success of local advocacy frequently depends on international funds and resources. International actors can pres-sure domestic governments and intergovernmental organizations to fund local efforts that ensure women's equal participation in their communities and in the formation of domestic law and policy. Inter-national organizations can also facilitate the formation of networks and the provision of human rights resources and tools so that advo-cates may share strategies, successes, and frustrations and move for-ward in solidarity.

12

Sexual Violence Against Women in War and Armed Conflict

Women remain uniquely vulnerable to violence and discrimination. War and armed conflicts compound this vulner-ability, intensifying the violations women suffer. Not only are women in conflict situations murdered, tortured, and attacked along with men, they also are subjected to rape and other forms of sexual violence. Men also are raped during wartime, but evidence shows that women are the more frequent targets. International humanitarian law—the law of war—has long prohibited rape during war and armed conflict.

Unfor-tunately, impunity for wartime rapists has just as long a history. Rape and other forms of sexual violence historically have not been con-demned, investigated, and prosecuted with the same intensity and fre-quency as other war crimes. Recently, however, wartime rape has begun to receive the attention it deserves. The International Criminal Tribunal for the former Yugoslavia and the International Criminal Tribunal for Rwanda have convicted individuals of rape as a war crime, an instru-ment of genocide, and a crime against humanity. Decisions such as these are necessary steps in a movement to end a culture of impunity for wartime rapists. Despite these encouraging steps, there remains much work yet to be done to eradicate the pervasive culture of impu-nity protecting those who inflict sexual violence on women during war or armed conflict.

This chapter considers the subject of women and war, focusing on the ways in which the laws of war have dealt with sexual violence against women during war and armed conflict.

THE LAWS OF WAR

Two branches of law govern war. The first, jus *ad bellum,* defines the legitimate reasons a state may engage in war, focusing on the criteria for characterizing a war as "just." The second, jus *in bello,* regulates how a war is conducted, requiring warring parties to adhere to a set of basic principles. This body of law, also referred to as international human-itarian law, relies primarily on treaties, but also comprises customary law, or recognized practices of war. Unlike human rights law, which applies to all people at all times, international humanitarian law ap-plies only during wartime and only to certain persons and situations. The principal documents that form the heart of international hu-manitarian law are the four Geneva Conventions of August 12,1949, and the two Additional Protocols of June 8,*1977.*

The Geneva Con-ventions relate to protection and assistance for victims of conflicts: the First protects the wounded and sick, the Second the shipwrecked, the Third prisoners of war, and the Fourth civilians in times of war. Common to all four Geneva Conventions is Article 3, which estab-lishes the minimum level of protection that must be provided in times of internal armed conflict. Common Article 3 applies to all parties to a noninternational conflict, including armed opposition forces. The Geneva Conventions codify many rules of the laws of armed conflict that were delineated in earlier treaties, and they are almost universally ratified. The First Additional Protocol completes and reinforces the provisions of the four Geneva Conventions.

The Second Additional Protocol further regulates the protection of victims of noninterna-tional armed conflicts, described in Common Article 3. It does not apply to situations of internal disturbances or tensions such as riots, which do not qualify as armed conflicts.

Various categories of crimes are prohibited during times of war and armed conflict. The Geneva Conventions codified one category of crime known as grave breaches. Grave breaches of the laws of war, as defined by the Geneva Conventions, include willful killing, torture or inhuman treatment, and willfully causing great suffering or seri-ous injury to body or health. Because of the serious nature of these crimes, states are obligated to prosecute those accused of grave breaches or extradite them to another country that is willing to do so. The grave breaches provisions apply only in international armed conflict and to acts committed against protected persons, as defined by the Geneva Conventions.

Another category of crime is war crimes, which are defined in the Geneva Conventions and by customary law. War crimes are commit-ted in times of war and are not subject to any statute of limitation. War crimes commonly include murder and ill treatment of the civilian population, killing of hostages, and murder or ill treatment of prison-ers of war.

Finally, there are crimes against humanity. Crimes against human-ity were first defined in the statute of the Nuremberg Tribunal, which was established to try members of the defeated armed forces after World War II. Unlike war crimes, crimes against humanity are not limited to wartime; they can occur in times of war or peace. Crimes against hu-manity generally encompass acts that involve or occur in a context in which widespread or systematic killing or mistreatment of civilians is occurring. In other words, the killing of a single civilian in isolation would not constitute a crime against humanity but could constitute a war crime. Crimes against humanity, like grave breaches, are subject to universal jurisdiction, which means that they can be prosecuted by an international tribunal or by the domestic courts of any country.

These categories of crime—grave breaches, war crimes, and crimes against humanity—overlap but are distinct crimes, with specific defi-nitions and legal elements. Historically, the international community has punished such crimes only on an ad hoc basis, establishing differ-ent international punishment mechanisms for each situation. Each mechanism consequently has yielded the formulation of different de-finitions of the crimes and different applications of the provisions of international humanitarian law. This has led to some inconsistency and inconclusiveness in the laws of war. Fortunately, the international com-munity is moving toward establishing more clarity in international hu-manitarian law. The establishment of the International Criminal Court (ICC) means an end to the ad hoc nature of international criminal jus-tice. The ICC is the first ever permanent, treaty-based, international criminal court developed to punish the perpetrators of the most seri-ous crimes of international concern. Unlike the ad hoc tribunals for the former Yugoslavia and Rwanda, which were set up within the framework of the United Nations, the ICC is a new international or-ganization that came into force on July 1,2002. It has jurisdiction, when certain conditions are met, over individuals accused of war crimes, genocide, crimes against humanity, and the crime of aggression. This jurisdiction extends only to crimes committed after the court came into existence. The ICC complements national judicial systems, prosecut-ing cases only if national courts are unwilling or unable to do so. By cre-ating the ICC, the international community has clarified and codified crimes under international humanitarian law and indicated its inten-tion to punish future perpetrators of those crimes.

RAPE AS A CRIME UNDER THE LAWS OF WAR PRIOR TO THE 1990S

The laws of war, both formal and customary, have prohibited rape for centuries. In 546 A.D. the Ostrogoth who captured Rome forbade his troops to rape Roman women (Brownmiller, 1975). Richard II's Or-dinances of War, issued in 1385, prohibited the rape of women and stipulated that offenders were to be punished by death (Meron, 1998; Brownmiller, 1975). The 1419 Nantes Ordinances of Henry V drew on these rules and also proscribed the rape of women (Meron, 1998). English ordinances issued in 1639,1640, and 1643 stated similar pro-hibitions on rape (Meron, 1998)7 Several scholars, including the Ital-ian Alberto Gentili (1552-1608) and Dutchman Hugo Grotius (1583– 1645) advocated the prohibition of rape in wartime and peacetime (Askin, 1997; Meron, 1998).

More recently, the Lieber Code of 1863 explicitly prohibited "all rape" and punished its commission with death. In the trials of World War II war criminals, the Nuremberg Tribunal received reports of sex-ual assault (Askin, 1997; Tompkins 1995). In addition, under Article 2 of Control Council No. 10, signed in 1945 by the four occupying powers of Germany, rape was explicitly listed as a crime against hu-manity (Askin, 1997). Most notably, at the Tokyo Tribunal, rape was prosecuted successfully as a war crime under prohibitions against "in-humane treatment," "ill-treatment," and "failure to respect family ho-nour and rights" (Askin, 1997). An unequivocal prohibition of rape was established in 1949 in the Fourth Geneva Convention, which char-acterizes rape as an attack on women's honor. Additional Protocols I and II to the Geneva

Conventions also protect women from rape, declaring that women deserve special respect and listing rape alongside other forms of attacks on dignity.

Despite these prohibitions, soldiers and combatants have commit-ted wartime rape with impunity for centuries. Indeed, the history of wartime rape reflects a tolerance for such actions. The founding of Rome began by the rape of the Sabine women. In ancient Greece, rape was "socially acceptable behavior well within the rules of warfare [and] an act without stigma for warriors." Christian rape and pillage of Mus-lims marked the Crusades (Brownmiller, 1975, pp. 33,34). Similarly, it was accepted, from the Age of Chivalry (1100 to 1500) through the Age of Napoleon (1792 to 1815), that if a town was taken by siege, women could be raped (Parker, 1994; Rothenberg, 1994). And although Henry V sought to protect women and impose discipline among his soldiers by issuing ordinances banning rape, there is evidence that he knew his rules were being breached and that his desired protection for inhabi-tants "remained largely unaccomplished" (Meron, 1998).

Rape continues to be accepted as an inevitable by-product of war and armed conflict. Examples of mass rape abound in modern wars and armed conflicts: in the actions of the Germans in World War I; by the German, Japanese, and Russians during World War II; in Bangladesh during the 1971 armed conflict; by Americans during the war in Viet-nam; and by the Indonesians in East Timor (Brownmiller, 1975; Meron, 1998; Tanaka, 1998; Habiba, 1998; Furusawa & Inglis, 1998). These crimes have gone largely unpunished, despite the written prohibitions and customs that penalize rape during war and armed conflict.

REASONS FOR THE CONTINUED EXISTENCE OF WARTIME RAPE

Although written and customary prohibitions of rape exist, they have not captured the true nature of this crime. Rather than identifying rape as a crime of violence, the prohibitions of rape classified it as an offense against women's honor. Defining rape in this way is problematic be-cause it inextricably links a woman's dignity to her sexuality. This con-trasts with other serious crimes like murder and torture, which are understood as violations of an individual's fundamental right to bod-ily integrity and security. Defining rape as a crime against honor means that "nowhere are the discriminatory and violent nature of the offence recognized" (Brunet & Rousseau, 1998; Erb, 1998). These definitions in international humanitarian law mischaracterize and obscure the crime of rape. Rape is more than merely a crime against a woman's honor, and it deserves the same condemnation and punishment as those war crimes that more commonly happen to men (Copelon, 1995). Unfortunately, because of the definition given rape in international hu-manitarian law, rape was placed on an unequal footing with other se-rious violations that occurred during war and armed conflict.

This insufficient definition of rape developed largely because of the absence of women's rights and perspectives within the framework of international human rights and humanitarian law. Feminists have decried international law as male dominated and reflective of a male point of view. One explanation for women's absence is that women's issues are seen as "private," whereas the "public" sphere "is regarded as the province of international law" (Charlesworth, Chinkin, & Wright, 1991, p. 625). Indeed, in international law, rape is often considered a private act by individual men, in contrast to the state violations of human rights, which are recognized and addressed at the international level (MacKinnon, 1993,1994a).

Because sexual violations against women were not afforded equal status, they similarly received unequal punishment. For example, the 1907 Hague Convention Respecting the Laws and Customs of War on Land does not list rape as a violation but rather provides general pro-tection for family honor and rights. This provision has rarely been interpreted to cover rape (Meron, 1998). In addition, although evi-dence of rape and sexual assaults was presented to the Nuremberg Tri-bunal after World War II, defendants were never charged with rape as a war crime (Askin, 1997). In fact, neither the Nuremberg Charter nor the Tokyo Tribunal Charter enumerated rape as a crime against hu-manity (Meron, 1998; Askin, 1997). Likewise, the Fourth Geneva Con-vention (Article 147), despite establishing an unequivocal prohibition of rape, does not explicitly include acts of sexual assault within its pro-vision on grave breaches, which are subject to universal jurisdiction (Meron, 1998). This failure to prioritize the punishment of wartime rapists created implied rules of war that permit, encourage, and con-done sexual violence against women. The willingness by states to tolerate sexual violence against women despite explicit prohibitions in international humanitarian law pro-vides soldiers with a "license to rape because of their military associ-ation" (United Nations, (1993). They are shielded from prosecution and provided with impunity because rape has proven to be a valuable war strategy. Rape is used in war as a means of vengeance, a tool of propaganda, a way to signify power to the opposing side, a reward for weary troops and a way to build morale, and, increasingly, a strate-gic tool of ethnic cleansing or genocide. Rape is an effective way to subjugate and terrorize a population and is a means of communication from conquering men to the conquered (Brownmiller, 1975; Mann, 1993). In this way, women as individuals are absent from the equation; their bodies are merely used to pass on a message or are seen as spoils of war.

The international community has finally begun to recognize the true nature of the crime of rape, signaling its intention to end the practice of using rape as a weapon of war by punishing the crime equally with oth-er war crimes. This change came about largely as a result of the alarm-ing prevalence of sexual violence inflicted on women in the former Yugoslavia and in Rwanda.

RAPE AS A WEAPON OF WAR: FORMER YUGOSLAVIA

The first rapes in the conflict of the former Yugoslavia occurred in 1991. They were thought to be isolated incidents and were largely ig-nored and disbelieved by the international community at that time. Repeated stories of mass rape continued to emerge in 1992 (Stiglmayer, 1994b; Gutman, 1992), at the same time that Serbian aggression against Bosnia and Herzegovina began in earnest, and eventually, the mass rapes began receiving the attention they deserved. Estimates of the num-ber of Bosnian Muslim rape victims range from twenty thousand to fifty thousand. Not only were women raped in their homes and vil-lages, but large numbers of women were forced into "rape camps" where they were held and raped repeatedly by various men.

There is substantial evidence of the widespread use of rape as an instrument of ethnic cleansing in the former Yugoslavia (United Nations, 1993). Women were raped by men who taunted them with ethnic slurs and stated their intention to forcibly impregnate them. Because lineage is passed from the father, forcibly impregnating Mus-lim women meant that they would bear Serbian children, thereby "ethnically cleansing" the former Yugoslavia. In the context of rape as ethnic cleansing, "rape has been used not only as an attack on the in-dividual victim, but is intended to humiliate, shame, degrade and ter-rify the entire ethnic group" (United Nations, 1993, para. 85). In the former Yugoslavia, it was rape with a particular political purpose; Serbs raped women publicly in front of friends, family, and neighbors, in a pattern of intimidation and abuse focused on forcing the Croatian or Bosnian population to flee (Ray, 1997; Amnesty International, 1993). This sent a clear message from Serbs that they were conquering the Muslim population and were leaving raped women as constant re-minders of Serb domination. In fact, there is evidence that soldiers were ordered to rape Muslim women and could be subjected to castration or death for refusing to do so (Gutman, 1992; Askin, 1997).

In addition, Muslim women were raped with knowledge of the cul-tural significance of rape. In patriarchal Muslim society, "when a man knows that a woman has been raped, he treats her badly.... People think she must have given the man occasion to rape her. Her life could be ruined by that." This sent another message to the community, since women who were raped brought shame and dishonor to their hus-bands and families. The rapes in the former Yugoslavia represent an example of women being targeted because of their multiple identities: as women, as Muslims, and as members of an ethnic group that was not dominant. By using rape to "ethnically cleanse" the Croatian and Bosnian population, the Serbian forces chose an effective and success-ful means of inflicting a reign of terror. The effect was the denigration of an ethnic group and the ostracism of raped women.

RAPE AS A WEAPON OF WAR: RWANDA

In 1994, genocide began in Rwanda. From April to July, between 500,000 and 1 million Rwandans were slaughtered in a catastrophic effort to eliminate the Tutsi minority and moderate Hutu sympathizers. Throughout that period, members of the Hutu militia groups known as Interhamwe, other civilians, and soldiers of the Rwandan Armed Forces subjected women to brutal sexual violence, including mass rape (Human Rights Watch/Africa, 1996). While it is impossible to determine the exact number of women who were raped, it is evi-dent from survivors' testimony that the rapes were widespread and systematic (Human Rights Watch/ Africa, 1996; United Nations, 1998). One estimate numbers anywhere from 250,000 to 500,000 rapes, based on the numbers of recorded pregnancies resulting from rapes. Doc-tors working in Rwanda have confirmed the existence of high numbers of rape survivors (Human Rights Watch/Africa, 1996). Other observers believe that almost every woman and adolescent girl who survived the genocide was raped (Human Rights Watch/Africa, 1996).

Mass rapes of Rwandan women were strategically used as a tool of genocide calculated to destroy the Tutsi population. This strategy was fostered by hate propaganda directed at Tutsi women, which "ex-horted Hutu to commit the genocide [and] specifically identified the sexuality of Tutsi women as a means through which the Tutsi commu-nity sought to infiltrate and control the Hutu community" (Human Rights Watch/Africa, 1996, p. 2). The propaganda therefore encour-aged sexual violence against Tutsi women as a way to subjugate and destroy the Tutsi population. As with the rapes in the former Yugo-slavia, the Rwandan women were targeted because of the intersection of their ethnicity and gender. They were individually raped, gang raped, and raped with objects. These brutal rapes often were inflicted on wom-en after they had witnessed the torture and killing of their relatives or after having been forced to kill their own children. A Rwandan wom-en's rights activist explained, "Rape was a strategy. They chose to rape. There were no mistakes. During this genocide, everything was orga-nized" (Human Rights Watch/Africa, 1996, p. 41).

LACK OF NATIONAL PROTECTION: FORMER YUGOSLAVIA

Although women were subjected to systematic rape as a weapon of war during the conflict in the former Yugoslavia, they were unable to access police protection and redress for the crimes perpetrated against them. In fact, after investigating the reports of rapes, a United Nations team of experts said that they "heard of no attempts made by anyone in a position of authority to try and stop the raping of women and girls" (United Nations, 1993, para. 48c). Human Rights Watch also claims that "there is no evidence that the Yugoslav Army or the Serbian Min-istry of

Interior made any attempt to apprehend or punish those re-sponsible for the attacks" (Human Rights Watch, 2000, p. 3). Some women reported the rapes to local authorities, who either dismissed the women, detained them, told the women that although they knew what was happening, they could do nothing about it (Amnesty International, 1993), or told them that there "wasn't any kind of power or law that could control [the rapists]." In this way, "practically speaking it was legal to rape Muslim women" (Stiglmayer, 1994a, p. 110). Indeed, the failure to punish rapists appears to be as consis-tent and widespread as the acts of rape. The local authorities were not just ignoring the mass rapes; some of those in power actively partici-pated in them. In the former Yugoslavia, the effective use of rape as a weapon of war was furthered by a lack of national prosecution or protection and by general impunity for rapists.

LACK OF NATIONAL PROTECTION: RWANDA

Women raped in the Rwandan genocide also faced a lack of interven-tion by authorities and tacit acceptance of the practice of mass rape as a tool of war. Despite laws on the books prohibiting rape and pro-viding for its prosecution under Rwandan criminal law, combatants used rape as a weapon with impunity during the genocide. In fact, those who orchestrated the genocide deliberately created and permit-ted an environment of lawlessness, in which "the government and military authorities gave the militias full license to commit egregious human rights abuses, including rape, with impunity" (Human Rights Watch/Africa, 1996, p. 40). Indeed, stories from survivors who were brutally raped by the militia are numerous and well chronicled (Hu-man Rights Watch/Africa, 1996). The military also encouraged or con-doned rape and violence by militia groups and others. In some cases, the soldiers or national policemen not only aided in attacks against the civilian population, but also were responsible for committing rapes themselves (Human Rights Watch/Africa, 1996). As a consequence of the involvement of the entire state apparatus and the militia of the rul-ing party in the genocide (United Nations, 1996), including rapes, it follows that the women would have had very little success had they tried to seek justice within the national system against their attackers. In this way, as in the former Yugoslavia, the weapon of rape was ef-fectively used as a tool in armed conflict.

EFFORTS TO PROHIBIT WARTIME RAPE

Partly in response to the reports of mass rape that came out of the for-mer Yugoslavia, public opinion mobilized around the issue of ensur-ing justice for victims of rape and other forms of sexual violence. At around the same time, the International Committee of the Red Cross (ICRC) adopted a broad construction of the existing Geneva Conven-tion that had neglected to include rape as a grave breach. The ICRC determined that the grave breach of "willfully causing great suffering or serious injury to body or health" could include rape (Meron, 1998).

Soon after the ICRC issued its interpretation, the U.S. Department of State confirmed its belief that under customary international law and the Geneva Conventions, rape was considered a war crime or grave breach and could be prosecuted accordingly. The letter referred to the situation in the former Yugoslavia, stating that "in our reports to the United Nations on human rights violations in the former Yu-goslavia, we have reported sexual assaults as grave breaches. We will continue to do so and will continue to press the international com-munity to respond to the terrible sexual atrocities in the former Yu-goslavia" (Meron, 1998, p. 208). It was within this framework—moving forward to punish wartime rape and increase the gravity with which rape was treated within international humanitarian law—that the stage was set for the creation of the international criminal tribunals for the former Yugoslavia and Rwanda.

THE INTERNATIONAL CRIMINAL TRIBUNALS

The specific intent to prosecute sexual assault crimes under the pro-posed International Criminal Tribunal for the Former Yugoslavia (ICTY) was evidenced by the 1993 report of the secretary general, who repeatedly condemned the systematic use of rape and urged liability for those responsible (Sellers & Okuizumi, 1997). Based on that re-port and strong public opinion, in 1993, the United Nations Security Council established the ICTY. The ICTY has jurisdiction over grave breaches of the Geneva Conventions of 1949, violations of the laws or customs of war, genocide, and crimes against humanity. Rape is specif-ically enumerated under Article 5 as a crime against humanity. The nonexhaustive list of the violations of the laws and customs of war (Article 3) also could permit the direct prosecution of rape. Since rape is not explicitly referred to in the grave breaches provision (Article 2) or in the genocide provision (Article 4), it cannot be explicitly and di-rectly alleged as a violation of those articles. The ICTY's prosecutor, however, determined that acts of sexual assault could be prosecuted implicitly under all four types of crimes within the tribunal's juris-diction (Sellers & Okuizumi, 1997).

On November 8, 1994, the United Nations Security Council, in Resolution 955 (1994) and acting under Chapter VII of the United Nations Charter, established the International Criminal Tribunal for Rwanda (ICTR). The ICTR's jurisdiction covers genocide, crimes against humanity, and, because of its internal nature, violations of Article 3 common to the Geneva Conventions and of Additional Protocol II. As in the ICTY statute, the ICTR statute includes rape as a crime against humanity. The ICTR statute goes one step further by incorporating Additional Protocol II' s explicit prohibition of rape into Article 4 of the statute.

Rape as Evidence of a Campaign of Terror

Although the first trial held by either tribunal was expected to be the first international war crimes trial to prosecute rape separately as a war crime, the prosecutor was forced to drop rape charges from two counts because the witness was afraid to testify (Askin, 1999; Marshall, 1996). The ICTY's decision in *Prosecutor v. Tadic (1997)* nevertheless offered some "absolute gems" in terms of prosecuting rape during wartime (Viseur-Sellers, 1998, p. 1509). One of these is the fact that the tribunal accepted testimony about the sexual violence that occurred and "the enormous pain and suffering endured by the women and girls and the community at large" from medical workers who did not witness the sexual violence (Askin, 1999, p. 102). The tribunal allowed this tes-timony under a hearsay exception and went on, in its decision, to quote that testimony at length. In addition, the tribunal interpreted testimony of rape as evidence of discriminatory intent ((Viseur-Sellers, 1998) and found that, based largely on the testimony of a rape survivor, "a policy to terrorize the non-Serb population... on discriminatory grounds is evident and that its implementation was widespread and systematic" *(Prosecutorv. Tadic,* 1997, para. 472). Although the prosecutor did not prove that Tadic himself had committed rape, Tadic was still held li-able for participating in a general campaign of terror, manifested by rape and other forms of violence. This decision signifies that anyone— including nonstate actors and low-level participants such as Tadic, who was a civilian traffic officer—can be convicted of aiding and abetting crimes of sexual violence through knowing participation in or tacit en-couragement of such crimes (Askin, 1999).

Rape as Genocide and a Crime Against Humanity

The ICTR decision in *Prosecutorv. Akayesu* (1998) has been hailed as historic in its treatment of rape within an internal conflict (Askin, 1999; Coalition on Women's Human Rights in Conflict Situations, 1998). It marked the first time an international court punished sexual violence in a civil war and the first time rape was found to be an instrument of genocide. Unfortunately, the rape allegations almost were ignored en-tirely.

When Jean-Paul Akayesu was charged in 1996, the indictment con-tained twelve counts, none of which included rape (Coalition on Wom-en's Human Rights in Conflict Situations, 1998). It was largely due to a concerted effort and heavy international pressure from women's rights groups that sexual violence charges were added to the indictment (Co-alition on Women's Human Rights in Conflict Situations, 1998; United Nations, 1998; Rosenberg, 1998; *Prosecutorv. Akayesu*, 1998). The ICTR acknowledged this in the final judgment: "The Chamber takes note of the interest shown in this issue by non-governmental organizations, which it considers as indicative of public concern over the historical exclusion of rape and other forms of sexual violence from the investi-gation and prosecution of war crimes. The investigation and presen-tation of evidence relating to sexual violence is in the interest of justice" *Prosecutorv. Akayesu*, 1998, para. 731)

It is important to note that at the time of the trial, there was no in-ternationally accepted definition of rape. When considering this fact, the ICTR clearly departed from restrictive definitions of rape that exist in national law. Instead, the chamber defined rape "as a physical invasion of a sexual nature, committed on a person under circumstances which are coercive." This is a broad definition of rape, unrestricted to one gen-der or to particular body parts. In fact, the chamber stated that "the cen-tral elements of the crime of rape cannot be captured in a mechanical description of objects and body parts" *(Prosecutorv. Akayesu*, 1998, para. 597,598). The chamber also found that force need not apply. Rather, coercive elements could include threats and intimidation. In addition to providing a broad definition of rape, the ICTR in-dicated its understanding of the true nature of the crime. It moved away from the view formerly held in international humanitarian law that rape is a crime against honor. Instead, the ICTR looked to inter-national definitions of torture. The ICTR declared that, like torture, "rape is used for such purposes as intimidation, degradation, humil-iation, discrimination, punishment, control or destruction of a per-son. Like torture, rape is a violation of personal dignity" *(Prosecutorv. Akayesu,* 1998, para. 597). By reconceptualizing rape, the ICTR placed rape on equal footing with other serious violations that occur dur-ing armed conflict. These groundbreaking steps—broadening the de-finition of rape and assigning it equal status—allowed the tribunal to recognize sexual violence as a form of genocide and a crime against hu-manity and to prosecute the crime accordingly.

In its decision, the ICTR recognized sexual violence as an essential component of the genocide and found Akayesu guilty of genocide for crimes that included sexual violence. Although gender is not one of the enumerated groups protected from genocide, the ICTR found that when rape was used as a method to destroy a protected group by caus-ing serious bodily or mental harm to the members thereof, it con-stituted an act of genocide. The ICTR found that in the Rwandan genocide, sexual violence was intimately linked to genocide and meant to destroy the spirit and will to live of its victim and the collective group. As the trial chamber declared in its judgment, "Sexual violence was an integral part of the process of destruction, specifically targeting Tutsi women and specifically contributing to their destruction and to the de-struction of the Tutsi group as a whole" *(Prosecutor v. Akayesu,* 1998, para. 731). The chamber also recognized rape and other forms of sex-ual violence as independent crimes constituting crimes against hu-manity. It found that the rapes had been systematic and carried out on a massive scale and that Akayesu had witnessed, and even encouraged, rapes of Tutsi women while serving as communal leader.

Akayesu was sentenced to three life terms plus eighty years. For geno-cide, he received a life term for each of the three counts. For rape as a crime against humanity, he received a fifteen-year sentence. This sen-tence was equal to sentences received for counts of murder, signaling the ICTR's recognition of rape as a crime of equal status to murder.

Through its broad definition of rape, its reconceptualization of the crime, its jurisprudence regarding genocide and crimes against hu-manity, and its sentencing, the ICTR began creating a paradigm shift concerning the crime of rape in war and armed conflict. Fortunately, the ICTY recognized the importance of this shift and carried it fur-ther in later decisions.

Rape as Torture

In the case *of Prosecutor v. Delalic et al.*, commonly referred to as the *Celebici* case, Zejnik Delalic, Zdravko Mucic, Esad Landzo, and Hazim Delic were charged with grave breaches and violations of the laws or customs of war, including torture. Some of the offenses charged were multiple rapes, public rape, gang rape, vaginal and anal intercourse, rape during interrogation, and multiple instances of rape. The judgment was rendered, in a nearly five-hundred-page document, on No-vember 16,1998. In considering the charge of rape as torture, the ICTY adopted the broad definition of rape provided by the ICTR in the *Akayesu* case.

In addition to accepting the ICTR's broad definition of rape, the ICTY also agreed with the ICTR's new understanding of the crime of rape. The trial chamber stated in its decision that it "considers the rape of any person to be a despicable act which strikes at the very core of hu-man dignity and physical integrity.... Rape causes severe pain and suffering, both physical and psychological" (*Prosecutor v. Delalic*, 1998, para. 495). This signified a further shift away from understanding rape as a crime against women's honor and instead recognized it as a vio-lation of integrity and a crime of violence.

In this way, building on the ICTR's *Akayesu* case, the ICTY recog-nized rape as torture (Askin, 1999). The tribunal stated that "there can be no question that acts of rape may constitute torture under custom-ary law" (*Prosecutor v. Delalic et al*, 1998). It then went on to find Hazim Delic guilty of rape as torture as both a grave breach of the Fourth Gen-eva Convention and a violation of the laws and customs of war. In its judgment, the principle of command responsibility also evolved; the tri-bunal found Zdravko Mucic, the camp commander, responsible for crimes committed at the camp, including gender-based crimes.

Rape as a War Crime

The trial of An to Furundzija, a local military commander, gave the ICTY a chance to play an important role in the movement toward es-tablishing rape as a serious violation of international humanitarian law. Furundzija was charged with a rape committed by his subordinate against a Bosnian Muslim woman during a single day of the conflict, which Furundzija witnessed and failed to disrupt or curtail *(Prosecu-torv. Anto Furundzija,* 1998; Askin, 1999).

The trial chamber, which delivered its decision on December 10, 1998, admitted that it was not possible to discern the elements of the crime of rape from international treaty or customary law, from gen-eral principles of international criminal law, or general principles of international law. It therefore concluded that it was necessary to look to major legal systems of the world in order to find common princi-ples of criminal law. After surveying municipal rape laws, the trial chamber found what it deemed a trend of broadening the definition of rape to include other forms of sexual assault. Although it did broad-en the definition of rape to include forced oral penetration, the trial chamber nevertheless delineated a surprisingly narrow and specific list of what it found to be the requisite elements of the offense of rape under international criminal law. Some have seen the trial chamber's elaboration of the elements of rape as a regression from the broad def-inition established by the ICTR in *Akayesu* (Askin, 1999)

Nevertheless, the trial chamber in *Furundzija* agreed with the ICTR that rape and other forms of sexual violence must be recognized for the serious violations they are. In its decision, the chamber stated, "The essence of the whole corpus of international humanitarian law as well as human rights law lies in the protection of the human dignity of every person, whatever his or her gender" *(Prosecutor v. Anto Furund-zija,* 1998, para. 183). The trial chamber also affirmed, "It is indisput-able that rape and other serious sexual assaults in armed conflict entail the criminal liability of the perpetrators" (para. 169). The ICTY there-fore acknowledged the true nature of the crime of rape and the ne-cessity of punishing perpetrators accordingly.

The trial chamber went on to find Furundzija guilty, under Article 3 of the ICTY statute, of violating the laws or customs of war for torture and for outrages upon personal dignity, including rape. He was sen-tenced to ten and eight years' imprisonment, respectively, which he was to serve concurrently. Although this was not a perfect decision, *Fu-rundzija* nevertheless served to move the treatment of wartime rape along its progressive trajectory by recognizing the violent nature of rape, recognizing a single incident of rape as a war crime, and further-ing the liability of those who aid and abet wartime rape.

Rape as the Sole Charge

The decision of the ICTY was hailed as a groundbreaking case. When the indictment was issued, an article on the front page of the *New York Times* asserted, "This is a landmark indictment because it focuses ex-clusively on sexual assaults, without including any other charges.... There is no precedent for this. It is of major legal significance because it illustrates the court's strategy to focus on gender-related crimes and give them their proper place in the prosecution of war crimes" (Simons, 1996, p. 1).

Indeed, this case represents the first time that an international tri-bunal brought charges solely for crimes of sexual violence against women. The indictment charged all of the accused with various counts of violations of the laws and customs of war and crimes against hu-manity, and charged Dragoljub Kunarac and Zoran Vukovic with grave breaches, all stemming from crimes of sexual violence.

In its decision, rendered on February 22, 2001, the ICTY took the opportunity to clarify the definition of rape in international law. It de-cided that part of the definition stated in the *Furundzija* decision was "more narrowly stated than is required by international law," in that it did not refer to factors other than coercion, force, or threat of force, "which would render an action of sexual penetration *non-consensual or non-voluntary* on the part of the victim." In order to develop a more appropriate definition of the crime in international law, the trial cham-ber determined that it must look to certain basic principles among the national legal systems. The trial chamber went on to say that the "true common denominator which unifies the various [national legal] sys-tems may be a wider or more basic principle of penalising violations of sexual *autonomy" (Prosecutorv. Kunarac, Kovac, and Vukovic,* para. 438,440).

The trial chamber then surveyed national legislation regarding three factors—force or threat of force; specific circumstances, which go to the vulnerability or deception of the victim; and absence of consent or vol-untary participation—to make clear its point about autonomy. The trial chamber determined that these factors indicate that in international law, "serious violations of sexual *autonomy* are to be penalised" (*Prosecutor* v. *Kunarac, Kovac, and Vukovic*, para. 457). The judgment then offered a slightly broader definition of rape than in *Furundzija*. This broader definition allowed for the rejection of Kunarac's claim that because one of the victims, D.B., took an active part in taking off his trousers and kissing him before having vaginal intercourse with him, she consented to sexual intercourse with him. Instead, the trial chamber found that D.B. did not in fact freely consent to any sexual intercourse with Ku-narac, given the context of the surrounding circumstances, and that Kunarac had full knowledge that she did not freely consent. In so de-ciding, the court made clear that sexual autonomy is intrinsically con-nected to human dignity and bodily integrity (Boon, 2001), furthering the paradigm shift in international humanitarian law.

In addition, this was the first time the ICTY found rape and sexual enslavement to be crimes against humanity. The trial chamber was satisfied that rape met the elements of a crime against humanity: it was a widespread and systematic attack directed against any civilian population during an armed conflict. Notably, the trial chamber stated that no nexus between the acts of the accused and the armed conflict was required: the "armed conflict requirement is satisfied by proof that there was an armed conflict at the relevant time and place" (*Prosecu-tor v. Kunarac, Kovac, and Vukovic*, para. 413). There was found to be an armed conflict and the underlying crimes were related to the armed conflict. In considering the charge of rape under the provisions gov-erning violations of the laws or customs of war, the trial chamber was satisfied that rape met the requirements for the application of Com-mon Article 3 of the Geneva Conventions, including that it is a seri-ous offense.

In its decision, the trial chamber convicted Kunarac, Radomir Ko-vac, and Vukovic of various counts of crimes against humanity and vi-olations of the laws or customs of war for rape, torture, or enslavement and sentenced them to twenty-eight, twenty, and twelve years' impris-onment, respectively. According to prosecutor Peggy Kuo, the prose-cution was "pleased with the court's decision because the sentences show that the court took the crimes very seriously" (Simons, 2001a, p. 1). The founder of a support group for women who have suffered trauma in war also praised the convictions: "I'm so glad, we've been waiting so long for such clear language and convictions" (Simons, 2001b, p. A1).

EFFECT OF THE TRIBUNALS' DECISIONS

These decisions from the ICTY and ICTR recognize the nature of sex-ual violence in armed conflict and signal that these crimes deserve un-relenting investigation and prosecution.

Giving Rape Equal Status and Equal Punishment

One important component of these decisions is the international def-inition of rape, which, due to the *Foca* decision, now links rape to a violation of women's autonomy. In this way, the international com-munity has acknowledged finally that rape should not be seen as a vi-olation of a woman's honor and thereby inextricably linked to her sexuality. Instead, the definition is cast from the victim's perspective, with rape as a violation of bodily integrity. This represents a major legal development as well, since prior to these cases, there was no stan-dard definition of rape in international law. The definitions developed by the ICTY and the ICTR will have a normative effect, informing other tribunals grappling with crimes of sexual violence during war and armed conflict. The *Foca* decision, which explicitly condemned rape and sexual violence and established, in clear and compelling language, that rape can constitute a war crime, genocide, and crime against human-ity, will lead the way.

Aside from the definition of rape, the tribunals' decisions also are remarkable for moving away from the idea of women as property to be taken as spoils of war. These decisions represent a paradigm shift in international humanitarian law. They indicate the international community's willingness to consider sexual violence where it belongs, on a par with other serious violations of individuals' rights. The eleva-tion of rape and other sexual violence to the level of other war crimes means that there should be no further uncertainty about how to han-dle evidence of rape during war and armed conflict. Rape is not to be ignored or tolerated as a tool of war. Rather, its thorough investigation and prosecution should occur with the same frequency as other seri-ous crimes committed during war.

This progress regarding the treatment of wartime rape is seen clearly in Sierra Leone, which currently is attempting to grapple with crimes committed during its decade-long conflict, which has been marked by an extraordinary level of brutal human rights abuses, in-cluding widespread sexual assault of women. Physicians for Human Rights (2002) estimates that approximately fifty thousand to sixty thou-sand internally displaced Sierra Leonean women may have suffered war-related sexual assaults. The Special Court for Sierra Leone, which was set up jointly by the United Nations and Sierra Leone, began its work in June 2002. The statute of the special court explicitly includes gender-based violence in its definition of several categories of crimes that the court has power to prosecute. Rape, sexual slavery, enforced prostitution, forced pregnancy, and any other form of sexual violence are listed in the article delineating crimes against humanity (Special Court for Sierra Leone, 2000). The court also expressly includes rape, enforced prostitution, and any other form of indecent assault as vio-lations of humanitarian law as enshrined in Common Article 3 and Additional Protocol II. The court has shown its willingness to treat rape and other forms of sexual violence as deserving of investigation and prosecution alongside other serious violations of humanitarian law. By the end of 2003, crimes of sexual violence were included in ten of the thirteen indictments issued. The court also has two full-time gender crimes investigators and has conducted gender sensitivity train-ing for all of its investigators (Jefferson, 2004).

Incorporating Women's Rights into International Humanitarian Law

Through the tribunals' decisions, the international community has become aware of gender-based atrocities in situations of war and armed conflict. This has helped not only to bring women's issues to the forefront but also to make women's voices audible. Indeed, the "opportunity to present rape in an international forum with the at-tendant media and world scrutiny offers women an unprecedented opportunity to try to tell the story of wartime rape from women's point of view" (Tompkins, 1995, p. 851). Once people listen to accounts of rape and the harm that accompanies such violations, they are more likely to understand the violation and seek to end the impunity that has served men so well in wars for centuries. One journalist eloquently described the impact of the *Foca* decision as "justice being done, but justice being played in a new, female key; painted in new, female col-ours that depicted rape as a tool of war and crime against humanity" (Vulliamy, 2001, p. 27). Women have largely been absent from inter-national law. The tribunals' decisions indicate a change in the opposite direction. It was women's groups that encouraged rape to be pursued in the tribunals to the extent documented in this chapter. Women's voices and concerns are now beginning to be heard and taken seri-ously in the international arena.

Indeed, this integration of women's rights into the international arena is seen clearly in the ICC. The statute of the ICC incorporates a gender-based perspective to ensure not only that women who are vic-tims of crimes during war and armed conflict receive justice, but also that women play an active role in the court itself. The ICC statute ex-plicitly recognizes rape and other forms of sexual violence as a crime against humanity and a war crime. It also clarifies the definition of rape as a war crime and a crime against humanity, providing defini-tions both broad enough to recognize other forms of sexual assault and coercive circumstances and specific enough to ensure that future perpetrators have advance notice. The ICC statute further incorpo-rates a gender-based perspective by requiring that the prosecutor and registrar, when hiring staff, take into account the need for fair repre-sentation of men and women, and that they appoint advisers with legal expertise on sexual and gender violence (Article 44[2]). It de-mands the same of states when electing judges (Articles 36[8a, 8b]). Out of the first eighteen judges elected to the court in 2003, seven are women. In this way, the international community has demonstrated its intention to clarify the crime of rape within international human-itarian law, place rape on an equal footing with other serious crimes, end impunity for perpetrators of wartime rape, and ensure gender equality and sensitivity within the ICC itself.

Further Challenges

Although the tribunals' decisions undoubtedly have led to an increased awareness of women's rights in international humanitarian law, it is important to examine how the decisions translate into the lives of women survivors of wartime rape.

ENSURING THE SAFETY OF VICTIMS AND WITNESSES

One of the most immediate issues is the safety of survivors. In Rwanda, for example, there have been consistent and increasing attacks on genocide sur-vivors who might serve as witnesses at trial ("'Survivors' Tell of Rwanda Revenge Killings," 1994; "Hutus May Be Targeting Witnesses," 1994; "Family of Six Assassinated," 1997; "Extremists Said Killing Witnesses to Genocide," 1997). Part of the problem is that many perpetrators are still free. The tribunals cannot hold hearings in absentia and have no power to force other states to turn over their citizens for trial (Atlas, 1994). Rather, the primary responsibility for seeking out and arrest-ing war criminals rests with the national states (Schiller, 1996). Un-fortunately, states have not been forthcoming in the arrest of their national criminals, so perpetrators remain at large, mixing with the citizen popul[illegible] that may include their prior victims. In the *Foca* case, for insta[illegible] of the eight men originally indicted, three were still at large when the decision came down (Human Rights Watch, 2001). In fact, shortly after the indictment was issued and had been hailed for its progressive view on punishing wartime rape, a journalist re-ported that the victims in the case "have little cause to celebrate the legal gain. If they returned to their hometown of Foca, they could not go to a grocery [store] or enter a café without the risk of bumping into the men they have accused of repeatedly raping them" (Ricchiardi, 1998). In Rwanda, one victim "moves from place to place, frightened of meeting some of the other perpetrators who are still wandering around freely" while at the same time being "threatened and perse-cuted" by the family of one person she testified against (United Na-tions, 1998). As long as those who are indicted remain at large, the women live in fear, and impunity for rapists remains.

Witnesses also fear reprisal because of their testimony. Unfortu-nately, the tribunals offer protection to witnesses only during their in-volvement at the tribunal. If someone is intent on retribution, the small period of protection might prove insufficient. For example, some Rwandan rape survivors told the UN special rapporteur on violence against women during her visit that they were afraid to travel to the ICTR to testify because they did not believe they would be adequately protected (United Nations, 1998). Witnesses in Rwanda voiced con-cern to the special rapporteur that the danger was not actually in Arusha, Tanzania, where the ICTR sits, but in Rwanda, where the wit-nesses returned after testifying. Because Arusha is remote from Rwanda, most feel that it is not possible for the ICTR to effectively protect wit-nesses on their return (United Nations, 1998). This has proven true; in 1997, a Hutu woman who had testified before the ICTR against Jean-Paul Akayesu was killed along with her husband, four of their own chil-dren, and three other children who were in the house at the time of the attack (Walsh, 2000; Softline Info., 1997; Woodruff, 1997).

This problem is no different at the ICTY, which sits in The Hague, a considerable distance from the atrocities in the former Yugoslavia. Witnesses travel to and from the ICTY without protection; the pro-tection offered by the ICTY begins only once the witnesses arrive in The Hague. Before arriving in The Hague or after leaving, a witness is dependent on the country of residence for protection. The ICTY, however, does not have reliable lines of communication with local po-lice in other countries. In addition, it has no legal enforcement au-thority within territories of other states and no practical means of implementing any measures of safety for victims and witnesses even if it wanted to do so.

Furthermore, the protection offered to witnesses at the tribunals is lacking in many respects. The special rapporteur found that "despite the enormous threat to women victims of violence and women witnesses, the ICTR has not really developed procedures concerning witness incog-nito" within the courtroom (United Nations, 1998). There have been similar problems with the ICTY. In fact, in the *Tadic* case *(Prosecutor v. Tadic,* 1995), there was a decision on the prosecutor's motion request-ing protective measures for victims and witnesses, which dealt with the issue of witness protection by means of confidentiality or anonymity. One witness eventually had to withdraw from the case because of threats made against her and her family, causing the prosecutors to drop rape charges against the accused (Askin, 1999; Marshall, 1996). Another problem is the leaking of identities of witnesses despite nondisclosure orders. In one case, information was leaked to the public; in another, the list of prosecution witnesses, including protected witnesses, was pub-lished in a newspaper alongside an interview with one of the accused. In neither case was the defense penalized (Murphy, 1999). It was not until April 2003 that the ICTY finally took action against someone for revealing the identity of a secret witness. Fortunately, the statute and rules of the ICC attempt to address many of the problems that witnesses at the two ad hoc tribunals face (see Articles 42,43,54[1][b], 57,64,68, 87[4]). As the ICC begins its work, the international community needs to guarantee the protections and services provided for in these articles and rules.

Providing services to survivors of sexual violence

Another dif-ficulty facing women survivors of wartime rape is the lack of coun-seling and medical services available to them. An abstract verdict in an international tribunal concerning rape as a crime against human-ity may not mean much for a woman who is trying to resume life after enduring rape. Women survivors of sexual violence need access to medical services, which can include screening for sexually transmit-ted diseases (STDs), access to abortion, and obstetrical and gyneco-logical services. Unfortunately, these services are not readily available in countries trying to recover from the devastation of war or internal conflict. In Rwanda, for instance, despite large numbers of rape sur-vivors and the massive injuries to reproductive organs that many of them endured, there were only five gynecologists in the country in 1998 (United Nations, 1998). Similarly, in the former Yugoslavia, "women are not being provided with the necessary gynaecological and STD screening that should be part of their overall care following rape" (United Nations, 1993, para. 36). Many victims of rape and other forms of sexual violence were infected with HIV and need access to HIV/ AIDS testing, counseling, and treatment.

In addition to medical traumas, victims sustain psychological trau-mas, which may be ignored or hidden as a result of the stigma attached to rape and the prioritizing of other war injuries. Survivors of sexual violence need access to mental health services in order to address the trauma to which they have been subjected. Unfortunately, because of the shame and disgrace associated with rape, especially in Rwandan and Muslim cultures, women may be reluctant to seek help (United Nations, 1993,1998). Those living with HIV face increased ostracism and alienation. Accessible, affordable psychological services and pro-grams are critical for the healthy resumption of victims' lives.

Because of the stigma attending sexual violence, many victims will find themselves in need of basic necessities, such as shelter and food. In the Balkans, "most of the rape victims have been cast out of their homes and left to fend for themselves... in battle zones without food, warm clothing or shelter" (Williams, 1992, p. A1). Humanitarian as-sistance in the form of economic assistance is necessary. Shelters, job training skills, and other forms of economic opportunities can help these women ensure their continued livelihood and assist their reintegration into society.

CONTINUED LACK OF POLITICAL WILL TO END IMPUNITY FOR WARTIME RAPE

The prohibitions against rape are now firmly developed in in-ternational humanitarian law, and jurisprudence around these issues has developed from the decisions of the ICTY and the ICTR. Statutes and jurisprudence condemning wartime rape and sexual violence will be effective, however, only if those in power use them in the future to prosecute perpetrators, thereby ending impunity. Unfortunately, the po-litical will to proceed with prosecutions of wartime rapists is lacking. Instead, combatants in conflicts around the world continue to effec-tively use rape as a weapon of war. In Liberia, for example, "more than 14 years of fighting... has made rape as common as looting or gunshot wounds" (Wax, 2003a, p. A16). There is no punishment for perpetra-tors. Similarly, in the eastern Congo, rapes have been widespread, sys-tematic, and brutal. Some aid groups estimate that one in every three women is a victim (Wax, 2003b). Unfortunately, as in the former Yu-goslavia and Rwanda, in the Congo, rape was turned "into a primary weapon of war.... Rape has even been encouraged by commanders as a way to gain control of such scarce resources as food, water and fire-wood, intimidating the women on a continent where women do nearly all the labor in the fields.... With Congo lacking a functioning court system, no one has been punished" (Wax 2003b, p. A17). This under-scores the fact that international courts cannot exist in a vacuum; they must be complemented by strong national systems. The international community must ensure that national institutions receive the proper instruction in prosecuting rape as a violation of international humani-tarian law, and receive gender-sensitivity training in order to allow them to do so in a way that respects the rights of survivors.

The lack of political will to prosecute rape is not only a domestic problem. It has plagued the ad hoc tribunals themselves. Since the ini-tial effort to investigate and prosecute sexual violence in the former Yugoslavia and Rwanda, the commitment of the tribunals to end im-punity for wartime rapists has waned. According to Human Rights Watch, the tribunals do not have an effective long-term prosecution strategy that acknowledges the degree of wartime sexual violence suf-fered by women (Jefferson, 2004). At the ICTR, for example, only one conviction involving sexual assault—that of Jean-Paul Akayesu—has survived appeal.

CONCLUSION

While the tribunals' indictments and decisions have begun to shape the future prosecution of gender-based violence by affording rape equal status and providing equal punishment, the tribunals cannot cease to continue prosecuting such crimes. Instead, all courts prose-cuting crimes committed during war and armed conflict—including the ICTR and ICTY, other ad hoc tribunals, the ICC, and national courts—must continue to ensure that the protections that have de-veloped against rape are real and effective, rather than theoretical and illusory, for women victims. These courts must prioritize the prose-cution of rape and redress its commission, thereby ending impunity for wartime rapists. If this occurs alongside an effort to create gender equity in international and national institutions, the practice of rape during war and armed conflict may cease altogether.

Bibliography

Allcock, R.S.: *Development Training: A Personal View*, Birmingham, Endeavour Training, 1988.

Berry, J. W.: *Human Ecology and Cognitive Style: Comparative Studies in Cultural and Psychological Adaptation*, New York, Sage, 1976.

Bowlby, J.: *A Secure Base: Parent-child Attachment and Healthy Human Development*, New York, Basic Books, 1990.

Burlew, K.A.: *African-American Psychology: Theory, Research, and Practice*, Newbury Park, SAGE, 1992.

Cox, Jr., T.: *Cultural Diversity in Organizations: Theory, Research & Practice*, San Francisco, Berrett-Koehler Publishers, 1993.

Damon, William: *Social and Personality Development: Infancy through Adolescence*, New York, Norton, 1983.

Denhardt, R. B.: *Managing Human Behavior in Public & Nonprofit Organizations*, Thousand Oaks, Sage, 2002.

Fine, M.: *Women with Disabilities: Essays in Psychology, Culture, and Politics*, Philadelphia, Temple University Press, 1988.

Glover, J.: *The Philosophy and Psychology of Personal Identity*, London, Penguin, 1988.

Greenaway, R.: *The Training and Development of Development Trainers*, Ambleside, Brathay Hall Trust, 1986.

Harvey, C.: *Understanding Diversity: Readings, Cases, and Exercises*, New York, HarperCollins College Publishers, 1995.

Jennifer, R.: *Divided Minds and Successive Selves: Ethical Issues in Disorders of Identity and Personality*, Cambridge, MIT/Bradford Press, 1996.

John, R.: *Subpersonalities: the People inside Us*, London, Routledge, 1990.

Johnson, C.: *Meeting the Ethical Challenges of Leadership*, Thousand Oaks, Sage, 2005.

Jones, R. J.: *Black Psychology*, Berkeley, Cobb & Henry, 1991.

Kathleen, V.: *Real People : Personal Identity without thought Experiments*, Oxford, Clarendon Press, 1988.

Kegan, R.: *In Over our Heads: The Mental Demands of Modern Life*, Cambridge, Harvard University Press, 1994.

Kenneth, R.: *Social, Emotional, and Personality Development*, New York, Wiley, 1998.

Levin, David Michael: *Pathologies of the Modern Self*, New York, NYU Press, 1988.

Mahler, Margaret: *The Psychological Birth of the Human Infant*, New York, Basic, 1975.

Matsumodo, D.: *People: Psychology from a Cultural Perspective*, Pacific Grove, Brooks/Cole, 1994.

Michael, S.: *Attachment in Adults: Clinical and Developmental Perspectives*, New York, Guilford Press, 1994.

Piaget, J., & Whelder, B.: *The Psychology of the Child*, New York, Basic Books, 1964.

Rubin, Kenneth: *Social, Emotional, and Personality Development*, New York, Wiley, 1998.

Schuster, C.: *The Process of Human Development*, Boston, Little, Brown & Co., 1980.

Stephen, L.: *The Unity of the Self*, Cambridge, MIT Press, 1991.

Walters, R. H.: *Social Learning and Personality Development*. New York, Holt, Rinehart, and Winston, 1963.

White, Stephen L.: *The Unity of the Self*, Cambridge, MIT Press, 1991.

Wiggins, Jerry: *The Five Factor Model of Personality: Theoretical Perspectives*, New York, Guilford Press, 1996.

Wilkes, Kathleen V.: *Real People : Personal Identity without thought Experiments*, Oxford, Clarendon Press, 1988.

William Berman: *Attachment in Adults: Clinical and Developmental Perspectives*, New York, Guilford Press, 1994.

William, Bukowski: *Social, Emotional, and Personality Development*, New York, Wiley, 1998.

William, D.: *Social and Personality Development: Infancy through Adolescence*, New York, Norton, 1983.

Index